AF324179

Save the Womanhood!

Save the Womanhood!

Vice, urban immorality and social control in Liverpool, *c*.1900–1976

Samantha Caslin

LIVERPOOL UNIVERSITY PRESS

First published 2018 by
Liverpool University Press
4 Cambridge Street
Liverpool
L69 7ZU

British Library Cataloguing-in-Publication data
A British Library CIP record is available

ISBN 978-1-78694-125-1 cased

Typeset by Carnegie Book Production, Lancaster
Printed and bound in Poland by BooksFactory.co.uk

Contents

List of Figures   vi

Acknowledgements   vii

List of Abbreviations   ix

Introduction   1

1   Experts in Womanhood: Morality and Social Order Before and During the First World War   14

2   Patrolling the Port: Interwar Moral Surveillance   41

3   Regulating Interwar Prostitution: National Debates and Local Issues   62

4   Finding Respectable Work for Women in Interwar Liverpool   85

5   White Slavery and Social Purists' Authority   106

6   Female 'Traffickers' and Urban Danger   125

7   Irish Girls in Liverpool (1): Interwar Moral Concerns   145

8   Irish Girls in Liverpool (2): The Second World War and the Post-War Years   162

9   A Changing of the Guard: Moral Order, Gender and Urban Space in the Post-War Years   183

Conclusion   210

Bibliography   217

Index   231

Figures

1 Liverpool Vigilance Association Badge   52

2 'Stranded': National Vigilance Association Charity Dinner
Pamphlet, November 1908   137

Acknowledgements

I want to thank staff in the Department of History at the University of Manchester as well as the Economic and Social Research Council who supported and funded the postgraduate research from which this book grew. My doctoral supervisors, Frank Mort and Carol Smart, were invaluable sources of insight, support and encouragement. I would also like to thank Mike Savage for his comments on early PhD chapter drafts, as well as others who offered advice, encouragement and interest along the way, especially Lucy Bland, Charlotte Wildman, Selina Todd, Caitríona Beaumont and Sally Sheard. My undergraduate tutors at the University of Liverpool were instrumental to the development of my interests in histories of gender and sexuality as well as urban sociology and social theory. I am very grateful to have been tutored by Matt Houlbrook, Paul Jones, Steve Miles, Stuart Wilks-Heeg and Peter Millward. I must give particular thanks to Andrew Davies, a former tutor and now colleague and friend, who never fails to inspire. My colleagues in the Department of History at the University of Liverpool have been great sources of support and advice during the writing of this monograph, especially Graeme Milne, as have the wonderful students that I have had the privilege of teaching.

I am very grateful to all of the archivists and librarians who assisted me while researching this book. The librarians and archivists that I have met at the Liverpool Metropolitan Cathedral Archive, Sydney Jones Library, the National Archives, the Lancashire Record Office and the Women's Library have all offered considerable help. A great deal of this research was conducted at the Liverpool Record Office; I am hugely grateful to their wonderful archives and records team.

Last but not least, I would like to thank my friends and family for supporting the development of this book at every stage, especially James Milton and my parents Paul Caslin and Amanda Pybis. I am also grateful to Elizabeth Pybis, an irrepressible Liverpudlian lady whose stories first began my interest in Liverpool women's history. My biggest thanks go to Duane, Alexander and Robert who have been beautiful sources of support, delight and much-needed distraction. Thank you.

Abbreviations

AMSH	Association for Moral and Social Hygiene
BVA	British Vigilance Association
CD Acts	Contagious Diseases Acts
CWL	Catholic Women's League
LVA	Liverpool Vigilance Association[1]
NVA	National Vigilance Association
PSS	Liverpool Personal Service Society
Wolfenden Committee	Departmental Committee on Homosexual Offences and Prostitution

1 Until 1921, the official title of the organization was The National Vigilance Association (Liverpool Branch). In 1921, this was changed to The Liverpool Society for the Prevention of International White Slave Traffic and from the late 1940s to the Liverpool Vigilance Association. For clarity, this organization is referred to throughout this book under its more commonly known title of the Liverpool Vigilance Association. See Chapter 5 for further clarification.

Introduction

The title of this book is taken from a statement made by a Liverpool-based women's refuge, the House of Help, in 1918. Having offered its services to women for two decades, the House of Help looked towards the end of the First World War with the hope that their organization could be part of the 'building' of a 'new world by helping to save the womanhood of our country'.[1] Their work providing temporary shelter to women who found themselves lost, stranded or penniless in Liverpool was just one element of local, social purity inspired philanthropic efforts to save young, typically working-class, women from the supposedly corrupting effects of urban life and the temptation to earn money via prostitution. This was a moral war, waged around the docks, the city's main train station at Lime Street, in city centre entertainment districts and in working-class neighbourhoods. Many of the women who stayed at the House of Help had been directed or brought there by women patrollers from the Liverpool Vigilance Association (LVA) and the local Women Police Patrols. Together, the activities of these patrollers and moral welfare workers proliferated a gendered sense of urban space that was predicated upon the idea that some women required moral guidance in order to deter them from the temptations of vice and sexual immorality.

The preventative agenda of Liverpool's social purists and moral welfare workers meant that they intervened in the lives of women according to vague and highly subjective ideas about immorality and vulnerability. As

1 House of Help, Annual Report 1918, p. 10. Liverpool Record Office, 362 HOU/3/28.

this book will show, these custodians of virtue employed definitions of immorality which disproportionally targeted women who were young, working class and/or Irish. Women in these social groups were subjected to the watchfulness of organizations like the LVA and the House of Help and their movements around Liverpool's streets were sometimes curtailed as a result of these observations. Despite being engaged in a campaign to highlight the skills and competence of women, even Liverpool's Women Police Patrols promoted the idea that women in these groups required moral surveillance. Through their associations with the LVA and the House of Help, the Women Police Patrols gave licence to and profited from the notion that young, working-class and immigrant women required matriarchal supervision from their moral and, in many cases, social superiors.

The twentieth-century practices of Liverpool's women patrollers, and their affiliates in organizations like the House of Help, were steeped in late nineteenth-century social purity traditions. One of the key points of continuity between the nineteenth and mid-twentieth centuries was the continuation of middle-class fears about the morality of the working class.[2] The idea that the working class could set their own moral codes of respectability was anathema to the majority of Victorian social purists. Participation in charitable endeavours afforded local elites an opportunity to address their anxieties about working-class unrest and bolster the security of their own social position.[3] Under the veneer of social inclusion, the 'respectable' poor were defined against a more threatening social residuum or underclass, a powerful strategy that had significant implications for debates about the extent to which it was legitimate or desirable for the law to impinge on the liberties of citizens. As Beverley Skeggs has argued, 'To not be respectable is to have little social value or legitimacy.'[4] Notions of civility and respectability had become synonymous with the middle class by the end of the

2   For more on the longevity of the nineteenth-century 'tradition' of 'social investigation' into the moral and sexual lives of the working class, see Peter Gurney, '"Intersex" and "Dirty Girls": Mass-Observation and Working-Class Sexuality in England in the 1930s', *Journal of the History of Sexuality*, 8:2 (1997), p. 258.

3   Derek Fraser, *The Evolution of the British Welfare State: A History of Social Policy since the Industrial Revolution*, 3rd edn (Basingstoke: Palgrave Macmillan, 2003), p. 137.

4   Beverley Skeggs, *Formations of Class and Gender* (London: Sage, 1997), p. 3.

nineteenth century, while the 'lower' classes were considered to be a threat to the morally ordered city.[5]

However, I do not want to suggest that the strategies of moral surveillance undertaken by organizations like the LVA and the Women Police Patrols were mere hangovers from the previous century. I want to show that concerns about moral order adapted in response to huge social changes in the lives of women. Nor do I want to suggest that working-class women were passive recipients of moral guidance. In many instances, tensions arose between patrollers and working-class women who felt scrutinized and patronized by patrollers' offers of assistance. Though I acknowledge that some women in need no doubt benefited from the welfare work performed by Liverpool's social purists and moral welfare workers, this book highlights the incongruousness of social purists' belief that they were engaged in a project to save the nation's womanhood. Organizations like the LVA and House of Help did not routinely work with those who had already been coerced into prostitution, nor did they aim to change the gendered culture of Britain's streets. To this end, I want to illuminate the way that, well into the twentieth century, the social purity rhetoric of saving women from prostitution actually served further to marginalize women deemed to be promiscuous or immoral.

Pioneering work by Judith Walkowitz in the 1980s and 90s opened up discussions about the cultural history of prostitution, though it is only in more recent years that historians have begun to turn their attention to the twentieth-century history of this issue.[6] Julia Laite's vital intervention into this field has used London as a case study for a wider exploration of

5   The Victorian concept of social order was tied to the condition of the streets. Order and peace on the streets were interpreted as signs of 'the urbanity of the citizens', while disorder on the streets was thought to threaten the very notion of 'civilisation'. See Andy Croll, 'Street Disorder, Surveillance and Shame: Regulating Behaviour in the Public Spaces of the Late Victorian British Town', *Social History*, 24:3 (1999), p. 252.

6   Judith Walkowitz, 'Going Public: Shopping, Street Harassment, and Street Walking in Late Victorian London', *Representations*, 62 (1998), pp. 1–30; Judith Walkowitz, 'The Politics of Prostitution', in Stevi Jackson and Sue Scott (eds), *Feminism and Sexuality: A Reader* (Edinburgh: Edinburgh University Press, 1996); Judith Walkowitz, *City of Dreadful Delight: Narratives of Sexual Danger in Late-Victorian London* (London: Virago, 1992); Judith Walkowitz, *Prostitution and Victorian Society: Women, Class, and the State* (Cambridge: Cambridge University Press, 1980).

the policing and processing of prostitutes through the criminal justice system.[7] Similarly, Stefan Slater has conducted detailed, useful research on London using Home Office and Metropolitan Police records.[8] There have also been moves to expand this field of research out beyond London. Simon Jenkins' work extends the geographical scope of this analysis to Cardiff, and he argues that we must take account of local specificities as well as broader issues in order to understand the anxieties that have surrounded vice.[9] Meanwhile, Louise Settle's recent work engages with the changing landscapes of interwar prostitution amid widespread social and technological change, highlighting how prostitutes in Edinburgh navigated the public sphere by using dance clubs to solicit furtively.[10]

This book adds to this scholarship by using the case study of Liverpool to explore overlaps between national debates about the *control* of prostitution and local efforts to *prevent* prostitution. This is not, therefore, a history of women who worked as prostitutes, rather it is a history of those who were concerned with saving and controlling young women perceived to be living on the precipice of urban immorality. I am concerned with examining the gendered power structures which were reinforced via the categorization of young, often working-class women as morally vulnerable while older, upper working-class and middle-class women were afforded roles as custodians of urban moral order. Although this work is about the policing of moral boundaries, rather than about prostitution per se, my approach is informed by earlier generations of feminist work which have criticized the law for using women working as prostitutes as examples to all other women of

7   Julia Laite, *Common Prostitutes and Ordinary Citizens: Commercial Sex in London, 1885–1960* (Basingstoke: Palgrave Macmillan, 2011).

8   Stefan Slater, 'Lady Astor and the Ladies of the Night: The Home Office, the Metropolitan Police and the Politics of the Street Offences Committee, 1927–28', *Law and History Review*, 30:2 (2012), pp. 533–73; Stefan Slater, 'Containment: Managing Street Prostitution in London, 1918–1959', *Journal of British Studies*, 49:2 (2010), pp. 332–57; Stefan Slater, 'Pimps, Police and Filles de Joie: Foreign Prostitution in Interwar London', *London Journal*, 32:1 (2007), pp. 53–74.

9   Simon Jenkins, 'Inherent Vice? Maltese Men and the Organization of Prostitution in Interwar Cardiff', *Journal of Social History*, 49:4 (2016), pp. 928–58; Simon Jenkins, 'Aliens and Predators: Miscegenation, Prostitution and Racial Identities in Cardiff, 1927–47', *Cultural and Social History*, 11:4 (2014), pp. 575–96.

10   Louise Settle, 'The Kosmo Club Case: Clandestine Prostitution during the Interwar Period', *Twentieth Century British History*, 25:4 (2014), pp. 562–84.

how not to behave.[11] My work is also influenced by current sociological studies on the way the criminalization of prostitution places sex workers in danger.[12] Indeed, it is pressing that critical approaches to the historically contingent moral discourses that have impacted prostitution regulation are addressed now. Sociologists Teela Sanders and Rosie Campbell argue that there has been, over the last decade, 'a re-entrenchment of a criminalization agenda' surrounding prostitution.[13] Yet their suggestion that the mid-twentieth-century legislation that followed the Wolfenden Committee was 'relatively liberal' when compared with the current climate requires examination.[14] I argue that the Wolfenden approach did not significantly depart from the previous strategies of social purists and moral philanthropists who categorized women working as prostitutes in terms of whether they were irredeemable or in need of rescuing.

Though some first- and second-hand accounts of young women's lives are used in this work, the stories of those considered to be morally vulnerable are predominantly told thorough the words of the social purists who categorized them in this way. In part, this is because marginalized voices are, by their very nature, often absent from the historical record, but my analysis of the way social purists and welfare workers infantilized and attempted to speak for the women that they helped allows me to focus on the far-reaching consequences of these philanthropic voices. I argue that social purists' well-meaning but often prejudiced ideas about respectable femininity and what it meant to be a good, well-behaved woman in the early to mid-twentieth-century city were taken up by some sections of the press and, crucially, by those with the power to influence the laws used to police prostitution. I provide a counterpoint to histories which seek to draw a line between the early twentieth century and the mid-twentieth

11   Carol Smart, *Law, Crime and Sexuality: Essays in Feminism* (London: Sage, 1995), p. 57. Indeed, Smart has argued that the law has had a role to play in defining not just the prostitute but female identities in general. Carol Smart, 'Law's Power, the Sexed Body, and Feminist Discourse', *Journal of Law and Society*, 17:2 (1990), p. 204.
12   Teela Sanders and Rosie Campbell, 'Criminalization, Protection and Rights: Global Tensions in the Governance of Commercial Sex', *Criminology & Criminal Justice*, 14:5 (2014), pp. 535–48.
13   Teela Sanders and Rosie Campbell, 'Criminalization, Protection and Rights', p. 536.
14   Teela Sanders and Rosie Campbell, 'Criminalization, Protection and Rights', p. 537.

century.[15] Certainly, there were significant cultural and social developments in women's lifestyles during these years, but these social changes must be balanced against long-standing moral anxieties and appeals to traditional gender ideologies.[16] For much of the twentieth century, perceptions of city streets as sites of moral disorder focused heavily on women's use of these environments. Nationally, police suggested that they struggled to tackle prostitution because they claimed they could no longer automatically assume that the women they saw dressed up and walking through streets were there to solicit.[17] To be sure, women throughout the twentieth century challenged social boundaries and claimed greater social and political freedom, but any progressive steps forward were almost routinely counterbalanced by the moral push-backs that they engendered.

The scale of social changes experienced by women during the course of the twentieth century has been a topic of critical analysis among historians. Carol Dyhouse's work has shown how, throughout the twentieth century, young women were consistently subjects of moral condemnation and panic, polarized into the categories of 'bad girl' and 'vulnerable girl', though she is ultimately optimistic about the gains women made during the period.[18] This overall optimism is less easily applied to the matter of prostitution, where notions of disreputability and victimhood dominated, and still dominate, popular understandings of the issue. I also want to add to new work on the intersections between moral regulation and criminal justice. Louise Jackson's work with Angela Bartie on post-war approaches to youth, morality and crime draws attention to the need for regional nuance in assessing official and unofficial forms of regulation. Their analysis of 'penal

15   For example, Samuel Hynes has suggested that the twentieth century did not begin in any cultural or imagined sense until almost two decades into its actual commencement. Samuel Hynes, *A War Imagined: The First World War and English Culture* (London: The Bodley Head, 1990).

16   This interpretation of the broad continuities between the Victorian era and the twentieth century is also supported by Lesley Hall, who has gone as far as to argue that such was the influence of late nineteenth-century understandings about gender and sexuality that 'a case can be made for "a long Victorian era" in Britain, which did not finally dissipate until around 1960'. Lesley A. Hall, *Sex, Gender and Social Change in Britain since 1880* (Basingstoke: Macmillan, 2000), p. 10.

17   See Chapter 3 of this book.

18   Carol Dyhouse, *Girl Trouble: Panic and Progress in the History of Young Women* (London: Zed Books, 2013).

welfarism' supports the stance taken in this book, which asserts that we need to recognize the lineages of Victorian moralism and how they coexisted with more progressive social changes well into the twentieth century.[19] However, I want to complicate their argument that while late-Victorian and Edwardian purity campaigners saw young women as potential victims, later moralists recast wayward young women as 'predatory'.[20] I argue that the coexistence of competing narratives was at play throughout much of the twentieth century. Interwar notions of white slavery utilized the idea of the 'trafficker' woman as a predator, while the image of the young woman as a potential victim of moral corruption remained potent in the post-war years. As such, the dichotomous figures of the woman out to corrupt and the woman liable to become a victim were constant features of the early twentieth-century *and* post-war rhetoric of those aiming to prevent prostitution.

The issue of place runs throughout this work, both in the sense that I explore Liverpool's experience of wider cultural anxieties and in the sense that I argue that moral uncertainty characterized understandings about women's relationship to urban space and city life. Judith Walkowitz's recent work on cosmopolitanism in London thematically explores the parallels between the panics about the peccadilloes of a specific locale and those concerns that resonated across the country, an approach also taken in this book.[21] The local examination of anxieties about female morality that I offer here highlights the relationship between the legal and cultural spheres of prostitution prevention and the production of regulatory discourses and practices governing women's sexual morality. That is not to say that the local picture simply represents a smaller-scale version of what was happening nationally. My examination of female morality and its social control in early and mid-twentieth-century Liverpool indicates that general anxieties about prostitution and promiscuity were played out in ways that were locally nuanced. Perceptions of Liverpool as a site of transience and as a magnet for the young, the Irish and the unemployed were implicated in the gendering of the city's streets. Consequently, my work heeds Graeme Milne's assertion that 'we should make some effort to

19   Louise Jackson with Angela Bartie, *Policing Youth, 1945–70* (Manchester: Manchester University Press, 2014), pp. 226–7.
20   Louise Jackson with Angela Bartie, *Policing Youth*, p. 119.
21   Judith Walkowitz, *Nights Out: Life in Cosmopolitan London* (New Haven, Conn.: Yale University Press, 2012).

study the "port city", rather than just the "port" or the "city"'.[22] I argue that Liverpool's role as a gateway to other parts of Britain clearly influenced understandings advanced by local social purity campaigners and moral welfare workers about the fragility of urban morality.

By concentrating on Liverpool, this book provides a point of comparison with histories of sexuality and gender that have used London to address nationally relevant social and sexual questions.[23] As John Belchem notes, Liverpool has typically thought of itself as a city apart from the rest of the nation, and this identity has fed into historiographical analysis of Liverpool's 'exceptionalism'.[24] Yet a closer look at women's experiences reveals that twentieth-century Liverpool was locked into broader moral debates about female sexuality. The attention that philanthropists, the press and some important police officials devoted to questions about women's geographic mobility and their use of public transport indicates that Liverpool's moral borders were understood to be highly permeable. Where the issue of sexual morality is concerned, I argue that Liverpool was not an unusual city, although there were certainly aspects to these anxieties that were locally nuanced by the presence of the port. Politicians, police and moralists expected the city to have problems with prostitution and these expecta-tions fed into the local culture of sexual surveillance. Liverpool's links with Irish immigration meant that this surveillance often targeted working-class Irish women. However, these were local inflections of a debate and sense of anxiety about the sexual freedom of women that ran through the country

22   Graeme J. Milne, 'Maritime Liverpool', in John Belchem (ed.), *Liverpool 800: Culture, Character and History* (Liverpool: Liverpool University Press, 2006), p. 257.

23   See, for example, Tony Henderson, *Disorderly Women in Eighteenth-Century London: Prostitution and Control in the Metropolis, 1730–1830* (London: Longman, 1999); Matt Houlbrook, *Queer London: Perils and Pleasures in the Sexual Metropolis, 1918–1957* (London: University of Chicago Press, 2006); Seth Koven, *Slumming: Sexual and Social Politics in Victorian London* (Princeton, NJ: Princeton University Press, 2004); Julia Laite, *Common Prostitutes and Ordinary Citizens*; Frank Mort, *Capital Affairs: London and the Making of the Permissive Society* (London: Yale University Press, 2010); Frank Mort, 'Mapping Sexual London: The Wolfenden Committee on Homosexual Offences and Prostitution 1954–57', *New Formations: Sexual Geographies*, 37 (1999), pp. 92–113; Stefan Slater, 'Containment'; Judith Walkowitz, *City of Dreadful Delight*.

24   John Belchem, *Merseypride: Essays in Liverpool Exceptionalism* (Liverpool: Liverpool University Press, 2006).

and right into Westminster. The upshot of this was that these local battles about who was a respectable woman and who was not actually informed discussions about the supposed necessity for prostitution policies to punish 'bad' women and save the vulnerable.

During the course of the twentieth century, Liverpool's economic fortunes and overall status faced significant challenges. In the 1880s, the city had been the 'gateway' of the Empire.[25] Despite Liverpool's population peaking in the 1930s, the signs of decline had already started to emerge in the early twentieth century, as southern ports increased their workloads.[26] In the post-war years, Liverpool benefited from some investment in manufacturing and the 1960s saw the city increase in status as a cultural centre, but the fortunes of the port remained precariously balanced.[27] As such, Liverpool makes for a particularly interesting case study of women's engagement with urban space and strategies of moral surveillance, not least because of the city's fluctuating status both in the national economy and in the national social imagination. Consistently imagined as a city struggling to meet the middle-class standards of respectability and civility befitting its national significance, the questionable moral status of Liverpool was an ever-present issue in wider public debate about its very real social problems.[28]

Though this work looks at the activities of a range of moral welfare workers in twentieth-century Liverpool, much of this book is focused upon the activities of the LVA. The LVA has clear links to earlier social purity groups (through its parent organization, the National Vigilance Association) and the Association's work indicates that national debates about the need to control prostitution were applied locally. The LVA's annual records detail the movements of women around the city and the migration habits of women entering and leaving Liverpool, providing close-up case studies of the sort of work that the organization was involved with on the streets. I

25   Krista Cowman, *'Mrs Brown is a Man and a Brother!' Women in Merseyside's Political Organisations 1890–1920* (Liverpool: Liverpool University Press, 2004), p. 15.
26   Olivier Sykes, Jonathan Brown, Matthew Cocks, David Shaw and Chris Couch, 'A City Profile of Liverpool', *Cities*, 35 (2013), pp. 300 and 307.
27   Olivier Sykes et al., 'A City Profile of Liverpool', p. 307.
28   Colin Pooley has argued that Liverpool has been considered a 'problem city' for almost two centuries because of its associations with poverty and immorality. Colin G. Pooley, 'Living in Liverpool: The Modern City', in John Belchem (ed.), *Liverpool 800: Culture, Character and History* (Liverpool: Liverpool University Press, 2006), p. 173.

also draw on a large collection of local newspaper cuttings kept in the LVA's archives in order to show how the organization was set up, the rationale for its creation and the messages the organization disseminated about its work. Nevertheless, we cannot understand the determination or longevity of the LVA without understanding their relationship to and interactions with other local agencies such as Liverpool's Women Police Patrols, the House of Help and purity associations around the country. Throughout the book I address the networks of moral welfare, assistance, surveillance and social control forged by these organizations in order to show how they worked together to foster a sense of urban space as inimical to any other type of respectable femininity but their own.

In the first chapter, I examine the origins, ideals and general practices of key Liverpool organizations aimed at protecting the moral and physical well-being of women during the early and mid-twentieth century. Alongside the activities of the LVA and the Women Police Patrols, I explore the much-neglected archives of organizations like the Liverpool House of Help and the Liverpool branch of the Catholic Women's League. It is my contention that these organizations performed complimentary works that intersected to create a complex network of surveillance and social control. These were organizations that were run primarily by women for women, but the social purists and welfare workers involved in these agencies did not readily associate themselves with the women that they 'saved'. In fashioning themselves as female experts on urban morality, the workers in these organizations set themselves apart from other women, whom they considered to be susceptible to being morally corrupted by the urban environment. In Chapter 2, I go on to analyse the preventative tactics used by moral welfare patrollers to compel young women to listen to them and argue that, despite not having any official powers, these watchful women were able to cultivate a sense of authority and purpose for themselves. Using various case studies from LVA and Women Police Patrols reports, I want to show that young women's travels around Liverpool were not only judged by social purity inspired philanthropists, they were circumscribed by them as well.

A national backdrop of moral panic about prostitution made it possible for local organizations to make the case for their own particular brands of informal moral policing. Chapter 3 considers evidence presented to the Street Offences Committee, formed in October 1927, and argues that, at national level, key officials gave credence to the idea that otherwise good women could be corrupted by being allowed to spend time in disreputable urban areas without moral chaperones like the LVA and the Women Police. The Street Offences Committee has yet to be analysed in detail by historians, save for an article by Stefan Slater on its formation and Julia Laite's analysis of the committee within the context of London trends on the policing of prostitutes.[29] The local evidence presented to the committee must be analysed if we are to avoid letting London speak for the provinces. Situating the Liverpool Women Police Patrol's testimony to the committee within a broader cultural context of moral policing, this chapter makes it clear that the regulation of prostitution during the interwar period was driven by the notion that a chaste, private and controlled female sexuality was integral to both official and unofficial approaches to the maintenance of social order.[30]

I want to show that these ideas had practical, lived outcomes in terms of social purists' and welfare workers' interactions with women. In Chapter 4, I note that the women met by moral welfare patrollers were not just directed off the streets, moved swiftly on to their destinations, sent home to their families or placed in hostels like the House of Help or the Women Police Patrol's Hostel for Girls. Each of these agencies also took an active role in finding work for working-class women in order to ensure that poverty did not encourage them to turn to prostitution. Organizations like the LVA and the House of Help saw work as a way of keeping women respectable, especially if the work involved supposedly feminine skills such as domestic service, but they did not trust women to find or to get new jobs without help.

Underneath this sense that young, working-class women in pursuit of jobs were naive about urban danger were allusions to sexual exploitation and attack. In Chapters 5 and 6, I explore how 'white slavery' was defined in the twentieth century and with what consequences for working-class women as they moved through city spaces. Carol Dyhouse notes that even before the First World War some feminists used the term 'white slavery' imprecisely to signify what they believed to be men's sexual dominance over women, but this broad definition gave oxygen to the rumoured cases

29   Julia Laite, 'The Association for Moral and Social Hygiene: Abolitionism and Prostitution Law in Britain (1915–1959)', *Women's History Review* 17:2 (2008), pp. 207–23; Stefan Slater, 'Lady Astor and the Ladies of the Night'.
30   This argument builds upon Judy Giles' research which suggests that working-class women were still expected to practise sexual restraint. See Judy Giles, '"Playing Hard to Get": Working-Class Women, Sexuality and Respectability in Britain, 1918–40', *Women's History Review*, 1:2 (1992), pp. 239–55.

of 'white slavery' as kidnap, which were largely unsubstantiated.[31] Dyhouse argues that the loose rhetoric of white slavery meant that young women who grew up in the early years of the twentieth century were encouraged to fear travel, despite the fact that these young women were much more likely to encounter a female voluntary patroller than a white slave trader at a port or train station.[32] I want to add to this by examining, in Chapter 5, how social purists used the rhetoric of white slavery as kidnap to bolster their moral authority and justify their surveillance of women's travel through and around Liverpool. I then proceed, in Chapter 6, to argue that social purists in Liverpool presented no evidence of organized trafficking in the city, so suspected madams and pimps and even local promiscuous young women suspected of prostitution were referred to within the context of white slavery and trafficking. The LVA deployed white slavery as a nebulous term and in such a way that the figure of the female trafficker furthered the notion that women could be divided into the categories of 'the disreputable' and 'the vulnerable'.

Chapters 7 and 8 focus on the issue of Irish female immigration in the interwar and post-war years. I want to show that Irish immigration was central to the LVA's work because their patrollers promoted a sense of Irish young women as sexually and socially naive, working class and unused to city life. These characteristics meant that Irish young women functioned as prime examples of feminine vulnerability. Yet this was about more than just imagery. Chapter 8 shows that during the Second World War, when travel between Ireland and Liverpool was reduced, the LVA's workload significantly declined. This dip in the LVA's workload testifies to the extent to which the organization was dependent on perceptions of these young women as vulnerable. When Irish female immigration levelled out again after the war, the LVA was once again ready to intervene in the travels and employment plans of these young women.

Well into the post-war years, the LVA and the House of Help expressed concern about the effects of city life upon the morality of young women. In Chapter 7, I argue that the decline of these organizations in the 1960s and 70s should not be taken as a sign that their ideas had been roundly rejected. I argue that the Wolfenden Committee, established in 1954, and the subsequent Street Offences Act 1959, saw the law clamp down upon prostitution precisely because it was perceived as undermining notions of

31   Carol Dyhouse, *Girl Trouble*, pp. 23–4.
32   Carol Dyhouse, *Girl Trouble*, p. 26.

female respectability and therefore threatening social order. At a local level, Liverpool certainly underwent significant changes during the post-war years. By the 1960s, social purists were concerned that young women were increasingly travelling to the city in search of excitement and glamour. But the decline of the LVA was not simply brought about by cultural change or a sense that young women were less likely to listen to their warnings. The Street Offences Act 1959 meant that the moral policing of prostitution had been incorporated into official responses to solicitation, making the street patrols of organizations like the LVA appear outdated. Nevertheless, the idea that urban spaces could have a morally corrupting effect upon women, and the idea that female respectability could be used as a barometer of social order, continued to inform attitudes towards prostitution and female sexuality in general long after these organizations had ceased to exist.

1

Experts in Womanhood
Morality and Social Order
Before and During the First World War

Despite the pioneering public roles performed by female philanthropists in Liverpool during the early twentieth century, the increasing confidence with which these women sought to shape public womanhood cannot be explained simply via the tropes of liberation, progress or emancipation. Instead, the story of these moral altruists was moulded in the intersections between class, ethnicity and gender and in the bifurcated distinction between the respectable and the fallen woman. Social purists, street patrollers and religiously motivated philanthropists reinforced the notion that public spaces had a corrosive effect upon working-class women's sense of morality. A number of women's organizations active in early twentieth-century Liverpool paradoxically upheld the belief that working-class women who ventured outside of the moral security of the domestic sphere required both help and surveillance. Their philanthropic activities were refracted through a lens of moral judgement about the seemingly problematic relationships between poor, immigrant and young women and the urban landscape. Social purists and moral welfare workers understood that it was impractical to expect working-class women to remain within the domestic sphere entirely; they understood that many women needed to work outside of the home in order to support their families. Yet such was the level of concern about the ability of working-class women to negotiate non-domesticated lifestyles, their urban excursions were subjected to the persistent moral guidance of watchful philanthropic women who were ready to offer their assistance, regardless of whether it was sought or welcomed by the recipients.

The interest that local social purists, religious philanthropists and street patrollers took in working-class women's presence in public was motivated by a complex mix of benevolence and the assumption that working-class communities were somehow intrinsically inclined towards moral disorder, requiring dedicated efforts to maintain public order and social control. There was also an important political and highly gendered outlook underpinning this work. Moira Martin argues that philanthropic welfare work in the early twentieth century enabled middle-class women to 'traverse the boundaries of class and gender without any loss of social status'.[1] By subscribing to and emphasizing fears about promiscuity and prostitution amongst working-class, Irish and transient young women, middle-class and upper-working-class women patrollers in Liverpool found fuel for their own efforts to establish themselves as women outside of the domestic sphere. They were able to use fears about disreputable women as a moral contagion in order to make the case for their own feminine expertise in dealing with matters of urban immorality. Street patrollers in the Liverpool Vigilance Association (LVA) and Women Police Patrols were particularly adept at reconfiguring aspects of maternally focused femininity to establish their potential practical function outside the domestic sphere. The acts of listening to, sheltering and even morally disciplining vulnerable women imbued the patroller with a respectable femininity and gave her an affinity with the domesticated matriarch, seemingly inoculating her from urban immorality and temptation. Altruism therefore served as a political tool for those women looking to branch out into the public sphere, though this was a freedom that came at the cost of other, more marginalized women.

While the task of engaging in welfare work broke down boundaries for the women offering the help, it paradoxically reinforced the boundaries used socially and morally to police poorer women. Certainly, moral welfare agencies did much to aid in individual cases where local and migrant women found themselves suffering the ill-effects of poverty, abandonment or disorientation in a new city. It was not unusual for these organizations to report having received letters of thanks from the women that they helped. In fact, Liverpool garnered a reputation in the early twentieth century for producing progressive and positive approaches to the welfare of the working class.[2] However, the cumulative effect of preventative

1   Moira Martin, 'Single Women and Philanthropy: A Case Study of Women's Associational Life in Bristol, 1880–1914', *Women's History Review*, 17:3 (2008), p. 395.
2   Margaret Simey noted that, at the end of the nineteenth and start of the twentieth centuries, Liverpool attracted welfare workers, such as the social policy

moral interventions, whereby working-class women were encouraged to accept help and advice in order to stay on the path of respectability, added weight and female concurrence to the notion that women of a higher social standing possessed greater moral fortitude than those who were poor. The notion that principles and good will would transform the lives of working-class women continued to be buttressed by the middle-classes' presumption of moral superiority over the poor.[3] The moral surveillance practised by social purists in the LVA, the didacticism of local religious groups such as the Catholic Women's League and the social welfare initiatives of the Women Police Patrols, however well-intentioned, impinged upon working-class women's moral agency, as the guidance and help on offer constituted forms of social control.

Concentrating on the period between the end of the nineteenth century and 1918, this chapter charts the creation, early years and wartime experiences of a number of active Liverpool welfare organizations concerned about urban immorality. The LVA, the House of Help, the Catholic Women's League and the Women Police Patrols all contended with concerns about prostitution and the moral effects of the First World War upon the city's young people. Any increases in working and social opportunities for women were traded off against the efforts of moralists to reassert the gender order of the pre-war years.[4] Alongside wartime social freedoms and calls for women to take up munitions work sat a competing gender construction, evident in both official and unofficial forms of propaganda, which situated domesticated, patriotic motherhood as central to

pioneer and cleric Frederic D'Aeth, who brought with them new and innovative approaches towards the poor. See Margaret Simey, *Charity Rediscovered: A Study of Philanthropic Effort in Nineteenth-Century Liverpool* (Liverpool: Liverpool University Press, 1992), p. 124 and Margaret Simey, *From Rhetoric to Reality: A Study of the Work of F.G. D'Aeth, Social Administrator*, edited by David Bingham (Liverpool: Liverpool University Press, 2005).

3   Margaret Simey, *Charity Rediscovered*, p. 129.

4   In his seminal social history of the war, Arthur Marwick notably suggested that the conflict altered the way women thought about themselves and transformed collective understandings about women's capabilities. See Arthur Marwick, *The Deluge*, 2nd edn (Basingstoke: Palgrave Macmillan, 2006 [1965]), especially p. 134. This chapter argues that this is only half the picture, with wartime concern about women's freedoms actually bolstering pre-existing practices and in some cases instituting new practices of moral surveillance at the local level aimed at controlling the behaviour of working-class women.

women's role in the war effort.[5] Meanwhile, the attempts of Liverpool's social purists and philanthropists to capitalize upon wartime moral panic prevented them from moving beyond the limitations of later-Victorian gender ideals.

That is not to say that women's lifestyles remained unchanged between the late-Victorian era and the early twentieth century, but alongside social change sat older ideologies and languages of gender that framed the new opportunities available to women with caution and anxiety about women's potential outside of the domestic sphere. Collectively, the work of the agencies explored in this chapter indicates that the early twentieth century did not witness a radical reshaping of dominant gender codes. Though many women did benefit from new opportunities, particularly during the war, changes in women's lifestyles were frequently understood and at times challenged via recourse to older ideas about the need for middle-class women to morally educate their working-class sisters.

As civil organizations, the groups examined in this chapter wielded a self-proclaimed social power over other women. Despite conducting patrols in the city, neither the LVA nor the Women Police Patrols had any legal authority. Neither organization possessed the ability to detain or arrest potential moral offenders. Similarly, the House of Help could not compel women to stay within its protection, but the women who did stay there were expected to abide by a strict moral regime. To some extent the House of Help drew its power to set rules and encourage compliance from its religious affiliations. Despite not existing to help Christian women specifically, the House of Help publicized its Christian beliefs in its annual reports. Similarly, the Catholic Women's League gained its authority through religion. Through its title and its organization, the Catholic Women's League made it known that it had the backing of the Church, and this was often enough to convince Catholic women that they should listen to the advice and moral guidance on offer. Consequently, by examining the pre-war origins, collective wartime experiences and urban politics of these organizations, this chapter argues that their combined practices of street patrolling, surveillance and moral instruction proliferated and even inculcated within working-class women the belief that a clear connection could be drawn between the scale of a woman's poverty and her susceptibility to urban moral corruption.

5 Nicoletta Gullace, *'The Blood of Our Sons': Men, Women and the Regulation of British Citizenship during the Great War* (Basingstoke: Palgrave Macmillan, 2002), chap. 3.

The House of Help

As a city with an active port, pockets of poverty and large numbers of transient, seafaring people passing though, late nineteenth- and early twentieth-century Liverpool was closely linked with debates about the behaviour of the urban poor, particularly in regard to prostitution. Local social purists called for practical intervention to prevent the spread of vice, while other organizations offered shelter and moral education under one roof. The Liverpool House of Help, a Victorian institution that survived well into the twentieth century, offered a combination of refuge and moral guardianship. Established in 1890, the home grew from a midnight mission that had been held in the schoolroom of St Matthew's church in Toxteth, an inner-city district of Liverpool, the previous year.[6] The House of Help offered temporary shelter to women and girls in need, some of whom also had young children and infants with them. The House helped women who found themselves lost, stranded or in financial difficulty, with typical cases including young runaways, domestic servants who suddenly found themselves unemployed and women who had missed trains to other parts of the country. Conflating the moral and physical well-being of these girls and women, the House of Help maintained traditional gender distinctions in its pursuit of urban welfare and moral reform. Save for the emblematic presence of male civic and religious figures as patrons and vice presidents, the House of Help was run mainly by women for women.[7] The female-centric nature of the organizing committee was born from the House's interest in 'issues affecting women and children, particularly those of health and morality'.[8]

The culture of the House of Help was matched in virtuosity by its strict adherence to rules and order. During the early part of the twentieth century it was made clear to women at the House that those who ran the home considered themselves to be moral role-models who intended to be emulated in decorum and values by the women and girls in their care. Well into the interwar years, the sense of social superiority about the workers at the refuge continued to leak out through the House's references to helping the 'destitute and unfortunate', the 'waifs and strays of

6   *Liverpool Mercury*, 8 December 1891.
7   Gaynor Diane Williams, 'Women in Public Life in Liverpool between the Wars', PhD thesis, University of Liverpool, 2000, p. 97.
8   Gaynor Diane Williams, 'Women in Public Life', p 97.

our city', and those who were 'victims of their **own** and **other's** sin and folly'.[9] To this end, the Victorian and Edwardian reformatory cultures of aligning material deprivation with moral fallibility proved to be remarkably enduring.[10]

Religious belief was both an important motivation and a source of authority for welfare workers in early twentieth-century Liverpool. In the years prior to the First World War, moralists in Liverpool expressed their concern for the welfare of working-class women by appealing to the religious imperative underpinning their work. The House of Help shared the support of religious patrons, such as the Church of England Lord Bishop of Liverpool, with other organizations like the LVA. Though Liverpool had a reputation for religious sectarianism, Krista Cowman argues that 'religion was not always a divisive factor in women's politics', nor, I would add, in women's philanthropy.[11] The board membership of the House of Help did tend to feature Protestant figures in prominent roles, but Catholic representatives were not discouraged from helping in the fight against vice, no doubt because Irish Catholic young women were considered to be some of the most morally vulnerable.[12] While there can be no doubt that the House of Help offered an important service for women in need, with their help came an education in Christian morality. In 1918, the House of Help included a prayer in its annual report, asking Jesus Christ to 'bless the endeavours of those who are seeking Thy lost sheep, in the wilderness of this sinful world'.[13] Here, the House of Help articulated through religious discourse the notion that working-class women struggled to navigate urban life without becoming lost or fallen, a theme that was common in philanthropic approaches to working-class women in early and mid-twentieth-century Liverpool.

9   House of Help, Annual Report 1933, p. 12 (original emphasis). Liverpool Record Office, 362/HOU/3/42.

10   See Jane Hamlett's work on the use within Victorian and Edwardian institutions of domestic routine and cleanliness to teach moral order. Jane Hamlett, *At Home in the Institution: Material Life in Asylums, Lodging Houses and Schools in Victorian and Edwardian England* (Basingstoke: Palgrave Macmillan, 2015), pp. 160–1.

11   Krista Cowman, *Mrs Brown is a Man and a Brother!*, p. 18.

12   See Chapters 7 and 8.

13   House of Help, Annual Report 1918, p. 2.

The Liverpool Vigilance Association

Links between social purists, local political figures and Christian religious leaders concerned about urban immorality had been driving forces in the creation of the LVA. Though the organization promoted itself as 'Non Sectarian', the initial meetings to establish vigilance work in the city appear to have been inclined more towards Protestantism, with guests at meetings including the Anglican Lord Bishop of Liverpool and his wife, and the Church of England Reverend John Wakeford.[14] However, it should be noted that while the Chairman of the LVA would become a role routinely held by the Church of England Rector of Liverpool, Catholic Archbishops were regularly given roles as Vice Presidents of the organization, indicating a degree of religious co-operation and a desire to be able to influence as many working-class women as possible.[15]

In late 1907, just months before the establishment of a local branch in the city, the National Vigilance Association (NVA) called a meeting in Liverpool to discuss the trafficking of women lured into prostitution via Liverpool's docks and wider transport links. Though the threat of 'white slavery' was exaggerated in Liverpool, fears about young white women being kidnapped and coerced into prostitution nonetheless provoked anxiety about the vulnerabilities of the city's young women.[16] Hosted in a drawing room at the Liverpool Town Hall, the Deputy Lord Mayor, Alderman Menlove, presided over the meeting in place of the Lord Mayor. Other notable local figures in attendance included the Lady Mayoress, a number of religious figures and the Hon. J.L. Griffiths, the American Consul in Liverpool.[17]

The discussion that occurred at the meeting made it clear that domesticity was still the gold standard of British femininity and the bedrock upon which social order was to be maintained. Full of support for the NVA's campaign against vice, the American Consul, Griffiths, believed that the NVA's work spoke directly to his wider fears about the moral degradation of

14   LVA Papers, 'Historical Notes', undated, Liverpool Record Office, 326 VIG/9; NVA Charity Dinner Notice, 5 November 1908. See LVA, Newspaper cuttings. Liverpool Record Office, M326 VIG/5/1.

15   See the committee listings in the LVA's Annual Reports 1916–75. Liverpool Record Office, M326 VIG/3.

16   For more on white slavery in Liverpool, see Chapters 5 and 6.

17   *Liverpool Daily Post*, 19 October 1907. See LVA, Newspaper cuttings. Liverpool Record Office, M326 VIG/5/1.

modern society. He argued that 'Civilisation … rested upon the sanctity of the home, the innocence of childhood, and the purity of womanhood.'[18] To 'Destroy that sanctity, innocence, and purity' would, he argued, bring about 'chaos'.[19] Concerned about the moral dangers of Liverpool's 'cheap attractive music-halls' and the 'well-dressed scoundrel[s]' who frequented such establishments for the purpose of luring girls into the 'maelstrom of vice', Griffiths played upon contemporary understandings of feminine naivety and urban contamination.[20] He feared that were it not for the crusades of organizations such as the NVA and its affiliates, even greater numbers of young women, especially those 'from the peace and quiet of the country', would become corrupted by the 'tumult and glamour of a great city'.[21] The peace of the home and the sanctity of the family were situated within this narrative as being at odds with urban lifestyles. If the countryside acted as a representation of an idyllic and unblemished domesticity then all the entertainment, noise, dirt, excitement and hedonism of the city stood for the imagined dangers of the public sphere.

The prevention of vice was about more than just stopping women from selling their bodies, it was about instilling confidence in the social order of the city by making sure that all of the women who lived, worked and travelled through Liverpool maintained their respectability. Drawing direct reference to the role of Liverpool in the white slave trade, Reverend John Wakeford spoke at the same meeting. He suggested that the NVA's agents 'had found that young girls were being waylaid on their way to Liverpool, and shipped from here to Buenos Ayres [*sic*] at £200 a head'.[22] Wakeford called for 'all the forces of Christian charity' to be pitted against the immorality of the traffickers and noted the importance of challenging organized trafficking through a counter-strategy.[23] The maintenance of women's morality was imagined as a crucial site in the battle to keep women out of the hands of would-be white slavers. Potential victims were crafted out of the young women who travelled in and out of Liverpool in search of

18   *Liverpool Courier*, 19 October 1907. See LVA, Newspaper cuttings. Liverpool Record Office, M326 VIG/5/1.
19   *Liverpool Courier*, 19 October 1907.
20   *Daily Dispatch*, 19 October 1907. See LVA, Newspaper cuttings. Liverpool Record Office, M326 VIG/5/1.
21   *Daily Dispatch*, 19 October 1907.
22   *Liverpool Daily Post*, 19 October 1907.
23   *Liverpool Daily Post*, 19 October 1907.

work, those who walked the streets in poor neighbourhoods and women who were thought to spend too much of their leisure time outside the family home. In this sense, the ongoing panic about young, white British girls becoming embroiled in an international vice ring was fuelled by the vigilance associations who tied concerns about trafficking to moral debates about the behaviour of young, working-class women in order to claim legitimacy and authority for themselves as protectors of *all* young women.

The proposed new LVA was to be an extension of their parent body's agenda.[24] The NVA had been formed in the wake of mass demonstrations in 1885 calling for a new Criminal Law Amendment Act to raise the age of consent (it rose to 16 as a result) and to give police more powers over brothel keepers. The moral protection of women against vice was at the centre of the NVA's campaign.[25] Outside of the NVA, there was debate amongst Victorian feminists about whether this moral protection would best be achieved by increased criminalization of prostitution or by non-legal efforts to challenge solicitation, with no one feminist perspective on the issue emerging.[26] Later, in the twentieth century, the LVA considered their work to have 'followed on from the wonderful work of Josephine Butler'.[27] A leading figure in the Victorian fight against the injustice of the Contagious Diseases Acts, which subjected women suspected of prostitution to physical examinations to check for venereal disease, Butler campaigned for the better treatment of prostitutes. However, the interventionist approach and imposition of morality favoured by the LVA makes their appropriation of Butler curious. Butler campaigned against the regulation of prostitution, but when the NVA took up its campaign against prostitution, it favoured greater regulation in law and the Association profiled the supposed immorality of working-class women in ways that were at odds with Butler's

---

24   LVA Papers, 'Notes on the Work of the Liverpool Vigilance Association for His Grace the Archbishop of York', undated, Liverpool Record Office, 326 VIG/9.
25   Frank Mort, *Dangerous Sexualities: Medico-Moral Politics in England since 1830*, 2nd edn (London: Routledge, 2000), pp. 81–2. See also Edward Bristow, *Vice and Vigilance: Purity Movements in Britain since 1700* (Dublin: Gill and Macmillan, 1977).
26   See Lise Shapiro Sanders, '"Equal Laws Based upon an Equal Standard": The Garrett Sisters, the Contagious Diseases Acts, and the Sexual Politics of Victorian and Edwardian Feminism Revisited', *Women's History Review*, 24:3 (2015), pp. 389–409.
27   LVA Papers, 'Notes on the Work of the Liverpool Vigilance Association for His Grace the Archbishop of York'.

approach.[28] Nevertheless, according to later members of the LVA, Butler had been a source of inspiration due to her campaign to 'get prostitutes treated as human beings with rights instead of creatures outside the law'.[29] Butler was also lauded for having 'forced a change in the attitude of public opinion' as a result of her 'serious attempts ... to deal with problems of sexual morality'. The members of the LVA acknowledged the gendered inequalities in Victorian attempts to tie the regulation of prostitution to efforts to control venereal disease, with control measures rendered 'entirely useless' because 'infected men [were] left untouched'.[30]

Yet the LVA still proceeded from the assumption that prostitution was a moral problem that represented a threat to all women and social order in general. In fact, even the Victorian feminist campaign against the Contagious Diseases Acts which so inspired the LVA had not been an entirely liberal affair grounded in achieving greater recognition of the rights of prostitutes. Some moral reformers voiced their disagreement with the Acts by arguing that they gave legitimacy to prostitution by making the trade in women's bodies safer for the men who wanted to buy them.[31] A continuation of the Victorian NVA's combined legal and moral approach to prostitution, the LVA conceived of the battle against vice as a battle against 'a girl's moral ruin'.[32]

From its inception, the LVA promoted the didactic potential of legislation and offered instruction on moral matters. In January 1908, a number of Liverpool's religious and political leaders met at the city's Town Hall in the company of NVA representatives. This time it was the Lady Mayoress who presided over the proceedings. The meeting had been called at the behest of the Liverpool branch of the Traveller's Aid Society to discuss the establishment of a local branch of the NVA in Liverpool.[33] In an effort to promote the virtues of his organization and cultivate support for the proposed Liverpool branch, the NVA National Secretary, William Alexander Coote, addressed those present. The 'object' of the new Association, he argued,

28   Julia Laite, *Common Prostitutes*, p. 123; Sheila Rowbotham, *Women in Movement: Feminism and Social Action* (London: Routledge, 1992), p. 96.
29   LVA Papers, 'Historical Notes'.
30   LVA Papers, 'Historical Notes'.
31   Julia Laite, *Common Prostitutes*, p. 7.
32   LVA Papers, 'Historical Notes'.
33   From an article in an unidentified Catholic newspaper, published 17 January 1908. See LVA, Newspaper cuttings. Liverpool Record Office, M326 VIG/5/1.

was to 'consolidate their work in Liverpool by placing qualified workers in the city to assist the local committee to look after girls who were leaving or arriving here from other parts of the world'.[34] Coote was subsequently praised for his 'wonderful spirit of earnestness and wisdom' by the Rector of Liverpool, who gave his full support to the initiative.[35]

The creation of a local branch proved popular with the other religious figures in attendance at the start-up meeting. The Anglican Reverend Canon Kempthorne volunteered his support, arguing that greater steps were needed in the 'organised attack upon a strongly organised evil – an organisation managed with Satanic ingenuity and persistency'.[36] Also in favour was the Catholic Reverend Father Pinnington, who took the opportunity to welcome the Liverpool branch 'on behalf of the Catholics of Liverpool'.[37] Pinnington echoed the concerns about the vulnerability of naive young women raised by Griffiths at the Town Hall meeting in late 1907, just three months prior. Pinnington commented that the formation of the Liverpool branch of the NVA had come at a time when Liverpool found itself increasingly playing host to 'simple and unsuspecting girls from country towns and villages', particularly those from rural Ireland.[38] With these girls in mind, Pinnington emphasized that the focus of the new local Vigilance Association should be on the uncorrupted, saveable girl. Though Pinnington acknowledged the efforts of organizations that dealt with the 'poor wrecks of humanity' and already 'fallen women', he stressed that the 'excellence of this Association consists in this – it is preventative'.[39] With these points having been discussed, support for the proposed local branch was unanimous, and Pinnington found himself appointed as a member on the new committee.

By the end of the meeting, a number of other significant local figures had been appointed to the board of the new Liverpool branch of the NVA. The Lord Mayor of Liverpool was made president, while the Mayors of Birkenhead, Bootle and Southport were appointed as vice presidents.[40]

34   *Liverpool Courier*, 11 January 1908. See LVA, Newspaper cuttings. Liverpool Record Office M326 VIG/5/1.
35   *Liverpool Courier*, 11 January 1908.
36   Unidentified Catholic newspaper, 17 January 1908. LVA, Newspaper cuttings.
37   Unidentified Catholic newspaper, 17 January 1908. LVA, Newspaper cuttings.
38   Unidentified Catholic newspaper, 17 January 1908. LVA, Newspaper cuttings.
39   Unidentified Catholic newspaper, 17 January 1908. LVA, Newspaper cuttings.
40   *Liverpool Courier*, 11 January 1908.

Others given positions on the committee included the Liverpool, Birkenhead, Bootle and Southport Mayoresses, the Reverend J. Collins Odgers, two Free Church Council representatives and a representative of the Travellers' Aid Society.[41] As Travelling Secretary of the NVA, Miss Edith Rose, 'one of the pioneers' of the vigilance movement, was also heavily involved in the activities of the Liverpool branch.[42] A recipient of the OBE following the First World War, Rose would go on to be an active member of the Liverpool branch.[43] Indeed, during the Second World War she was singled out for praise by the Rector of Liverpool, the Reverend Ambrose Reeves, who proclaimed that 'were it not for the untiring zeal and energy of Miss Rose it is difficult to see how the work of the Society could have been preserved these last years'.[44]

That the NVA was able to continue expanding into new, localized settings indicates the extent to which Victorian discourses about vice and female morality persisted into the twentieth century. Older strategies of moral welfare continued to shape legislative debate, particularly where prostitution was concerned. When the sensationalist journalist W.T. Stead, who had been part of the successful campaign to enact the 1885 Criminal Law Amendment Bill raising the age of consent to 16, was killed on the *Titanic* in 1912, his death gave a significant boost to a new, much-debated White Slave Traffic Bill; there were calls to enact the bill in tribute to his work.[45] When the bill was passed, in December 1912, the new Criminal Law Amendment, which included the NVA among its supporters, meant that those suspected of procuring women could be arrested without a warrant.[46] However, its clause that landlords must evict women convicted of prostitution in their dwellings was less welcomed amongst feminists.[47] Overall, the new Act's use against trafficking, which received much strategic support amongst social purity feminists, disappointed once it was enacted. Many women were concerned about the extent to which the Act simply gave police further

41   *Liverpool Courier*, 11 January 1908.

42   Untitled LVA notes on history of the National Vigilance Association, undated, 326 VIG/9.

43   LVA, Annual Report 1919–20, p. 2. Liverpool Record Office, M326 VIG/3.

44   LVA, Annual Report 1942–43, p. 2. Liverpool Record Office, M326 VIG/3.

45   Lucy Bland, *Banishing the Beast: Feminism, Sex and Morality* (London: Tauris Parke Paperbacks, 2001), pp. 297–8.

46   Lucy Bland, *Banishing the Beast*, p. 302.

47   Lucy Bland, *Banishing the Beast*, p. 302.

powers to increase their surveillance of prostitutes.[48] However, neither the NVA nor the LVA was overly concerned with the liberty of the prostitute in their battle against vice; rather their overriding concern was with the moral surveillance of women in public.

Both the NVA and LVA were united in the belief that moral education was key to maintaining respectability amongst working-class young women. In 1911, the *Catholic Herald* published an article entitled 'Dangers to Girls', in which the Catholic Bishop of Liverpool, the LVA's vice president, congratulated his organization as a 'class of charity superior to others'.[49] The elevated status he afforded the Association was born, according to the Bishop, from the vigilance workers' explicit interest in thwarting 'moral evil', a social problem for the 'community as well as the individual'. The article suggested that 'the soul affected by moral evil was more important than the body affected by physical evil'. Rather than expending energy on curative approaches that were likely to prove fruitless, it was argued that 'prevention' was needed in the form of 'moral training', instilling in 'the young' the virtues of honesty, purity and 'reverence to authority'.[50] For both the NVA and LVA, their own particular brand of moral custodianship was vital in this respect. The *Catholic Herald* article contrasted two classes of individuals that vigilance workers regularly encountered. The first group was made up of 'young women, innocent and virtuous, who, through necessity or otherwise, had to travel, and to whom danger came in the utter loneliness and helplessness of foreign cities, want of means and difficulties as to destination.'[51] Abroad in urban settings that were strange and new to them, it was felt that the innocence of these young women left them without the appropriate social and economic tools to negotiate the moral dangers presented by city life. According to social purists, the naivety of these young women left them open to unscrupulous characters who would seek to manipulate them, and it was in this regard that the article presented the second class of individuals dealt with by the vigilance workers. These were the 'victimisers – men and women of infamous character', who sought out 'the young and innocent' and 'determined to ruin [them]', and in fact 'cared very little if they ruined them body and soul'. Situating the fragility of

<hr>

48   Lucy Bland, *Banishing the Beast*, pp. 302–3.
49   *Liverpool Catholic Herald*, 21 October 1911. See LVA, Newspaper cuttings. Liverpool Record Office, M326 VIG 5/1.
50   *Liverpool Catholic Herald*, 21 October 1911.
51   *Liverpool Catholic Herald*, 21 October 1911.

feminine decency in opposition to such predatory characters, the LVA and its affiliated Christian supporters established themselves as moral arbiters, there to identify the good and the vulnerable and to protect them from the bad and impure. The LVA put late nineteenth-century moral welfare ideas into practice in the twentieth century. By their own estimations, members of the LVA worked morally and practically to prevent what they considered to be the pollution of female respectability in urban public spaces.

The Catholic Women's League

The LVA and the House of Help were not the only philanthropic organizations applying older ideas about class, gender and urban immorality to the lives and experiences of women in twentieth-century Liverpool. The Catholic Women's League (CWL) had been established in 1906 and in 1911, just three years after the LVA was formed, Liverpool got its own local branch of the CWL, focused on offering physical and moral protection to the city's Catholic women and girls. Caitríona Beaumont notes that the CWL did not involve itself in women's suffrage campaigning and the organization was careful to seek approval for policy matters from the upper echelons of the Catholic Church, meaning that it was essentially 'answerable to a male hierarchy'.[52] Moreover, despite its only stipulation being that members be Catholic, the culture of philanthropic intervention practised by the CWL meant that its membership was skewed towards middle-class women.[53]

When the Liverpool branch of the CWL was founded, the local organization quickly set about establishing itself as a key agency in maintaining the safe emigration of girls from Liverpool to other parts of the world. As part of this work, the Liverpool branch 'furnished a hostel under the care of the Sisters of Charity of St. Vincent de Paul', with 'shelter and supervision thus being afforded to Catholic girls while in Liverpool', and a matron accompanied groups of emigrants on boats bound for Canada in order to ensure their safe reception there.[54] Although they were concerned with the

52   Caitríona Beaumont, *Housewives and Citizens: Domesticity and the Women's Movement in England, 1928–64* (Manchester: Manchester University Press, 2013), p. 16.

53   Caitríona Beaumont, *Housewives and Citizens*, p. 17.

54   Catholic Women's League Liverpool Archdiocesan Branch, Twenty First Report, 1932, Liverpool Metropolitan Cathedral Archive, RAS/S3/1/ABC (Series 3, Box R7, File 9).

religion of those helped, the local CWL did not segregate themselves from non-Catholic welfare organizations in Liverpool. The LVA, the House of Help, CWL and, a little later, local Women Police Patrols, were all aware of and in contact with one another. During the interwar years, the CWL's Miss Walmsley sat concurrently on the committees of the LVA, the Women Police and the House of Help. Mrs Richard Yates, Secretary of the Liverpool Branch of the CWL, also spent time on the LVA Committee.

Even when the First World War 'necessarily brought Emigration activities to a standstill', other aspects of the CWL's work continued apace.[55] In many ways, the CWL actually 'gain[ed] momentum during the war years'.[56] In 1932, the committee recalled proudly that an 'account of the League's work in Liverpool would not be complete unless some mention were made of the work done during the years of the Great War'.[57] It was noted that the CWL helped over 276 Belgian refugees between August 1914 and March 1919 and that a total of £741 was raised for their care. As a direct result of the CWL's work, these refugees were given shelter in convents and in the private homes of families, and houses were loaned to them.[58] The CWL was also involved in work with soldiers. The CWL's Liverpool, Salford and Preston Joint Hut Committee funded a £1,300 Chapel and Soldiers' Recreation Hut at Yorkshire's Catterick Camp, with 'most of the workers being drawn from Liverpool and district'.[59] Additionally, 'Some members worked in the C.W.L. Huts in France' and the 'china for the first C.W.L. Hut at Boulogne was provided by the Liverpool Branch'.[60] CWL members also visited military hospitals and distributed clothing to the men at the Front ('over 500 pairs of socks were sent in the first year of the War').[61]

For the women of the CWL, tending to the welfare of refugees and soldiers allowed them to participate in the war effort without unsettling gendered codes of citizenship, which defined fighting as a masculine endeavour. Active and organized in their willingness to help, the women of

55   CWL Liverpool Archdiocesan Branch, Twenty First Report, 1932.
56   Letter to Mrs Ryan on the history of the CWL, from the CWL Liverpool Branch, dated 8 December 1977. Liverpool Metropolitan Cathedral Archive, RAS/S3/1/ABC (Series 3, Box R7, File 9).
57   CWL Liverpool Archdiocesan Branch, Twenty First Report, 1932.
58   CWL Liverpool Archdiocesan Branch, Twenty First Report, 1932.
59   CWL Liverpool Archdiocesan Branch, Twenty First Report, 1932.
60   CWL Liverpool Archdiocesan Branch, Twenty First Report, 1932.
61   CWL Liverpool Archdiocesan Branch, Twenty First Report, 1932.

the CWL set about redeploying the feminine skills of the domestic sphere in service to the nation. Just four days after war was declared, the Liverpool branch of the CWL opened a Women's War Service Bureau, a centre where women could go to volunteer to help in the war effort.[62] Volunteers made clothes for refugees and rolled bandages, while maternity packages were provided for the wives of servicemen. The Bureau was also used to employ the services of the 'unfortunate' women who had lost their regular employment as a result of the war; these women used their skills in 'work rooms' where they made shirts, suits and hospital dressing gowns to order.[63] Significantly, then, the CWL supported the employment of working-class women and were 'deeply concerned' about the plight of unemployed women.[64] However, the CWL's employment of women was more about recognizing the economic necessity of women's work rather than an attempt to shift perceptions of women's capabilities. Women's movement from the domestic to the public sphere was tied to fears that the war was eroding all sense of sexual morality in urban space. Therefore, by occupying women in ways that utilized supposedly *feminine* skills, the CWL's activities did not significantly challenge traditional gender roles.

Women Police Patrols

Though some female moral welfare workers were trying to challenge traditional gender roles insofar as they wanted to see their own work professionalized, their work did not necessarily challenge restrictive gender roles where other women were concerned. So powerful were concerns about the habits and vulnerabilities of local women that Liverpool's own Women Police Patrols, formed in direct response to the war, had more in common with social purists and religious charitable workers than with the city's official (male) police force. Established in November 1914, using 'large numbers' of female volunteers, the work of the Liverpool Women Police Patrols indicates the degree to which moral supervision of the streets was felt to be necessary during wartime conditions.[65] In all, 69 women

---

62   Untitled CWL Notes, undated, Liverpool Metropolitan Cathedral Archive, RAS/S3/1/ABC (Series 3, Box R7, File 9).
63   Untitled CWL Notes, undated, Liverpool Metropolitan Cathedral Archive.
64   Untitled CWL Notes, undated, Liverpool Metropolitan Cathedral Archive.
65   Liverpool Women Police Patrols, Annual Report 1933, p. 5. Liverpool Record Office, 365 WOM/18/1–19.

undertook wartime patrol work with the Liverpool Women Police.[66] Initially, the Liverpool patrols began in conjunction with the National Council of Women and were funded partly by the National Union of Women's Suffrage Societies and partly by public donations.[67] Concern about the sexual behaviour of young women drove the creation of the patrols. In 1915, the Birkenhead Sub-Committee of the Patrols explained that the work had been started owing to the 'presence of so many girls in the neighbourhood of newly formed camps'.[68] It was suggested that this had led to 'undesirable conduct' from the girls, 'many of them quite young…[and] excited by the unaccustomed presence of many soldiers and recruits'.[69] As a result, the Women Police Patrols were part of the wider process, also supported by the likes of the LVA and the CWL, of defining acceptable public womanhood in narrow terms that typically excluded working-class women. Where working-class young women frequented the streets, their sense of morality and decorum was viewed with suspicion; where middle-class, philanthropic women patrollers walked the streets, they retained their sense of respectability by virtue of their self-styled function as the apparently sobering antidote to the frivolousness of young, working-class women.

Armed with a card bearing the Chief Constable's signature, a map, a guidebook, an armlet and a badge, Liverpool's Women Police patrolled working-class areas such as Scotland Road, an area of poverty with a significant Irish Catholic population.[70] It should be noted that although the Women Police did also venture into the more middle-class area of Blundellsands, much of their time patrolling was spent monitoring the city's public transport districts close to the Landing Stage and Lime Street train station, the docklands and around various military camps in places

---

66   Gaynor Diane Williams, 'Women in Public Life', p. 123.

67   Liverpool Women Police Patrols, Annual Report 1933, p. 3.

68   National Union of Women Workers, Birkenhead Patrol Sub-Committee, Report for 1914–15, Liverpool Record Office, H364/5 (719) WOM.

69   National Union of Women Workers, Birkenhead Patrol Sub-Committee, Report for 1914–15.

70   Charlotte Wildman notes that many Irish immigrants chose to settle in this area, despite levels of material deprivation, because of the social support networks that existed among the Irish community there. See Charlotte Wildman, *Urban Redevelopment and Modernity in Liverpool and Manchester, 1918–1939* (London: Bloomsbury, 2016), p. 169. For more on this community, see also Pat O'Mara, *The Autobiography of a Liverpool Slummy* (Liverpool: Bluecoat Press, 1994).

like Litherland, Seaforth and Knotty Ash.[71] In addition to patrolling, the Women Police Patrols sought to ingratiate themselves into the domestic lives of working-class parents and children. In the course of their work they offered counselling to local parents, performed home visits and helped vulnerable girls into hostels.[72] Consequently, their approach had much more in common with the strategies of surveillance practised by social purity groups than it did with official police work. Just as the NVA performed unofficial duties that complemented the activities of the Metropolitan Police in London, women police in Liverpool operated in a similar way to female-dominated purity organizations, such as the LVA, in their work alongside the Liverpool police force.[73]

It was not unusual for the Women Police Patrols to rely on the same welfare networks as the LVA.[74] Due to their shared interest in monitoring the presence of women as they moved through Liverpool, the Women Police Patrols were aware of and in contact with the LVA: Edith Rose, Secretary of the LVA, sat on the Women Police Patrol's Committee throughout the interwar years.[75] Indeed, a number of local figures interested in cultivating their standing as philanthropists took up board positions in both organizations. Sir J. Sandeman Allen MP was both vice-chairman of the LVA and a member of the Women Police Patrol's General Council, and both organizations also shared the support of a number of high status figures drawn from the local religious community. The President of the Free Church Council was a vice president of the LVA and Women Police Patrols, as was the Reverend Frampton, a senior Jewish minister. Additionally, the Anglican Lord Bishop of Liverpool and the Roman Catholic Archbishop of Liverpool took up vice president roles in both organizations.[76]

71   Gaynor Diane Williams, 'Women in Public Life', p. 123.
72   Gaynor Diane Williams, 'Women in Public Life', p. 123.
73   Gaynor Diane Williams, 'Women in Public Life', p. 121.
74   Liverpool Women Police Patrols, Annual Report 1928, p. 2. Liverpool Record Office, 365 WOM/18/1–19.
75   See Liverpool Women Police Patrols, Annual Reports, Liverpool Record Office, 365 WOM/18/1–19.
76   See Liverpool Women Police Patrols, Annual Report 1928 and LVA, Annual Report 1928–29, Liverpool Record Office, M326 VIG/3. This plethora of religious representation suggests that, despite being influenced by Judeo-Christian moral traditions, women's preventative work in Liverpool was not necessarily used to promote or convert those that were 'saved'.

Re-establishing Gender Boundaries During the War

Together, the organizations examined in this chapter were careful to ameliorate concern about changes in women's lives in ways that tacitly reinforced the link between respectable femininity and the domestic sphere. For the NVA, the social conditions of the First World War exacerbated the problem of moral laxity and, as a result, they took to their preventative patrol work with young women with renewed vigour. In 1916, the Liverpool branch proudly informed readers of its annual report of the 'godly work' carried out by the organization. Maintaining watches over the city's main transport stations – the Landing Stage at the docks and Lime Street train station – its report noted that the LVA workers were on hand to investigate the circumstances of women as they arrived in Liverpool.[77] Full of pride about their war work, the LVA reflected in 1920 on their efforts to maintain women's morality under difficult conditions during the war. They argued that although the number of travellers passing through Liverpool had been 'much reduced' by the 'special conditions and difficulties' of war, their Landing Stage and railway station patrols 'had regularly to be maintained'.[78]

During the war, women across the classes worked in support of the war effort and in support of their families while their husbands were enlisted.[79] Women's war work challenged spatial distinctions between 'home' and the 'front'.[80] Judy Giles suggests that 'Financial independence, increased job opportunities, educational opportunities and the mobilities occasioned by the First World War had made women visible as never before in the public spaces of all large cities.'[81] As women entered these new sectors of social and economic life, the networks that they used to negotiate city spaces expanded. Susan Kingsley Kent argues that by 1915 women's active

---

77   LVA, Annual Report 1916, p. 2. Liverpool Record Office, M326 VIG/3.

78   LVA, Annual Report 1919–20, p. 2.

79   David Monger, 'Nothing Special? Propaganda and Women's Roles in Late First World War Britain', *Women's History Review*, 23:4 (2014), pp. 518–42; Deborah Thom, *Nice Girls and Rude Girls: Women Workers in World War I* (London: IB Tauris Publishers, 1998); Angela Woollacott, *On Her Their Lives Depend: Munitions Workers in the Great War* (Berkeley: University of California Press, 1994).

80   Krisztina Robert, 'Constructions of "Home", "Front", and Women's Military Employment in First World War Britain: A Spatial Interpretation', *History and Theory*, 52 (2013), pp. 319–43.

81   Judy Giles, *Women, Identity and Private Life in Britain, 1900–50* (London: Macmillan, 1995), p. 102.

participation in the war effort had begun to threaten the 'perceived gender system of the Victorian and Edwardian periods'.[82] Distinctions between prostitute women and working-class women were increasingly difficult to sustain. Across the classes, women were entering public spaces as shoppers and patrons of entertainment venues. In moving around in new ways and seeking out new opportunities, women challenged and changed the meanings attached to particular spaces, destabilizing previously held assumptions and the presumed absolutisms about the gendered nature of the city. This proved to be an 'exhilarating' experience, particularly for many middle-class women.[83] The public and private distinction that had once confined them to the domestic sphere was partly undermined.[84]

Certainly, the war enabled women to move into areas of work that had previously been closed to them. Marwick's argument that the war dramatically accelerated societal recognition of women's capabilities is based upon his assessment of the large increases in women working in non-traditional employment. He notes, for example, that the number of women working in transport in 1914 stood at 18,000; by 1918 there were 117,000 women working in this area.[85] But this experience was not universal. The situation in Liverpool suggests that we must not overstate the extent to which women's wartime participation within the public sphere was welcomed or encouraged. In Liverpool there were complaints about employers' reluctance to recruit women into non-traditional occupations, or even into traditional occupations if the women applicants were over 25 years of age. Emma Mahler, of the Liverpool Women's Industrial Council and the Women's Employment department at the Soldiers' and Sailors' Families Association, publicly complained in 1915 that there 'does not seem to be the much-spoken-of demand for women as well as for girls in Liverpool'.[86] In the same month, a member of the public wrote to the *Liverpool Echo* to protest, 'I do not think it is too much to say that the majority of employers in Liverpool have made no sustained and serious effort to use the female labour in unaccustomed occupations.'[87]

---

82   Susan Kingsley Kent, *Gender and Power in Britain, 1640–1990* (London: Routledge, 1999), p. 277.
83   Judy Giles, *Women, Identity and Private Life in Britain*, p. 102.
84   Judy Giles, *Women, Identity and Private Life in Britain*, p. 102.
85   Arthur Marwick, *The Deluge*, p. 131.
86   Emma Mahler, letter to *Liverpool Echo*, 14 October 1914.
87   Anon., letter to *Liverpool Echo*, 6 October 1915.

When, on 3 November 1915, the *Liverpool Echo* reported that the city was finally to get female tram conductors due to war conditions having 'overcome all opposition', the local newspaper explained that the Trams Committee had hoped to avoid this measure not because of 'antipathy towards women' but because Liverpool was 'considered a difficult city for tram traffic, calling for cool heads at both ends of the car'.[88] The notion that a woman was as capable of performing this job as a man was not readily or easily accepted by local officials, who still subscribed to the belief that women were inherently more emotional and less rational than men. Moreover, where women were able to find war work in munitions this only added to concerns about the numbers of transient, young, working-class women arriving in Liverpool. Although the emigration work of the CWL was largely put on hold during the war, calls for munitions workers meant that Irish young women continued to flow into the city. In 1916, the CWL opened a 'Residential Club' to provide accommodation for these workers. Providing refuge for Catholic women workers and travellers was to be a key part of the CWL's philanthropic work within the community.[89]

The war had a direct impact upon the lived experience of city spaces, with the movement of women between different parts of the country and even between different neighbourhoods coming under increasing scrutiny. According to the LVA, the war years induced girls to 'abnormal excitement ... accentuated the moral dangers [and] made special vigilance necessary for the safeguarding of girls and young women'.[90] As much as young women endeavoured to traverse the city with greater purpose and confidence, social purists, philanthropists and even concerned members of the public considered the war to present particular urban problems and moral difficulties. In October 1915, one citizen wrote to the *Liverpool Echo* to note how the drawing in of the winter nights, when combined with lighting restrictions, had left the city feeling like 'an unknown country. Familiar streets and buildings take on weird unaccustomed shapes. The few lighted street lamps only seem to make the darkness visible, and one has not a little difficulty ascertaining where one is.' In search of a silver

88   'Women on the Cars', *Liverpool Echo*, 3 November 1915.
89   The Residential Club had closed in 1919, but just two years later another hostel was opened. It remained open until 1959. See letter to Mrs Ryan on the history of the CWL, from the CWL Liverpool Branch, dated 8 December 1977.
90   LVA, Annual Report 1919–20, p. 2.

lining, the letter-writer hoped that the darkness would at least keep young women off the streets, reasoning 'It is considered "not nice" for young girls to be out in such conditions', meaning that 'Miss Flapper' had to 'be in much earlier than she used to be'.[91] The condescending reference to Miss Flapper emphasized the extent to which young women were thought to be naive to the dangers of wandering in public. According to the letter-writer, it was only once the city had become so dark as to feel alien, for negotiation of the streets to have become so utterly impractical, that the Flapper would return to the safety of her home.

While middle-class women, especially those engaged in philanthropy and efforts to maintain the moral welfare of the working class, considered themselves able to handle their increased urban freedom with their integrity intact, the women that they identified as being most at risk of moral degradation were less empowered by changes in women's use of public space. The Liverpool experience indicates that alongside changing social practices sat scepticism about working-class women's ability to traverse public space without losing their sense of moral virtue. The idea that promiscuous women were setting negative examples to other women and thereby threatening the war effort began to permeate the thinking of social purity campaigners and the public. From the outset, the war generated concerns about young, working-class women's sexual interest in the soldiers. Training bases had been established in a number of towns and cities, meaning that men in uniform were now highly visible. A wave of panic surrounding young women's efforts sexually to 'entice dutiful and sober soldier-men' in a frenzy of 'khaki fever' illustrated the extent of Britain's cultural anxiety about the immoral practices of its youth.[92] Angela Woollacott has argued that, for young women keen to help with the war effort but with no actual outlet for their patriotic desires, khaki fever became a vicarious means of getting involved in what was happening.[93] Nevertheless, the power that these young women were perceived to have over soldiers seemed to represent a perversion of patriotic national pride.

Khaki fever girls were considered 'blatant, aggressive and overt in their

---

91   Letter to *Liverpool Echo*, 11 October, 1915.
92   Philippa Levine, '"Walking the Streets in a Way no Decent Woman Should": Women Police in World War I', *Journal of Modern History*, 66 (1994), p. 43.
93   Angela Woollacott, '"Khaki Fever" and its Control: Gender, Class, Age and Sexual Morality on the British Homefront in the First World War', *Journal of Contemporary History*, 29 (1994), pp. 325–47.

harassment of soldiers'.[94] Their active, predatory female sexual agency threatened established gender codes and produced new categories of sexual transgression, as the boundaries between promiscuity and prostitution became less and less distinct.[95] The excesses of youth and leisure were hypersexualized by onlookers concerned about effects of the war upon British social order. Alex Rock notes that, in London, cinemas functioned as sites where the moral panic about khaki fever could be played out, both by the young, working-class patrons of these venues and by the social purists who identified cinemas as dark, closely confined spaces of dangerous excitement.[96] In Liverpool, suspicion surrounded the young women who made the acquaintance of soldiers. One worried citizen wrote to the *Liverpool Echo* to complain about girls who would walk for miles to soldiers' camps to 'make eyes at the boys'.[97] With respectable womanhood tied to notions of sexual purity, the libidinous behaviour of these girls was used to signal insolence and ill-discipline among young women. The letter claimed that warning young women against immorality only encouraged them to pursue the soldiers more fervently.[98]

It was amid this climate that the LVA argued that wartime social conditions and a loosening of morals had made it all the more necessary for them to patrol the urban landscape. Far from rendering the gender and class ideologies of Victorian philanthropy and social purity obsolete, the war allowed associations between working-class women, prostitution and wider social disorder to be publicly rearticulated. Although social purists and moralists in Liverpool had to tailor their work to wartime conditions, they remained resolute in their fears about the potential for young, working-class women to become corrupted by the iniquity of urban spaces. In 1916, the LVA noted, 'During the War our work at this Port has greatly increased as we have been specially privileged to continue it without hinderance.' With 'cordial assistance' from 'Cunard, White Star, American Line, Allan Line, Canadian and Pacific Railway, Pacific and Royal Mail, Irish and other

94   Angela Woollacott, '"Khaki Fever" and its Control', p. 326.
95   Helen J. Self, *Prostitution, Women and Misuse of the Law: The Fallen Daughters of Eve* (London: Frank Cass, 2003), p. 53.
96   Alex Rock, 'The "Khaki Fever" Moral Panic: Women's Patrols and the Policing of Cinemas in London, 1913–19', *Early Popular Visual Culture*, 12:1 (2014), pp. 57–72.
97   Letter to *Liverpool Echo*, 30 March 1915.
98   Letter to *Liverpool Echo*, 30 March 1915.

Shipping Companies, the Mersey Dock Board' and the local authorities, the patrollers met with women arriving at and leaving the city for other parts of the world. Out of the 1,280 women helped in 1916, 780 were under the age of 21, a figure that excluded a smaller number of young children aged between 3 and 13 travelling alone under the watch of 'officials on board the ship or at the station'.[99]

Concerned that young women would not always take the help and advice on offer, the LVA patrollers were shrewd and persistent in their approach. When one vigilance patroller met two young women disembarking from an Irish boat on their way to a Midlands munitions factory, she made it her duty to prevent them from fulfilling their intention to continue on their journey in the company of soldiers who they had met on the boat.[100] Approaching the soldiers, rather than the young women, the patroller made sure that they 'promised that they would not detain the girls on the journey', a guarantee that they apparently upheld.[101] That the worker approached the servicemen in this case speaks to the extent to which young women were thought to be enthralled by soldiers. It was assumed that the young women would not listen to the vigilance worker and, as such, it was considered easier to appeal to the respectability of the men in uniform.

In a similar case from the same year, an LVA patroller intervened in the journey of two Irish girls, aged 17 and 14, who arrived in Liverpool from the Holyhead train in the company of a soldier and a sailor.[102] Rather than attempting to stop the girls herself, the patroller asked the ticket collector to 'detain the girls and allow the men to go on'.[103] With local port and railway co-operation often aiding the LVA in their duties, the ticket collector carried out the request.[104] Once alone, the vigilance worker spoke to the girls and found that they were 'most indignant and refused to give any information at first'.[105] After a time the younger girl confessed that they had met the men at Holyhead. Despite having tickets to Manchester, where they had

<hr>

99   LVA, Annual Report 1916, pp. 2–3.
100   LVA, Annual Report 1917–18, p. 6. Liverpool Record Office, M326 VIG/3.
101   LVA, Annual Report 1917–18, p. 6.
102   LVA, Annual Report 1917–18, p. 9.
103   LVA, Annual Report 1917–18, p. 9.
104   The LVA suggested that their work was appreciated by 'Shipping Offices Staff, the Railway Staff, and the Police, as well as by the travelling public'. LVA, Annual Report 1927–28, p. 5. Liverpool Record Office, M326 VIG/3.
105   LVA, Annual Report 1917–18, p. 9.

originally intended to stay in a house where the elder girl worked, the girls had taken the men up on an offer to travel with them to Liverpool. With the girls separated from the sailor and solider, the vigilance worker was able to see them on the train to Manchester, but not before 'talking seriously to them'.[106] For the LVA, these incidents were a clear indication that young women were too ready to make the acquaintance of servicemen.

This extra sexual agency afforded to promiscuous young women during the war gave added impetus to the idea that uncontrolled female sexual desire threatened social order. With wartime propaganda promoting images of 'patriotic motherhood' (the notion that the domesticated mother figure could and should sustain the nation's military), female citizenship was still defined primarily in relation to women's roles within the private sphere.[107] Alongside the image of the British Tommy as a chivalrous protector of women and the home sat his feminine counterpart, the dutiful, virtuous and domesticated woman.[108] Female permissiveness was therefore situated in direct opposition to military success, with sexually adventurous women and prostitutes blamed for the number of soldiers suffering from venereal diseases. In contrast, the military absolved soldiers from blame for using the services of prostitutes because it was felt that men physically needed sexual release in ways that women did not; the women were believed to be taking advantage of this weakness in men's nature.[109]

During the war the government took legislative action aimed at maintaining a clear boundary between *respectable* women and those who were thought to present sexual and moral dangers to the troops. Under Regulation 13a of the Defence of the Realm Act 1914 (DORA), a woman convicted of 'a prostitution-related offence' was not permitted to enter 'the vicinity of any place where His Majesty's Troops were stationed'.[110] Moreover, alongside the common prostitute, her close relative the 'promiscuous woman' was also targeted. When Regulation 40d of DORA made it a crime for a woman to solicit or have sex with a serviceman if she suffered

106   LVA, Annual Report 1917–18, p. 9.
107   For more on 'patriotic motherhood', see Nicoletta Gullace, *The Blood of Our Sons*, chapter 3.
108   Nicoletta Gullace, *The Blood of Our Sons*, p. 54.
109   For more on the acceptability of soldiers' use of prostitutes, see Clare Makepeace, 'Male Heterosexuality and Prostitution during the Great War', *Cultural and Social History*, 9:1 (2012), p. 67.
110   Julia Laite, 'The Association for Moral and Social Hygiene', p. 212.

from a venereal disease, it worked with the assumption that promiscuous women alone were responsible for sexual disease.[111] In this way regulations 40d and 13a of DORA recalled the sexual regulation and gender difference previously enacted by the controversial Contagious Diseases Acts of the 1860s.[112]

While the state sought to regulate female promiscuity with policy, on the ground social purists and moral welfare workers used the war to justify their interventions into the lives of young, working-class women. The Women Police Patrols and the patrollers in the LVA reacted to the social and spatial freedoms that women experienced as a result of the war. Indeed, the work of organizations like the LVA, the Women Police, the House of Help and the CWL set the tone for future decades of philanthropic work in Liverpool. Their activities and ideologies were at once complex and contradictory, with their efforts to facilitate safe female travel paradoxically underpinned by fundamental mistrust of working-class women's ability to comport themselves respectably. The moral codes proliferated by social purists and moral welfare organizations in early twentieth-century Liverpool did not merely weather the effects of the First World War upon British society; instead they found new expression and purchase, as British society was perceived to be under threat not just from the conflict abroad but also from immorality within. In an effort to distinguish themselves from the working-class women who they helped, Liverpool's women social purists and the Women Police Patrols attempted to assuage concern about their active,

111   Julia Laite, 'The Association for Moral and Social Hygiene', p. 212.

112   The Contagious Diseases Acts (CD Acts) did not apply in Liverpool. However, in 1871, it was reported by the *British Medical Journal* that there had been discussions amongst Liverpool's medical population about the potential merits of extending the CD Acts to 'the civil population'. The report suggested that there was no consensus on the issue, but it was noted that support for the regulation of prostitutes was in evidence amongst Liverpool medics. It was suggested that 'any well-devised … measure' with 'a reasonable prospect of diminishing the spread of syphilis amongst the community … would receive the support of at least a majority of the profession'. See 'The Contagious Diseases Acts', *British Medical Journal*, 1:538 (22 April 1871), p. 427. Moreover, it has been suggested that were it not for the success of the repeal campaign (and Liverpool being the hometown of repealer Josephine Butler), then the CD Acts would most likely have been extended to cover the city. See Philip Howell, David Beckingham and Francesca Moore, 'Managed Zones for Sex Workers in Liverpool: Contemporary Proposals, Victorian Parallels', *Transactions of the Institute of British Geographers*, New Series, 33 (2008), p. 238.

non-domesticated womanhood by reiterating their own respectability as caring women of higher social status. The LVA and Women Police Patrols were able to claim legitimacy as women in public on the basis that they were above the temptations of the street in ways that *ordinary* working-class women were not.

The LVA had clear links to earlier traditions of moral anxiety and social purity, while the House of Help continued to function as a reminder of late nineteenth-century attitudes towards the supposed moral fragility of the urban working class. Together with newer organizations like the CWL and the Women Police Patrols these agencies, set up primarily to look after the interests of other women, promoted cultures of surveillance and concern about women in public that undermined changing gender dynamics. This evidence of a long continuity of nineteenth-century moral welfarism in twentieth-century Liverpool does not necessarily mean that there was little new about the activities of those women who sought to influence the moral character of the streets. The Women Police Patrols attempted to fashion themselves in reference to contemporary debates about the professionalization of this type of women's work and the philanthropic work of social purists and welfare workers did, at least, promote the idea that *feminine* skills like caring, watchfulness and attentiveness could be utilized outside of the domestic sphere. Nevertheless, even where the Women Police were concerned, their gendered practice of street-patrolling and their discourses of urban female vulnerability were part of a much longer tradition of understanding public space as inimical to respectable femininity. The next chapter argues that these practices and discourses had real, ground-level, practical implications for women trying to make their way around Liverpool after the First World War. The notion that working-class women were morally vulnerable and under threat from white slavers and other dangerous characters when outside of the home meant that the interwar freedoms of urban working-class women were tempered by the maternal supervision of more respectable ladies engaged in philanthropic observation and intervention.

2

Patrolling the Port
Interwar Moral Surveillance

In early twentieth-century and interwar Liverpool, women's patrol work was used as an important means of morally policing the city's public spaces. Both the LVA and the Women Police Patrols sent women patrollers out onto the streets in a bid to deter misbehaviour and maintain a sense of public order. The women who patrolled Liverpool's streets were afforded informal, though not legal, powers over the actions of young women who were thought to be in need of physical protection and good advice. Authoritative and respectable, the presence of these women patrollers was intended to prevent naive young women from engaging in disreputable sexual practices or venturing into notorious areas. Focusing on the practicalities of patrolling, observing and interacting with women deemed to be morally vulnerable, this chapter considers how social purists and moral welfare workers continued to view urban space as antithetical to respectable femininity even after the First World War was over.

Across the nation, idleness amongst the young, time spent socializing on the streets and the influence of glamorous aspects of consumer culture were seen as significant threats to morality. Yet this was more than a straightforward case of social elders fretting about the mores of youth. The questions asked of interwar teenagers and young adults were heavily gendered. Idealized notions of femininity still placed women in sexually passive roles within the domestic sphere. Apprehension about changes in young women's lifestyles, fears about a rise in promiscuity and a perceived rise in *amateur* prostitution all continued to be underpinned by the presumption that the boundary between the public and private spheres had to be maintained if social order were to be preserved.[1]

Though interwar society considered itself transformed from the comparatively strait-laced ideals of the Victorian era, the gendered notion of public and private spheres was reworked rather than abandoned after the war.[2] The nineteenth-century conceptualization of male and female realms in terms of public and private spheres had positioned respectable women in contradistinction to *street women*, who were defined as dangerous and transgressive.[3] Moreover, ideal notions of femininity had been defined in direct opposition to the prostitute.[4] In this regard, there was considerable continuity between interwar, cross-class gender ideals and late nineteenth-century ideas about gender. Andrew Davies suggests that in late-Victorian Manchester and Salford 'working-class notions of respectability incorporated central components of the middle-class ideal of womanhood'.[5] Though the middle-class ideal of domesticated womanhood was often at odds with the realities of working-class life, where many women needed to

1   See Philippa Levine, "Walking the Streets in a Way no Decent Woman Should", pp. 34–78; Samantha Caslin, 'Flappers, Amateurs and Professionals: The Spectrum of Promiscuity in 1920s Britain', in Kate Hardy, Sarah Kingston and Teela Sanders (eds), *New Sociologies of Sex Work* (Farnham: Ashgate Publishing, 2010), pp. 11–22. See also Susan Kingsley Kent, who has argued that the First World War and its impact on women's lifestyles challenged ongoing Victorian gender ideals. Kent, *Gender and Power in Britain*, p. 277.
2   Judy Giles, 'A Home of One's Own: Women and Domesticity in England 1918–1950', *Women's Studies International Forum*, 16:3 (1993), p. 244.
3   Caroline Arni and Claudia Honegger have argued that the separation of the public and private spheres, with women being assigned to the domestic sphere, has its origins before the Victorian period. They have suggested that the domestic role afforded to women came amid a '[f]ear of disintegration' following the social and intellectual changes wrought by the French Revolution. See Caroline Arni and Claudia Honegger, 'The Modernity of Women: Jenny P. d'Hericourt's Contribution to Social Theory (1809–1875)', *Journal of Classical Sociology*, 8:1 (2008), p. 60. However, though the distinction between the public and private spheres appeared prior to the Victorian period, what I am interested in examining here are the continuities between the way Victorian social purists understood this distinction and the way it was understood later, in the twentieth century.
4   See Judith Walkowitz, *City of Dreadful Delight*, p. 21.
5   Andrew Davies, '"These Viragoes are No Less Cruel than the Lads": Young Women, Gangs and Violence in Late Victorian Manchester and Salford', *British Journal of Criminology*, 39:1 (1999), p. 76.

work outside the home, the low status and low pay of non-skilled and semi-skilled work meant that marriage and domesticity still proved compelling even in the post-First World War age of the flapper and the modern woman.[6] Judy Giles argues that the consolidation of a working-class housewife identity after the First World War was brought about by working-class women themselves, as they sought legitimacy for and greater recognition of the homemaking labour that they performed.[7]

The story of Liverpool's street patrollers is not, therefore, simply one of middle-class women subordinating working-class girls with archaic, moral ideas about distinctions between public and private. The patrollers afforded themselves a special role in renegotiating the limits of public and private morality, and the women that they interacted with were often receptive to the domestic message because it genuinely appealed to them. Nevertheless, organizations like the LVA and Women Police Patrols were not concerned with the construction of new forms of working-class female agency. Though they considered themselves to be able to stand strong against the moral dangers of public life, these organizations showed no such confidence in young, working-class women.

According to these organizations, the increasing presence and visibility of young women in public space undermined female virtue. In an effort to strengthen moral order, vulnerable, young, working-class women were encouraged to retreat into feminine positions in domestic service and the ideal of domesticated womanhood was reasserted.[8] Nationally, various housewives' associations and middle-class philanthropists avoided the political feminism of suffrage-orientated societies and instead sought to enhance the social status of women by emphasizing the importance of women's domestic work to wider society.[9] In Liverpool, moral philanthropists and social purists sought to re-establish themselves after the First World War as key stakeholders in the maintenance of social order, presenting themselves as having particular expertise in holding the immoral tendencies of the working class in check. Street patrollers in the LVA and

---

6 Lucy Bland, *Modern Women on Trial: Sexual Transgression in the Age of the Flapper* (Manchester: Manchester University Press, 2013). For more on the importance of women's work to family economics, see Selina Todd, *Young Women, Work, and Family in England 1918–1950* (Oxford: Oxford University Press, 2005).

7 Judy Giles, 'A Home of One's Own', p. 245.

8 Susan Kingsley Kent, *Gender and Power in Britain*, pp. 298–9.

9 Caitríona Beaumont, *Housewives and Citizens*, pp. 33–4.

Women Police Patrols monitored public spaces for signs of indiscretion and female vulnerability, while other organizations such as the CWL and the Liverpool House of Help reinforced and supplemented this particular brand of urban morality by diverting young women's attentions away from immoral influences. The local branch of the CWL attempted to cleanse Liverpool's urban spaces of signs of indecency, while the House of Help was ready to offer accommodation and domesticated moral guidance to women directed to their refuge by workers from the LVA, the Women Police Patrols and other organizations within the city.

Though their patrols were distinct from one another, the presence of both women police and the LVA patrollers on the streets of Liverpool during the interwar period suggests that there was a significant degree of shared concern about the moral order of the city's public spaces. Collectively, these organizations promoted a specific moral optic, and their watchfulness on the streets enacted a distinctive form of control over the activities of young women. By drawing associations between the welfare of women travelling through the docks and on the rail network, the moral dangers of promiscuity, and both amateur and professional prostitution, patrollers set themselves up as bastions of purity in Liverpool. The influence of these women's organizations over Liverpool's urban spaces served to reaffirm the notion that the city landscape posed very real threats to the moral purity of young, working-class women.

Urban Danger

After the war, cities were increasingly imagined as sites of hedonistic consumerism with the potential to destabilize traditional gender behaviours and moral codes. Notions of the 'modern woman' and the 'flapper' came to symbolize the habits of fashionable ladies with keen interests in leisure pursuits, such as visiting dance halls, going to the theatre and smoking.[10]

---

10   Lucy Bland, 'The Trials and Tribulations of Edith Thompson: The Capital Crime of Sexual Incitement in 1920s England', *Journal of British Studies*, 47:3 (2008), p. 628. Also, Laura Doan has noted that the term 'flapper' was used in the 1890s to refer to a young prostitute. This shift in the word's definition illustrates the extent to which boundaries between prostitute women and other women had become less distinct by the early twentieth century. See Laura Doan, 'Passing Fashions: Reading Female Masculinities in the 1920s', *Feminist Studies*, 24:3 (1998), p. 670.

Indeed, smoking increasingly became a part of female consumer culture during the interwar years.[11] Moreover, Adrian Bingham balances the poor representation of women in the House of Commons, discrimination in the workplace and the Restoration of Pre-War Practices Act (1919) against the opportunities available to women in the world of leisure and via public discourse about sexuality and birth control.[12]

Yet there was concern about the effects of these opportunities upon women's morality. Lucy Bland has examined how fears about the 'modern woman' coalesced around the sensational trials of Edith Thompson and Marguerite Fahmy who were each prosecuted for murder, in 1922 and 1923 respectively. Both fashionable women, Bland argues that Thompson was found guilty due to her supposed sexual excesses, while Fahmy was found not guilty because she had been represented by her defence as sexually passive and victimized.[13] Press discussion of the trials focused on the appearance of the defendants and on the way the female public seemed to be enthralled by the cases.[14] Women's interest in these fashionable women was, itself, a source of anxiety, as women used fashion to transgress and challenge established codes of social order. In 1934, the novelist J.B. Priestley notably observed that 'factory girls' had started to achieve the look of 'actresses'.[15] Carol Dyhouse argues that women's interest in fashion

11   Penny Tinkler, 'Rebellion, Modernity, and Romance: Smoking as a Gendered Practice in Popular Young Women's Magazines, Britain 1918–1939', *Women's Studies International Forum*, 24:1 (2001), pp. 111–22.

12   Adrian Bingham, '"An Era of Domesticity?" Histories of Women and Gender in Interwar Britain', *Cultural and Social History*, 1:2 (2004), pp. 227–8. However, Kate Fisher notes that advancements in birth control were not necessarily gender-progressive, with men often still taking responsibility for contraception in relationships and many couples still relying upon traditional methods. See Kate Fisher, *Birth Control, Sex, and Marriage in Britain 1918–1960* (Oxford: Oxford University Press, 2006), p. 5.

13   Lucy Bland, *Modern Women on Trial*, p. 213.

14   Lucy Bland, *Modern Women on Trial*, pp. 213–14.

15   See Rebecca Conway on J.B. Priestley in Rebecca Conway, 'Making the Mill Girl Modern?: Beauty, Industry, and the Popular Newspaper in 1930s England', *Twentieth Century British History*, 24:4 (2013), p. 519. Also, Liz Conor's conclusions about female visibility in 1920s Australia are applicable to Britain in this regard. She has argued that the flapper 'embodied the scandal attached to women's new public visibility' more than 'any other type of Modern Woman'. See Liz Conor, *The Spectacular Modern Woman: Feminine Visibility in the 1920s* (Bloomington: Indiana University Press, 2004), p. 209.

and consumer culture led to women who looked 'too glamourous' facing 'social disapproval'.[16]

There was an important spatial dimension to this female consumerism too. John Belchem's research has suggested that, despite the economic instability in the city during the interwar years, Liverpool was able to offer opportunities for consumers, with the Church Street and Bold Street areas of the city establishing themselves as quality retail districts.[17] With a specific focus on gendered experiences of urban culture, Charlotte Wildman has examined the development of interwar Liverpool as a site of consumer pleasure. She argues that local consumers, women in particular, used shopping to construct their own identities and, in doing so, blurred class distinctions.[18] Moreover, the post-1918 period saw considerable anxiety around gender roles, with many working-class women embracing new jobs, new fashions and in some cases even embarking upon criminal careers in a bid for 'self-improvement'.[19]

These developments meant that the physical identifiers used to categorize the prostitute – such as clothing and the patronization of particular city spaces – were losing their meaning and specificity.[20] For Liverpool's House of Help, this blurring of both class and gender boundaries meant that the refuge had to adapt to the demands of a very different social climate from the one into which it had been born. In 1930, the organization suggested 'Social conditions have changed during the last 40 years' and staff at the refuge lamented interwar society's 'lack of discipline, the loosening of moral restraints, and the greater freedom which girls now enjoy'.[21] Reflecting upon their work within this social context, the House of Help lauded their work

16   Carol Dyhouse, *Girl Trouble*, p. 94.

17   John Belchem, 'Introduction: Celebrating Liverpool', in John Belchem (ed.), *Liverpool 800: Culture, Character and History* (Liverpool: Liverpool University Press, 2006), p. 41.

18   Charlotte Wildman, 'The "Spectacle" of Interwar Manchester and Liverpool: Urban Fantasies, Consumer Cultures and Gendered Identities', PhD thesis, University of Manchester (2007), p. 23.

19   Charlotte Wildman, 'Miss Moriarty, the Adventuress and the Crime Queen: The Rise of the Modern Female Criminal in Britain, 1918–1939', *Contemporary British History*, 30:1 (2016), p. 75.

20   This argument is supported by the work of Julia Laite. See Julia Laite, 'Taking Nellie Johnson's Fingerprints: Prostitutes and Legal Identity in Early Twentieth Century London', *History Workshop Journal*, 65 (2008), p. 103.

21   House of Help, Annual Report 1930, p. 7. Liverpool Record Office, 362/HOU/3/39.

as a 'first stepping stone to a new and happier life, or to the recovery of that which has been lost', with the House presented as a moral haven in direct opposition to the urban dangers outwith.[22]

The anxieties that House of Help expressed about the moral state of Britain in the years after the First World War were shared by others. In 1927, a member of Liverpool's Women Police Patrols took a cutting from a newspaper article which declared:

> never were our parks and gardens so much frequented; never were there such large numbers of unemployed men and women, youths and maidens, walking our streets and lounging in public spaces; never were there such temptations and problem plays, suggestive pictures, dances.[23]

The message in the extract resonated with the moral concerns of the local patrollers. After the war, moral welfare workers seized upon the idea that their work was more important than ever. Nationally, numbers of women police significantly declined during the 1920s, but support for a women police service that could complete adjunct, specialist *feminine* tasks was still in evidence amongst members of the government, moralists and feminists.[24] The idea that 'public' spaces were increasingly being used for illicit interactions between 'youths and maidens' served to reinforce the necessity of the women police and their preventative patrol work in cities like Liverpool. In 1924, the Women Police Patrols presented the efforts of a temporary patroller to monitor an area known as the Recreation Ground and some nearby 'waste land' in the area of Clubmoor as a 'special feature' of their work that year.[25] The Women Police Patrols suggested that this was a district requiring 'careful supervision', with the patroller's work said to have gone some way towards reducing the 'extreme misconduct frequently occurring among couples' in the area.[26]

22   House of Help, Annual Report 1930, p. 7.
23   Unidentified newspaper, 7 July 1927. See newspaper cuttings relating to Women Police, Liverpool Record Office, 365 WOM/17/1–15.
24   Louise A. Jackson, *Women Police: Gender, Welfare and Surveillance in the Twentieth Century* (Manchester: Manchester University Press, 2006), p. 19.
25   Liverpool Women Police Patrols, Annual Report 1924, p. 6. Liverpool Record Office, H364/5 WOM.
26   Liverpool Women Police Patrols, Annual Report 1924, p. 6.

Social purists in the LVA expressed similar anxieties about the moral condition of urban environments after the war. Much to their chagrin, the LVA believed interwar Liverpool to have popular appeal among the young as a 'gateway to adventure'.[27] For naive youngsters, Liverpool was believed to act as 'a sort of magnet to them, and [excite] their imaginations'.[28] During the early 1920s, the LVA promoted an imagined urban landscape that presented Liverpool as an intrinsically problematic city due to its associations with transport and travel. Acting as chairman of the LVA's organizing committee, G.W. Hockley, the Rector of Liverpool, wrote: 'The conditions of a great seaport such as Liverpool demand increasing watchfulness on the part of those concerned for the moral welfare of the women and girls passing through its gates.'[29] Liverpool's role as a port meant that the city itself became synonymous with boundary-crossing, in terms of population transience, fluctuations in employment and a perceived culture of sexual transgression which challenged distinctions between public and private.

Managing the Streets

When taken together, the patrols conducted by the LVA and Women Police Patrols formed an unofficial network of moral welfare surveillance. Separately, the LVA and Women Police Patrols claimed authority over significant parts of the city's public spaces, particularly around the docks and the central railway station. From its establishment in 1908, the LVA had conducted patrols to meet boats at the Liverpool Landing Stage and trains at Lime Street station. Seven days a week, at 6 a.m., a patrol worker was on hand to guide and advise the young women who passed through the city.[30] LVA representatives would approach women as they disembarked from boats or trains and enquire about the purpose of their visit to the city. If the woman was intending to stay in the local area, the LVA representative would ask whether the woman had secured *respectable* accommodation and a *respectable* job. If any of these measures were found to be lacking from the woman's plans then the LVA would offer assistance by, for example, taking the woman to a hostel, arranging job interviews or planning for her to return home to her family.

27   LVA, Annual Report 1927–28, p. 3.
28   LVA, Annual Report 1927–28, p. 3.
29   LVA, Annual Report 1923–24, p. 3. Liverpool Record Office, M326 VIG/3.
30   LVA, Annual Report 1916, p. 2.

Acting with the agreement of officials from the shipping and railway companies, the LVA received recognition as a local expert authority on the protection of female travellers. The LVA insisted that their presence at the docks and the city's main train station was essential; women travelling alone, especially young, working-class women, were perceived to be morally vulnerable and thus in need of guidance. The vigilance workers who patrolled these areas of the city considered themselves to be respectable and, unlike the young women that they helped, able to negotiate Liverpool's streets without succumbing to immorality. The LVA explained that they had a 'duty' to protect women from the 'enemy', from the white slave traffickers, criminals and immoral men and women who sought to corrupt and exploit the young women that the LVA 'saved'.[31] Even so, the LVA was not a *rescue* organization. Most of the Association's work involved preventing young women from ever falling into immoral hands rather than saving those who had already been taken. Preventative patrol work formed the main part of the LVA's strategy for maintaining the morality of young, women travellers. To this end, managing young, working-class women's use of public space occupied the greatest amount of the LVA's time and attention.

Though the Women Police Patrols functioned in a similar fashion to the patrols of the LVA, there was an extra degree of professional motivation underpinning the work of the Women Police: members of the Women Police Patrols were part of an organized campaign to receive official policewoman status. Their patrolling was shaped by their own professional politics as much as it was by concerns about women's welfare. Liverpool's Women Police Patrols remained separate from the official police force until 1948.[32] Campaigning for official status, the women police used their interwar patrol work to try to stake a claim for themselves in the public sphere, without necessarily alienating constituents of the local population uncomfortable with feminism or the increased emancipation of women. Just like the LVA, the Women Police Patrols paradoxically encouraged women to idealize domesticity, despite the women police being *public* women themselves. Emphasizing their *feminine* skills in caring, the Women Police Patrols constructed for themselves an almost matriarchal authority that promoted their moral role in urban life; they argued that their work helped maintain 'order and decency' in the city.[33] Much of their work took the

31   LVA, Annual Report 1916, p. 2.
32   Gaynor Diane Williams, 'Women in Public Life', p. 119.
33   Liverpool Women Police, Annual Report 1928, p. 4.

form of patrolling the streets looking out for children, teenagers and young women in need of assistance or guidance.

Yet by conducting themselves in very similar ways to the social purity organizations like the LVA, the Women Police Patrols inadvertently hindered the assertion that their work should be official and attested. The 1924 Report of the Departmental Committee on the Employment of Policewomen suggested that there still existed 'a great difference of opinion as to whether the work [of women police] can be better done by policewomen than by members of voluntary organisations'.[34] However, the war work of the Women Police Patrols meant that they did enter the interwar years with a degree of public recognition. During 1918, their patrols were granted a £200 expenses grant by the Liverpool Watch Committee and this was increased to £600 in 1919 and £2,000 in 1921.[35] That the local authority was willing partly to fund these patrols indicates the extent to which the moral concerns promoted by the LVA and utilized by women police campaigners were recognized at the level of the local state. Their patrols were part of a culture of unofficial (though officially condoned) street policing which aimed to prevent women falling into prostitution on Liverpool's streets. The LVA and the Women Police Patrols saw city spaces as morally dangerous, and each organization set about carving out their roles as experts in maintaining female morality and, thus, social order in Liverpool. In this sense, patrolling was culturally significant as a female public endeavour that did not necessarily contravene traditional ideas about women being better suited to the home and the protection of the private sphere.

Watching the Runaways

Social purists and moral welfare workers defined many of the young women who they encountered on the streets of Liverpool as having run away, though the women themselves may have described their situations differently. Restoring these runaways to their families or finding them work in domestic service were common options taken by patrollers in Liverpool. In 1922, the House of Help declared that the 'Runaway girls' helped by their organization were usually 'restored to their homes or otherwise dealt with',

---

34 *Report of the Departmental Committee on the Employment of Policewomen* (1924), Home Office, p. 6. Preserved in Employment of Women Police: Publications, 1908–48, Women's Library, 3AMS/B/12/04.
35 Liverpool Women Police, Annual Report 1933, p. 5.

though the House was dismissive of the reasons why these young women left home in the first place.[36] Runaways were presented as naive, insolent girls often led to distraction by lust, immorality or false promises. The House of Help explained that runaways tended to be 'girls who have left home in a fit of temper, or who have done something wrong and are afraid of being found out, or who have been tempted away by some young man and then deserted.'[37]

The LVA was similarly sceptical of the reasons why many of the young women that they encountered had been moved to abandon their family homes in search of new lives. Rather than focusing their attentions upon the living conditions, lack of working opportunities or the potential abuses that these young women were trying to get away from, the LVA was instead preoccupied with the idea that young, working-class women were motivated to run away as a result of ill-thought-out flights of fancy. The Association's concerns with 'runaway girls' intent on 'stowing away on some outgoing steamer', young women looking for employment and, more worryingly, those in search of 'pleasure', grew from the organization's perception of urban moral danger being exacerbated by Liverpool's role as a port city.[38]

Perceiving young women's urban adventure, travel and transience as potentially subversive acts, the LVA mapped the crossing of geographical boundaries onto their ideas about moral boundary-crossing. In doing so, the organization justified their surveillance of women's use of the port and railway networks as necessary to the maintenance of social order. For the LVA, young, working-class women travelling alone or without adequate supervision were of paramount importance. It was feared that many young women who arrived in the city, especially those from Ireland, were not experienced in navigating the overwhelming temptations and dangers of city life. Without sufficient funds, geographical knowledge of the area or familial support, patrollers believed these young women to be especially vulnerable to being accosted by unscrupulous characters seeking to recruit them into vice, criminality and even white slavery.

That the LVA were able to convince young women to follow their instruction speaks to the determination of their workers and their shrewd use of culturally recognizable tropes of authority and officialdom. Despite having

36   House of Help, Annual Report 1922, p. 9. Liverpool Record Office, 362/HOU/3/31.

37   House of Help, Annual Report 1922, p. 9.

38   LVA, Annual Report 1929–30, pp. 6–7. Liverpool Record Office, M326 VIG/3.

Figure 1   Liverpool Vigilance Association Badge
(Liverpool Record Office, Liverpool Libraries)

no legal powers over those in whose journeys they intervened, the LVA's references to their patrol work as a 'duty' gave their work a formal veneer.[39] Using established visual cues, they projected their importance by casting themselves in the light of other recognizable authorities. Unlike the Women Police Patrols, who undertook uniformed patrols, the LVA workers had no uniform. However, their use of a badge (Figure 1), imitating the insignia of the police force, provided the LVA with cultural power by proxy.[40]

Though the badge held no official significance because it did not connote any form of objective authority, it served to differentiate LVA workers from ordinary members of the public. As an emblem of trust and guardianship, it conveyed a sense of the LVA workers as experts in matters of urban guidance, local transport and, most importantly, morality. The badge was intended to provide vital symbolic proof that the wearer was inoculated against vice and temptation. Though the women involved in the LVA understood Liverpool's streets as spaces of danger for young women, the badge explained that the patroller was specially qualified to navigate moral danger and to

39   LVA, Annual Report 1917–18, p. 9.
40   See LVA, Annual Report 1916, p. 16.

protect other, more vulnerable women. The LVA patrollers' public position as knowledgeable urban guides did not, therefore, detract from their own respectability as women. Just like the Liverpool Women Police Patrols, the LVA workers presented themselves as having gender-specific skills in the associated fields of welfare and moral rescue. Unlike the professional prostitute, the street-walker, the LVA and Women Police Patrols implied that their patrollers were drawn to urban spaces precisely because patrol work enabled them to make use of their reputable, feminine, caring skills and it gave them opportunities to exercise their maternal instincts towards women (and children) in need.

Though all young women who walked in the neighbourhoods patrolled by the women police or who passed by the LVA patroller at the docks and station were potential subjects of this culture of watchfulness, there were a number of clues that these organizations looked for when deciding whether or not they considered a young woman to be in need of help. Typical signs of vulnerability included their youth, any evidence of economic hardship, or a readiness to talk to strange men. Of course, the greatest indicator of immoral intention was a refusal to accept the assistance of a patroller. The LVA reported on such instances carefully throughout the 1920s and 30s. On the one hand, they did not want to fill their annual reports with examples of how young women found them annoying and interfering. On the other hand, these cases could be used sparingly to remind their supporters of the frivolousness of young women. For example, in 1938, a couple of teenage 'runaways' left their Manchester homes to walk and catch lifts to Liverpool.[41] According to the LVA, the girls 'wanted work as waitresses, and had at one time been in Pantomime at a Liverpool theatre'. The girls' interest in theatrical work would have immediately been interpreted by the LVA as a sign that they were vulnerable to the seduction of dubious characters who might try to offer them unreliable, *glamourous* occupations.[42] Upon encountering the LVA, the girls were placed in a hostel while the Association sought work for them. The LVA found that the girls 'soon proved to be dishonest, stealing money and running away', and it transpired that they had provided false addresses for their parents. The LVA subsequently had to report the girls to the police as 'missing'.[43] As such, it would be inaccurate to suggest that the

41   LVA, Annual Report 1938–39, p. 10. Liverpool Record Office, M326 VIG/3.
42   As will be seen in Chapter 4, the LVA showed an extra level of concern about the moral vulnerability of young women who were interested in theatrical work.
43   LVA, Annual Report 1938–39, p. 10.

LVA were able to wield unchallenged power over the young, working-class women that they attempted to take into their charge.

Girls and young women would, in fact, go to great lengths to ensure that their travels through interwar city spaces were unimpeded by the interventions of those who sought to interfere in their plans. In their 1928–29 annual report, the LVA recounted the case of two young girls named Mollie and Dorothy.[44] Aged just 14 and 15, the girls had run away from their home town in the Midlands, with grand ideas and an elaborate plan to stow away in a liner's lifeboat to seek out domestic work abroad. After sending postcards to each of their parents explaining their intentions to leave the country, Mollie and Dorothy dressed themselves in boys' clothing and set off on their foreign adventure. By cloaking themselves in masculine disguises, the girls' plan reflected the significance of gender in young women's negotiation of Britain's cities during the period. Dressed as boys, the girls intended that their movements be inconspicuous. Although it is unlikely that those who paid close attention to the girls would have been fooled by their attire, their plan to avoid such scrutiny was, for a time, successful. At least one of their fellow travellers had been taken in by their disguise. The LVA noted that the girls had been 'quite elated when an elderly gentleman in the same carriage said to one "Hop out, Sonny" on arrival at Central Station about midnight'.[45]

The gender-crossing of Mollie and Dorothy was not intended to be provocative: quite the opposite in fact. Yet by attempting to pass as male in order to navigate their way across the country, the girls were engaged, however much they themselves were aware of it, in a deeply political act. Their new masculine identities allowed Mollie and Dorothy unhindered access to sites that would otherwise have been denied to them, as two young girls travelling unaccompanied. Their experience exemplifies the extent to which public spaces were still understood as sites of masculinity. At the same time, their plan was indicative of an increasing dissolution of the boundaries between the masculine and the feminine. Women who rejected the stereotypical tropes of femininity in preference for a more masculine appearance were considered 'profoundly disturbing' during the mid-twentieth century.[46] Trends in post-First World War fashion focused

44   LVA, Annual Report 1928–29, p. 6.

45   LVA, Annual Report 1928–29, p. 6.

46   Penny Summerfield, 'Gender and War in the Twentieth Century', *International History Review*, 19:1 (1997), p. 7.

attention on women's clothing as a symbol of transgression and modernism. The short hair and boyish-figure of the flapper, the most famous of female cultural archetypes from the period, created a sense of the modern woman as freer from the ideological gender constraints of earlier generations.[47] Though neither Mollie nor Dorothy was dressed as a flapper, their plan to assume male identities through disguise was informed by continued associations between masculinity and public space, and by this new sense of fashionable androgyny.

Mollie and Dorothy's plan to leave the country ultimately ended in Liverpool. How they found themselves under the charge of the LVA is not clear, though it is significant that Mollie and Dorothy were only subject to adult intervention once they had dispensed with their masculine disguises and given their clothes to some poor young boys.[48] This gesture of generosity and care for those possibly less fortunate than themselves influenced the sympathetic light in which the LVA viewed the girls. For the LVA, the transgressive activities of Mollie and Dorothy did not necessarily signify any irredeemable or unscrupulous qualities on the part of the girls. Said to be 'well-educated, nicely spoken and well mannered', the LVA received the girls with sympathy and understanding. The LVA did not unilaterally judge women who wanted or needed to work outside the home, so long as the employment that they sought fit the organization's notions of respectability. Both girls explained that they intended to take up posts in domestic service to fund their ambitions to become nurses. This undoubtedly mitigated any unease that the LVA might have felt about the determined ambition of these two young girls.

Domestic service and nursing could be reconciled with traditional ideas about women's social roles emanating from the private sphere, relying as they did on the attributes of home management and philanthropy. As welfare workers themselves, the workers of the LVA may even have been able to identify with the ambitions of Mollie and Dorothy. Where the LVA representatives considered themselves different from these girls, of course, was in their age and experience. In the fight against vice, the LVA placed a premium upon their interactions with characters like Mollie and Dorothy. Both girls 'looked several years older' than their actual ages and the LVA feared that

47   See Susan Kingsley Kent, *Gender and Power in Britain*, p. 286. See also Adrian Bingham, *Gender, Modernity and the Popular Press in Inter-War Britain* (Oxford: Clarendon Press, 2004), p. 48.
48   LVA, Annual Report 1928–29, p. 6.

they would be prime candidates for an 'undesirable man or woman' seeking to trap innocent young women into immorality.[49] Mollie and Dorothy were not considered to be immoral or boisterous girls, but they were presented as naive individuals who had acted out of a desire to 'show they could be self-reliant and independent of their parents'.[50] As such, the girls' dangerous adventure and their ill-considered ambitions were framed in direct opposition to the safety and succour of the domestic sphere.

Return to Domesticity

Local philanthropic activities were frequently articulated during the interwar years in relation to both women's supposed suitability to work within the home (either their own or someone else's as domestic servant) and the importance of female morality to the maintenance of the family unit. By promoting domesticated womanhood, both the CWL and the House of Help reinforced the public-and-private/immoral-and-moral dichotomy upheld by the street patrollers in the LVA and Women Police Patrols. The CWL promoted a version of women's citizenship that was grounded in the relationship between respectable femininity and domesticity, with increased state support for women's roles as wives, mothers and homemakers being a key goal of the organization.[51] But conservative and religious ideals continued to be prioritized in the discourse of women's rights that emerged from this political mobilization of the domestic sphere. The CWL's efforts positively to ally motherhood with citizenship, for example, did not translate into a sense that women should have better access to birth control. In 1924, the CWL protested against birth control lectures by Marie Stopes at the Liverpool Philharmonic Hall.[52] Moreover, the CWL were cautious about the types of entertainment that women and children enjoyed during the interwar years, despite most plots rarely challenging the status of the male breadwinner and his doting wife.[53] During the interwar years, the CWL were involved in

49   LVA, Annual Report 1928–29, p. 6.
50   LVA, Annual Report 1928–29, p. 6.
51   Caitríona Beaumont, *Housewives and Citizens*, pp. 19 and 33.
52   Letter to Mrs Ryan on the history of the CWL, from the CWL Liverpool Branch, dated 8 December 1977.
53   Christine Grandy, 'Paying for Love: Women's Work and Love in Popular Film in Interwar Britain', *Journal of the History of Sexuality*, 19:3 (2010), pp. 486–7.

a successful campaign calling upon magistrates to continue to prevent children attending 'A', i.e. 'Adult', films.[54]

Liverpool's House of Help refuge was similarly concerned to cleanse women of the temptations and dangers that were to be found in public life. Focusing on the culture of the streets, the House was critical of 'the irresponsible way in which people wander about' and remained sceptical about the morality of many of the women helped at the refuge.[55] Those who stayed there were offered education and induction into the ways of moral respectability via the discipline that was to be found in domesticated chores. Though the House provided free accommodation, it encouraged 'inmates or their friends … to make some contribution towards their board'.[56] The women helped did not stay long in the House of Help; one of the rules of the House stated, 'no inmate shall remain for more than one week … without the permission of the House Committee'. Nevertheless, the women who stayed were expected to assist in the maintenance of the refuge by taking 'a share in the domestic work of the House under the direction of the Matron'.[57]

Indeed, the role of the Matron was central to keeping the House of Help running and to the redemptive work of the home. In 1924, the House of Help suggested that some of the women helped came to 'look upon the Matron as their best friend'.[58] But this was not a friendship of equals, with the young women helped sometimes cast in ways that suggested that the House viewed them as creatures that needed to be tamed, civilized and domesticated. In 1922, the House encountered a 'waif', a 'wild undisciplined untruthful scraggy little girl of 14'. She had been sent by her mother to Dublin to find her aunt, but the girl had simply come back 'without making any effort to find the aunt, [and] somehow drifted into the House of Help', who sent her to a training home where she 'did well'.[59] Cases like this were highlighted by the House to illustrate its role in reforming the character of problem women and girls. The House of Help informed its subscribers, who were a vital source of revenue for the under-funded home, 'we are making a real contribution to the welfare and uplifting of the

---

54 CWL Liverpool Archdiocesan Branch, Twenty First Report, 1932.

55 House of Help, Annual Report 1922, p. 8.

56 House of Help, Annual Report 1918, p. 4.

57 House of Help, Annual Report 1918, p. 4.

58 House of Help, Annual Report 1924, pp. 7–8. Liverpool Record Office, 362 HOU/3/33.

59 House of Help, Annual Report 1922, p. 10.

womanhood of our city'.[60] Though 'a few' of the women encountered were 'rude, ungrateful' and 'very unpleasant', the 'majority' were said 'fully [to] appreciate the kindness and help received'.[61] In this way, the House of Help promoted itself as a vital refuge for young, working-class women who lived their lives on the edge of moral ruin.

Certainly, there can be no doubt that the House of Help did offer vital assistance to some of the women who stayed there. The Matron would investigate and source employment for women in need of work and she provided women with donated clothes and boots. Nevertheless, there were clear moral and gendered dimensions to the work of this refuge. Just as with the work of the LVA, the CWL and the Women Police Patrols, the House of Help exhibited fear about the influence of the streets upon women's morality and the refuge supported the notion that poor women were especially susceptible to corruption. The imaginary moral gulf between the figures of the disreputable, poverty-stricken girl and the more affluent woman was drawn into stark relief in 1925 when the House of Help introduced a private, fee-paying room for 'respectable women'.[62] The policy appears to have been only moderately successful at improving the House's income. The House reported a roughly £10 increase in annual income from inmate payments/room rents when compared with the previous two years.[63] In part, then, this was a pragmatic approach to revenue-raising, but it was also a solution that sprang from philanthropists' tendencies to carve distinctions between the respectable working class and an underclass, or social residuum of the poor.[64]

The House of Help considered that it had a vital role to play in urban moral politics, first with regards to preventing slippage from working-class

60   House of Help, Annual Report 1920, p. 9. Liverpool Record Office, 362 HOU/3/29.

61   House of Help, Annual Report 1925, p. 8. Liverpool Record Office, 362 HOU/3/34.

62   House of Help, Annual Report 1925, pp. 8, 8–9.

63   The House of Help was not consistent in the way it recorded information on income and expenditure. The money earned through board and lodging in 1923 was £25; in 1924, the House recorded inmate payments of £11, plus a further £14 for rent on a large room; in 1925, inmate payments were recorded as £35. See House of Help, Annual Reports for 1923 (Liverpool Record Office, 362 HOU/3/32), 1924, 1925.

64   Lydia Morris, *Dangerous Classes: The Underclass and Social Citizenship* (London: Routledge, 1994), p. 16; John Welshman, *Underclass: A History of the Excluded Since 1880* (London: Hambledon, 2006).

respectability, and, secondly, in encouraging redemption where the boundaries of decency had already been transgressed. In 1925, the House reported its success with a 21-year-old woman who had been 'placed in a convent on probation after being charged with theft'.[65] When the woman absconded from the convent the House of Help applied to the magistrate 'to be allowed to give her another chance'. Later, the environment and discipline of the refuge apparently reformed the woman, with the House reporting that she made 'good use of the opportunity given to her'; she lived at the Home while undertaking 'regular daily work'.[66] Indeed, for street patrollers in organizations like the LVA and the Women Police Patrols, refuges like the House of Help were invaluable for getting women in seemingly immediate moral danger into respectable accommodation at short notice, while more long-term solutions to their individual predicaments could be sought. For each year from 1920 to 1939, between 10 per cent and 22 per cent of women who stayed at the House of Help had been referred there by the Women Police Patrols, although there was a peak of 32 per cent in 1933.[67]

The Women Police Patrols also had their own Hostel, set up in Knotty Ash, the suburban location apparently chosen since it was thought that 'a few days in peaceful surroundings' would 'work wonders for some girls in difficulties'.[68] The Hostel provided shelter specifically for teenage girls and young women. The focus on this young age group was explained in terms of the Hostel's ability to provide 'constant skilled observation … combined with more supervision than is possible where older women are also taken'.[69] The 'Hostel for Girls, Knotty Ash' was described as imperative to the Women Police Patrols' 'preventative work among the younger girls' and it was argued by the Women Police that 'the Patrols would be seriously handicapped had they not the Hostel to fall back upon'.[70] Available to young women for an

---

65   House of Help, Annual Report 1925, p. 9.

66   House of Help, Annual Report 1925, p. 9.

67   Liverpool House of Help, Annual Reports, 1920–39. Liverpool Record Office, 362 HOU/3.

68   Hostel for Girls, Knotty Ash: Liverpool Women Police Patrols and Training Centre, Annual Report 1925, p. 3. Liverpool Record Office, H364/5 WOM.

69   Hostel for Girls, Knotty Ash: Liverpool Women Police Patrols and Training Centre for Women Police, Annual Report 1929, p. 3. Liverpool Record Office, H364/5 WOM.

70   Hostel for Girls, Knotty Ash: Liverpool Women Police Patrols and Training Centre, Annual Report 1922, p. 1. Liverpool Record Office, H364/5 WOM.

'indefinite time', the 'happiness' experienced by young women at the Hostel was attributed to 'Matron's motherly care and sympathy'.[71] Aping the tropes of an idealized domesticity, the Hostel functioned as a sanctuary where vulnerable young women were brought back from 'the brink of disaster'.[72]

Such was the belief that domesticity represented the best place for young, working-class women that it was not unusual for runaways to be returned to families to which they clearly did not want to belong. In 1929, the House of Help referred a 20-year-old woman to the Women Police Patrol's Hostel for shelter. Investigations revealed that the woman had come to Liverpool in search of work after being left by a husband who 'neglected her'.[73] Before travelling she had left their child in the care of its grandmother. Despite this difficult and unhappy marital background, the hostel workers made arrangements for the woman to return to her home. They concluded their notes on her case with the at best naive and at worst cajoling sentiment that 'It was hoped that husband and wife would come together again'.[74] No details were offered on the neglect that the woman had suffered or whether she in fact shared the hostel's hopes about the future of her marriage.

Restoration to the family unit was a common way for these organizations to handle such cases. Other options, such as sending young women on to more permanent independent lodgings, helping to find them work in domestic service or locating them in mother and baby homes, were considered in cases where the domestic situation was itself thought to be obviously immoral because of, for example, sexual abuse, illegitimacy or alcoholism within the home. But dissatisfaction within family units and potential emotional abuse were not thought to be reasons to facilitate a woman's efforts to leave her domestic situation. In a case from 1923, the LVA encountered a 'poor girl' on Liverpool's Landing Stage who explained that she had left her Lancashire home to look for work on a ship because she no longer wanted to live with her 'exacting' mother and 'very unkind' father.[75] The LVA boasted of telegraphing the girl's parents and sending her back to them via train, all within 24 hours. According to the LVA, the 'child' was later said to have been 'most penitent and sorry that she had been

---

71   Hostel for Girls, Knotty Ash, Annual Report 1922, p. 1.
72   Hostel for Girls, Knotty Ash, Annual Report 1922, p. 2.
73   Hostel for Girls, Knotty Ash, Annual Report 1929, p. 4.
74   Hostel for Girls, Knotty Ash, Annual Report 1929, p. 4.
75   LVA, Annual Report 1923–24, p. 8.

so hasty in leaving home'.[76] Nevertheless, the speed with which the LVA dealt with the girl's case suggests that they did not use their self-publicized powers of investigation and surveillance in order to make a considered assessment of the conditions that this girl said that she was trying to escape. Instead, investigation and interrogation tended to focus upon testing and highlighting the frivolity of young women's travel and employment plans in a bid to encourage them to return to the assumed moral and physical safety of the home.

The work of women patrollers in Liverpool *did* help women who became lost and stranded as they travelled through the port in search of work or relatives. However, an over-arching concern with maintaining the respectability of women in public meant that street patrolling was not so much about campaigning to make the streets safer for women as it was about reinforcing the idea that working-class women required moral chaperoning. The street patrolling of the LVA and Women Police Patrols represented a form of public womanhood that was far less controversial than that exhibited by the young, working-class woman who used the streets for work, entertainment and socializing. Augmented and reinforced by the moral guardianship of the CWL and the domestic refuge offered by hostels like the House of Help and the Women Police Patrols' Hostel for Girls in Knotty Ash, street patrolling gave added cultural purchase to the idea that young, working-class women could not be trusted to travel or walk the streets without significant risk to their virtue. Though the Women Police Patrols and LVA were pioneering in the sense that they were run by women striving to fashion public roles for themselves, the notions of class, gender and respectability that they subscribed to ultimately supported the proposition that working-class women needed to be watched and that, where possible, they should be encouraged to find pleasure and purpose in the duties of domestic service and homemaking.

The next chapter will examine the ways these anxieties about urban space and female morality were played out in the city in relation to the specific problems posed by prostitution. The Women Police Patrols became involved in national debates about the role of the law in maintaining the respectability of the streets. Such was the level of interwar concern about the decency of young, working-class women living in cities like Liverpool that street patrolling by agencies like the LVA and Women Police was increasingly framed as a legitimate strategy for preventing prostitution.

76   LVA, Annual Report 1923–24, p. 8.

3

Regulating Interwar Prostitution
National Debates and Local Issues

During the early and mid-twentieth century, prostitution was subject to considerable moral panic and cultural anxiety. The legal status of the common prostitute as a criminal was the result of her failure to conform to traditional codes of respectable female behaviour, that is to say, of her lack of sexual innocence and moral purity. Legally and socially, the female prostitute was supposed to be demarcated from all other women, ring-fenced in law as a distinct category of woman offender so that she may be exhibited as an example of the need to hold women's sexual morality in check. Official efforts to confirm this perception of the prostitute as 'other' were rooted in Victorian jurisprudence, which supported the criminalization of these women on the assumption that prostitution was predicated upon female disreputability and a man's struggle to control his own sexual urges. In 1871, when a Royal Commission rejected the suggestion that the male clients of prostitutes should face criminalization, it did so infamously on the grounds that the prostitute committed an offence 'as a matter of gain', while her male client was guilty only of an 'irregular indulgence of a natural impulse'.[1] Consequently, the prostitute was credited with a sense of sexual moral agency that the man, at the mercy of his own biology, was not. According to this gendered view of sexual relations, male sexuality was understood to be unruly; it required taming and tempering in relationships with respectable women. By igniting male passions, the prostitute was therefore charged with undermining the seemingly functionalist basis

1 Keith Thomas, 'The Double Standard', *Journal of the History of Ideas*, 20:2 (1959), p. 198.

of personal relationships between men and women. A visibly disreputable woman, the criminalization of the prostitute was justified by this idea that she represented a threat to male sexual sensibility and urban social order itself.

Yet, by the interwar years, a perceived rise in promiscuity and increasing social freedoms for women meant that distinctions between the prostitute and the sexually adventurous modern woman were fraught with both social and legal uncertainties. After the First World War, the prostitute was joined by a cast of others (the flappers, the 'modern' girls, the amateur prostitutes) who also stood accused of sexual provocation.[2] Although the idea of the prostitute as other was still very much in existence during the early twentieth century, there was concern about the utter dependence of the solicitation laws upon the notion that the prostitute's offences were particular to *her* character and *her* trade. Precisely what made a prostitute so distinctive from the promiscuous woman or the amateur prostitute was up for debate, as were the ways the police attempted to utilize these apparent differences in their day-to-day street work. Moreover, the considerable discretion and inconsistency involved in the policing of prostitution was compounded by the lack of clarity in the law on this matter. Prostitution was not illegal, but various laws had long since made it difficult for prostitutes to operate without becoming criminalized. London's Metropolitan Police Act 1839 and the provincial Town Police Clauses Act 1847 both made it illegal to solicit to the annoyance of passers-by, with police testimony alone being enough to secure a conviction.[3]

Paying particular attention to the Street Offences Committee, this chapter will show that the legislative debate surrounding prostitution in the 1920s was shaped at least as much by a cultural discourse which cast the prostitute as an other as it was by legal considerations relating to issues of public order. Indeed, since the Victorian period, concerns about promiscuity have been significant in legal definitions of prostitution.[4] Interwar uncertainty about the efficacy, legitimacy and application of the solicitation laws was not prompted by a change in attitudes towards prostitution. Instead, the debate about the solicitation laws was concerned with how appropriate it was to legally define the common prostitute as a

2   Samantha Caslin, 'Flappers, Amateurs and Professionals'.

3   Samantha Caslin, 'Flappers, Amateurs and Professionals', pp. 15–16.

4   Elizabeth Clement, 'Prostitution', in H.G. Cocks and Matt Houlbrook (eds), *The Modern History of Sexuality* (Basingstoke: Palgrave Macmillan, 2006), p. 209.

distinct category of woman, given her increasing conflation with promiscuous women. Focusing on the testimony provided to the committee by Liverpool-based experts, particularly that of representatives of the Women Police Patrols, the evidence presented in this chapter reveals the extent to which moral condemnation of the prostitute as a transgressive other and concerns about her links to promiscuity remained central to the thinking of officials across England and Wales. Witness testimony given to the committee by Liverpool's Stipendiary Magistrate and Chief Constable also makes explicit official attitudes towards prostitutes as a source of social disorder and moral danger.

The Street Offences Committee's efforts to meet with local figures was indicative of their desire to avoid accusations that they understood prostitution only in philosophical or moral terms, with little knowledge about solicitation as it actually occurred on the streets. However, practical street-level concerns relating to prostitution were in fact sidelined in the committee's discussions in favour of overarching concerns with female respectability and social order. The committee's recommendation to repeal the legal category of the common prostitute did not necessarily mean that they no longer regarded the prostitute as socially and morally unacceptable. As the evidence explored in this chapter will show, prostitution was still considered to be part of a spectrum of disreputable female behaviour which ranged from sex outside of marriage, to promiscuity and occasional prostitution, to the professional sale of sex for money.

Prostitution in Liverpool

By the 1920s, port and army towns already had historical reputations as areas of significant prostitution-related activity.[5] Large cities like Liverpool were identified as places where young and poor women would prostitute themselves in order to earn money, and the more destitute parts of urban Britain came to be seen as chief sources of prostitution. However, official statistics on the extent of prostitution in these areas are problematic. The level of police discretion involved in the application of the solicitation laws meant that it was difficult to ascertain how prevalent street prostitution

---

5   Paula Bartley has argued that during the late-Victorian period these localities were 'commonly accepted' as having the greatest number of prostitutes. See Paula Bartley, *Prostitution: Prevention and Reform in England, 1860–1914* (London: Routledge, 2000), p. 3.

actually was during the late nineteenth and early twentieth centuries. Arrest rates tell a story about policing activities and moral panics rather than revealing the true nature of prostitution. In her examination of the later nineteenth-century records, Paula Bartley notes substantial discrepancies in the figures collected because of the many ways prostitution and prostitution-related activities were recorded. Some records employed exceptionally broad definitions of prostitution, including single mothers and women cohabiting with men in this category, while others included only those women prosecuted for prostitution.[6]

Similar problems of categorization and recording are also evident in the statistics available for the early twentieth century. In Liverpool, Stipendiary Magistrate Stuart Deacon struggled to explain why the number of arrests for prostitution had diminished from 1772 in 1907 to just 316 in 1927.[7] When asked about these figures by the Street Offences Committee in 1928, Deacon was uncertain whether this decrease could be explained by 'improved morals'.[8] Jeffrey Weeks has suggested that there may, in fact, have been a real decline in prostitution offences during the early part of the twentieth century as a result of there being less rowdiness and drunkenness on the streets, increased employment opportunities for women and greater opportunities for premarital, casual sex for men who may otherwise have used the service of a prostitute. However, Weeks also suggests that prostitution may simply have been less visible during this period as it had migrated into nightclubs.[9] Stuart Deacon suggested to the Street Offences Committee that a range of factors, from better social conditions on the streets to restricted opening hours for licensed houses, could have affected the arrest rate. He also proposed that a decision taken by the Deputy Recorder in Liverpool in 1909 not to apply the Vagrancy Act to prostitution might have given the appearance that there were fewer cases of prostitution, although the fact that there was an increase in prosecutions for prostitution between 1909 and 1910 means that even this suggestion does not fully explain the overall downward trend in arrests between 1907 and 1927.[10]

6   Paula Bartley, *Prostitution*, p. 2.
7   Stuart Deacon, Transcript of Evidence, Departmental Committee on Street Offences, 14 January 1928, p. 4. The National Archives, HO 45/12663.
8   Stuart Deacon, Transcript of Evidence, p. 4.
9   Jeffrey Weeks, *Sex, Politics and Society: The Regulation of Sexuality since 1800*, 2nd edn (London: Longman, 1989), p. 208.
10   Stuart Deacon, Transcript of Evidence, p. 4.

One possibility that the Stipendiary Magistrate did not suggest to the Street Offences Committee was that the decrease in arrests may have reflected a change in police attitudes towards solicitation. Indeed, police figures relating to prostitution often reflected a local force's interests in and attitudes towards immorality rather than the actual extent of prostitution in an area. Bartley has suggested that during the late nineteenth century Liverpool's Chief Constable was concerned that there were excessive levels of local prostitution, while Sheffield's Chief Constable made the doubtful claim that there was not a single brothel in his jurisdiction, and in Manchester one superintendent distorted evidence to show an actual decrease in prostitution.[11] In his history of the police, Michael Brogden has argued that, even prior to the outbreak of the First World War, the force in Liverpool had become increasingly autonomous from the local Watch Committee, suggesting that the police were able to act with greater political independence in deciding when and where it was appropriate to target prostitutes.[12] These difficulties in policing prostitution based on the subjective reading of precisely which women the law should be aimed at, which areas should be policed and which solicitation laws should be used in which particular cases had significant implications for the status of the solicitation laws.

The Street Offences Committee

With public debate over the solicitation laws growing in the 1920s, the Home Office began to face calls from all sides for an inquiry into street solicitation. For social purists in the NVA, the parent body of the LVA, an inquiry was necessary because they believed that more needed to be done to quell the corrupting influence of female prostitutes on urban morality and social order. However, not everyone favoured the criminalization of women working as prostitutes. The Association for Moral and Social Hygiene (AMSH), who had campaigned for a repeal of the solicitation laws since being formed in 1915, also pressed for the setting up of a government committee.[13] Between 1923 and 1926, the Public Places

11   Paula Bartley, *Prostitution*, p. 3.
12   Michael Brogden, *The Police: Autonomy and Consent* (London: Academic Press, 1982), pp. 70–1.
13   For more on the formation and history of the AMSH, see Julia Laite, 'The Association for Moral and Social Hygiene'.

(Order) Bill, which had been drawn up by the AMSH, was introduced to Parliament on a number of occasions.[14] The bill proposed to replace the solicitation laws with a more gender-neutral approach to the problem of social and moral order.

The purpose of the Public Places (Order) Bill, as it was aired in 1926, was, first: 'To repeal the provisions in the existing law which refer to solicitation by common prostitutes, and other provisions which do not explicitly refer to solicitation but are sometimes used for dealing with such conduct.'[15] Secondly, the Bill proposed, 'To substitute [the solicitation laws with] a simple provision, which substantially covers the same ground as the existing law, but applies to all persons alike.' Lastly, the Bill proposed, 'To enact that proceedings shall only be taken on complaint by or on behalf of the party aggrieved.'[16] In this way, the Bill responded directly to widespread concerns about inconsistencies in the policing of prostitution and promoted feminist concerns that the law singled out prostitute women for punishment, while her male client went ignored.

In 1922, George W. Johnson, the vice-chairman of the AMSH, published a pamphlet entitled *The Need for Repealing the Present Solicitation Laws*.[17] For Johnson, a supporter of the women's suffrage movement like many other members of the AMSH, the issue was one of gender inequality.[18] It was obvious that the law took far more interest in the regulation and condemnation of female prostitutes than it did their male customers. Addressing the gender imbalance exhibited by the regulation of prostitution, he wrote:

> Apart from the other miseries and evils of prison life, many of these women and girl prisoners feel the injustice of having to bear the penalty, when the man who was morally a partner in their offence goes entirely free; for in many cases a woman only solicits when she sees that the man is looking out for it. Every man knows that he is

14   Julia Laite, 'The Association for Moral and Social Hygiene', p. 217.
15   Public Places (Order) Bill Memorandum, Received by the Home Office, 24 November 1926. The National Archives, HO 45/12663.
16   Public Places (Order) Bill Memorandum, 24 November 1926.
17   George W. Johnson, *The Need for Repealing the Present Solicitation Laws* (London: Association for Moral and Social Hygiene, 1922), p. 4. Preserved in Records of the Public Places (Order) Bill 1924, Women's Library, 3AMS/B/04/06.
18   Julia Laite, 'The Association for Moral and Social Hygiene', p. 210.

rarely solicited, unless he is himself loitering for the purpose, or at the women whom he passes.[19]

In this way, Johnson's pamphlet reflected the AMSH's long-standing concern with removing the sexual double standard from legislation, while protecting individual liberties from unnecessary state intervention.[20]

Scepticism about the law's ability to distinguish between the chaste, moral woman and her prostitute 'other' was not limited to the AMSH. Significantly, the AMSH was able to garner support from other organizations who agreed that the increasing visibility of young women in urban spaces made existing laws all the more unsuitable. Miss Picton Turbervill, of the Young Women's Christian Association, argued:

> twenty years ago no respectable young girl would be found walking down Regent Street at night and it was comparatively easy to know the character of women found walking in such a street. But today all that had been altered by the different habits prevailing amongst women and girls.[21]

Similarly, Mrs Bramwell Booth of the Salvation Army also told the Home Secretary that the law as it stood was unfair. She explained that 'the dividing of the community into three classes – men, women and prostitutes – was unjust and a grave injustice to the women'.[22]

When Lord Balfour introduced the second reading of the Public Places (Order) Bill to the House of Lords in December 1926, he stressed that the potential for discrepancies in policing was one of his key objections to the solicitation laws as they stood. He argued that while he admired the police and the work that they did, he did not 'regard them as ideal custodians of public morality', and proposed that 'the sooner they [were] relieved of their duties in this respect the better it [would] be for their own reputation and the safety of women lawfully using the

19   George Johnson, *The Need for Repealing the Present Solicitation Laws*, p. 6.

20   Julia Laite, 'The Association for Moral and Social Hygiene', p. 213.

21   Miss Picton Turbervill paraphrased in Minutes of AMSH deputation to the Home Office (Home Office ref. 483.171/21), 13 November 1925, p. 4. The National Archives, HO 45/12663.

22   Mrs Bramwell Booth paraphrased in Minutes of AMSH deputation to the Home Office (Home Office ref. 483.171/21), 13 November 1925, p. 3.

public streets'.[23] The inference that law-abiding women were not safe under the solicitation laws clearly pointed towards concerns that so-called respectable women could not be easily distinguished from prostitute women by signifiers such as clothing or their presence in a particular public space.

At this same reading of the Bill, Lord Desborough announced that he was able to 'state ... the position of the Government', informing his fellow peers that the debate about the solicitation laws had interested the Home Office and the Home Secretary, William Joynson-Hicks, 'for some considerable time'.[24] According to Desborough, the Home Secretary was keen to accommodate calls for an inquiry into the effectiveness of the solicitation laws, but the Home Office had been 'overworked', with the General Strike and disputes with those in the mining industry having taken precedence.[25] Nevertheless, Desborough insisted that the 'importance of the matter and the wide divergence of views in different quarters' meant that the Home Secretary had in fact 'been considering the question of an inquiry'.[26] Desborough informed the Lords that the Government did not necessarily oppose the Public Places (Order) Bill but did not want to 'tie themselves down to the letter of the Bill or perhaps even some of its main provisions as drafted'.[27] Certainly, had the Bill been made law it would have meant making important changes to those who could be charged with solicitation. It was thought that the removal of the category of the common prostitute would bring about greater gender equality in the laws used to control solicitation and bring about greater legal clarity, to the benefit of those involved in the policing of this particular offence.

Amid this wave of contemporary concern, Joynson-Hicks finally formed a committee of inquiry into the solicitation laws in October 1927, ten months after the second reading of the Public Places (Order) Bill in the House of Lords. Under the chairmanship of Hugh Macmillan, the remit of

23   Parliamentary Debates, House of Lords, 9 December 1926, Official Report, Vol. 65, No. 88, para. 1398. The National Archives, HO 45/12663.
24   Parliamentary Debates, House of Lords, 9 December 1926, Vol. 65, No. 88, paras 1400–1.
25   Parliamentary Debates, House of Lords, 9 December 1926, Vol. 65, No. 88, para. 1400.
26   Parliamentary Debates, House of Lords, 9 December 1926, Vol. 65, No. 88, para 1402.
27   Parliamentary Debates, House of Lords, 9 December 1926, Vol. 65, No. 88, para 1401.

the committee was to examine 'the law and practice ... in connection with prostitution and solicitation for immoral purposes in streets and public places'.[28] The government wanted the Street Offences Committee to assess whether the laws against these and 'other offences against decency and good order' required changing.[29] The Home Office's entire approach to the committee illustrated the extent to which central government considered sexual 'decency' to be inextricably connected to the maintenance of social 'order'. By pushing street-based forms of prostitution to the fore of the committee's agenda, the government acted on the assumption that the visibility of the disreputable woman was the most socially threatening aspect of prostitution.

The committee considered that, while it was not within the scope of the law to regulate personal, moral issues between citizens, prostitution presented a public problem. During the course of their discussions with witnesses, members of the Street Offences Committee sought to clarify precisely why prostitution was approached as a criminal rather than a moral matter. In an effort to justify why the law was used to criminalize female prostitutes, the committee endeavoured to separate notions of private sexual conduct from concerns about public order. However, even with public order being used as the justification for the control and criminalization of prostitution, issues of personal sexual morality were ever-present within the committee's considerations and, in fact, their report. The very idea that solicitation was dangerous to public order was based on moral understandings about what behaviours were harmful to society.

Those who sat on the Street Offences Committee represented the overlap between legal debate and moral concerns about prostitution, with legal professionals, such as Miss E.H. Kelly JP and Sir Charles Biron serving alongside religious figures such as the Lord Bishop of Durham and the Reverend R.C. Gillie. Also serving on the committee was Sir Leonard Dunning, a 67-year-old Inspector of Constabulary at the Home Office and a former Assistant Head Constable of Liverpool.[30] The Home Secretary's personal influence was very much in evidence in the composition of the

28   Home Office, 'Notice Issued to the Press', 14 October 1927. The National Archive, HO 45/12663.

29   Home Office, 'Notice Issued to the Press', 14 October 1927.

30   'Dunning, Sir Leonard', *Who Was Who* (London: A & C Black, 1920–2016; online edition, Oxford University Press) [Accessed May 2016].

committee. Out of a total of 15, just five members of the committee were women, with one of them being his wife, Lady Joynson-Hicks.[31] This Home Office influence meant that the committee faced criticism about its lack of political representativeness. Ramsay MacDonald criticized the Home Secretary's decision to appoint a Departmental Committee rather than a Parliamentary Select Committee, complaining in a letter to Joynson-Hicks that, 'Had it been a Home Secretary of ours who had appointed the committee I should certainly have insisted upon his consulting you, had you been an ex-Home Secretary belonging to the Opposition'.[32] Joynson-Hicks defended his decision, arguing that he did not think that party politics were relevant to the enquiry and that he had brought together 'a body of men and women representative of various types of experience who would bring entirely fresh opinions and open minds'.[33]

The Home Secretary overstated his taste for impartiality and innovation where the Street Offences Committee was concerned. Stefan Slater argues that there were concerns that the committee had been stacked in a 'deliberate Home Office ruse to ensure the findings that it wanted'.[34] Certainly, Joynson-Hicks already favoured a social purist approach to prostitution even before he established the committee, and this was not the first instance where Joynson-Hicks took a purist interest in matters of public morality. During his time as Home Secretary he also opposed the publication of pornographic literature and supported the efforts of the Metropolitan Police in their ongoing campaign against nightclubs.[35] Jeffrey Weeks suggests that contemporary social purists were able to influence a number of high-profile individuals, such as Sir Thomas Inskip (the Solicitor-General),

31   William Joynson-Hicks, letter to Lady Joynson-Hicks on her Appointment to the Street Offences Committee, 14 October 1927. The National Archives, HO 45/12663.

32   Ramsay MacDonald, letter to William Joynson-Hicks on the composition of the Street Offences Committee, 17 October 1927. The National Archives, HO 45/12663.

33   William Joynson-Hicks, letter to Ramsay MacDonald on the composition of the Street Offences Committee, 19 October 1927. The National Archives, HO 45/12663.

34   Stefan Slater, 'Lady Astor and the Ladies of the Night', p. 542.

35   See H.G. Cocks, 'Saucy Stories: Pornography, Sexology and the Marketing of Sexual Knowledge in Britain, c.1918–70', *Social History*, 29:4 (2004), p. 475; Heather Shore, '"Constable Dances with Instructress": The Police and the Queen of Nightclubs in Inter-War London', *Social History*, 38:2 (2013), p. 184.

Sir Archibald Bodkin (the Director of Public Prosecutions) and, crucially, Joynson-Hicks himself.[36]

It was clear from the outset that the NVA had influenced the opinions of the Home Office and that the Street Offences Committee were keen to pay attention to purity concerns. In a Home Office report on the Public Places (Order) Bill, it was explained that 'representations have been received from many quarters that the present law is not satisfactory' and that the 'wide divergence of view in different quarters' had given the Home Secretary cause to consider an 'inquiry'.[37] Significantly, this report revealed that the Home Office was already sceptical about the measures outlined in the Public Places (Order) Bill. It noted, 'Many of the societies which are interested in public morals are also of the opinion that the Bill as it stands might be harmful'.[38] The NVA was privileged in the document as a particularly prominent group opposed to the Bill and one that was believed by the Home Office to have 'exceptional experience of this problem'.[39]

The recognition that the Home Office afforded to the NVA's objections to the Bill points to the Association's ongoing power and influence during the interwar years. Home Office documents suggest that, even before he had agreed to form a committee, the Home Secretary strongly favoured the NVA's interest in continuing to use the law to combat prostitution. A Home Office report describing events at an AMSH-organized deputation calling for an enquiry into the solicitation laws suggested that the Home Secretary had told those present that he was 'keenly interested in social conditions', and that he was 'in favour of any practical steps for improving the condition of the streets' and combating the 'evil of prostitution'.[40] Distancing himself from one of the central complaints of the solicitation

36   Jeffrey Weeks, *Sex, Politics and Society*, p. 218.
37   Home Office Report, 'Public Places (Order) Bill' (*c*.1926), unpublished. The National Archives, HO 45/12663.
38   Home Office Report, 'Public Places (Order) Bill' (*c*.1926).
39   Home Office Report, 'Public Places (Order) Bill' (*c*.1926).
40   Minutes of AMSH deputation to the Home Office (Home Office ref. 483.171/21), 13 November 1925, p. 6. Also, a letter from Alison Neilans, Secretary of the AMSH, to the Home Secretary suggests that this deputation was introduced by Lord Muir Mackenzie and was attended by, amongst others, George Johnson of the AMSH and Mrs Bramwell Booth JP of the Salvation Army. See Alison Neilans, letter to William Joynson Hicks, 6 November 1925. The National Archives, HO 45/12663.

law abolitionists in the AMSH, the Home Secretary appeared unconcerned that the law targeted female prostitutes while their male clients were ignored. He argued that 'morally the man might be as bad or worse but the moral offence of which the man was guilty was not an offence of which the law had hitherto taken cognizance as a legal offence'.[41] Joynson-Hicks went on to explain to the deputation that because the man 'was not selling his own body ... his position from a legal point of view was different'.[42] In fact, the Home Secretary did not accept that laws targeting prostitutes were problematic, claiming that it was 'not true to say that what one woman can do another cannot'. The Home Office report made clear that Joynson-Hicks considered the 'use of the streets as a public market' to be 'the scandal at which the law is aimed'.[43] As such, the Home Secretary showed himself to be reluctant to accept the notion that prostitutes were being singled out for special regulation based upon gendered, moral judgements about their behaviour.

Much of what Joynson-Hicks told the AMSH deputation echoed arguments made by the social purity movement. In the late nineteenth and early twentieth centuries, purists in the NVA, as well as in local branches such as the LVA, attempted to intervene in the lives of women thought to be at risk of becoming prostitutes. With so many purity campaigners located in the middle classes, feminist social purity concerns were frequently rooted in fears about the dangers of working-class culture.[44] The social purity movement's efforts to intervene in the lives of the working class reflected their desire to inculcate in the poor a sense of middle-class moral respectability.[45] Purity campaigners articulated their desires to see the law brought to bear on the more disruptive aspects of life in Britain's cities via the debate about street prostitution. In the discourse of legal rights that emerged from this debate, the prostitute woman was imagined as distinct from all other women and the maintenance of her liberty was rejected as inimical to the advancement of women's moral and social protection.

41   Minutes of AMSH deputation to the Home Office (Home Office ref. 483. 171/21), 13 November 1925, p. 7.

42   Minutes of AMSH deputation to the Home Office (Home Office ref. 483. 171/21), 13 November 1925, p. 7.

43   Minutes of AMSH deputation to the Home Office (Home Office ref. 483. 171/21), 13 November 1925, p. 6.

44   Lucy Bland, *Banishing the Beast*, p. 97.

45   Lucy Bland, *Banishing the Beast*, p. 97.

Lady Laura Riding made the point explicitly in her address to the National Union of Women Workers (NUWW) in 1912.[46] Riding argued that any legal infringement of a prostitute's liberties came as a result of her decision to work as she did. For Riding, the prostitute might be pitied but no more: 'It is not a trade that should be specially protected', she told the NUWW.[47] Riding's comments made clear that Victorian feminists' moral and political concerns about female sexuality and social purity endured into the twentieth century.

Women Police Patrols and Moral Control

The conflation of the law with matters of personal sexual morality was an issue that greatly concerned the Street Offences Committee. Tasked with making recommendations regarding changes to the solicitation laws, the committee wanted to avoid the appearance of suggesting that the law should intervene in private sexual conduct between consenting individuals. In fact, they wanted to construct an objective legal response to the issue of solicitation that was as disassociated from moral considerations about prostitution as possible. But the task of deciding what was criminal about solicitation and the harm it might inflict upon the solicited person or society at large necessarily involved making moral decisions about the impact of prostitution upon social order and individual liberty. As a result, the committee struggled to decide which aspects of the prostitute's supposed immorality should come under the jurisdiction of the law. Members of the Street Offences Committee were very keen to be clear that they did not personally condone prostitution while at the same time trying to maintain distinctions between morality and law. This tension was particularly evident in the discussions that took place between the Street Offences Committee and Mabel Cowlin on 20 April 1928, not least because Cowlin took the view that solicitation *was* a moral rather than a criminal offence.[48] It was a stance with which some members of the committee who favoured legal controls struggled.

As the former leader of the Women Police Patrols in Liverpool, Mabel Cowlin was introduced to the committee as a 'pioneer', a title that she

46   Frank Mort, *Dangerous Sexualities*, p. 112.
47   Frank Mort, *Dangerous Sexualities*, p. 112.
48   Mabel Cowlin and L.D. Potter, Transcript of Evidence, Departmental Committee on Street Offences, 20 April 1928. The National Archives, HO 326/7.

readily acknowledged.[49] Her experience of working to improve conditions on the streets was extensive: the Director of the Women Patrols and Training School in Liverpool, she had worked on the Women Police Patrols since January 1915, until her retirement in 1927.[50] Cowlin described the patrols in her evidence as a 'voluntary organisation' established 'at the beginning of the war to deal with the street problem'.[51] Cowlin's belief in the importance of these patrols was evident in her assertion that the Patrols carried out 'very skilled work required on the streets'.[52] Such was her determination and involvement in campaigning for greater female involvement in public life, Cowlin would go on to become President of the Bristol Branch of the National Council of Women (NCW) and a magistrate. She believed firmly in the 'right of women to share in the administration of public service' and, in her work with the NCW, she encouraged women to take up places on the boards of hospitals and asylums, as well as calling for the appointment of female magistrates and promoting the right of women to serve on juries.[53] In 1937, when she returned to her former school, Redland High, for a prize-giving, Cowlin told an audience of pupils, 'If you want to live your life to the full you will have to serve your generation to the best of your ability'.[54] She urged the girls to seek out work upon leaving school, explaining that women could make a valuable contribution to social services, as magistrates and on the city council.

Cowlin's testimony to the Street Offences Committee in 1928 was already coloured by her professional politics insofar as she endeavoured to legitimate and advocate the importance of the Women Police Patrols. She drew parallels between official police work and that conducted by her own organization, though she was careful to note that the only women working in Liverpool's police force at the time were 'uniformed women working privately', one of whom took statements from 'women and children'.[55] Cowlin explained that, despite their unofficial status, the Women Police Patrols also wore a uniform and understood themselves to be an official

49   Mabel Cowlin and L.D. Potter, Transcript of Evidence, p. 10.
50   Mabel Cowlin and L.D. Potter, Transcript of Evidence, p. 10.
51   Mabel Cowlin and L.D. Potter, Transcript of Evidence, p. 10.
52   Mabel Cowlin and L.D. Potter, Transcript of Evidence, p. 10.
53   *Western Daily Press and Bristol Mirror*, 23 July 1945.
54   *Western Daily Press and Bristol Mirror*, 25 November 1937.
55   Mabel Cowlin and L.D. Potter, Transcript of Evidence, p. 10.

body, very much in the same mould as the police force.[56] Talking about the patrols, Cowlin said:

> They do what the policemen do. They work in the streets very much on the lines of the police. When we are in uniform we represent to the public an official body, we are always open to be questioned on anything we do. Of course we are out to help and protect young people, and to raise the standard of conduct in the streets; that is the objective of the patrols.[57]

Cowlin's suggestion that the women in Liverpool's Women Police Patrols performed the same role as male police officers was an effort on her part to gain more recognition for women police. In actual fact, women police did not do exactly as male officers did. Louise Jackson's characterization of post-war policing is also applicable to interwar Liverpool, with women police doing preventative work while policemen carried out arrests and investigations into prostitution.[58]

Cowlin's own evidence contradicted her assurances of the similarities between male and female police work. In highlighting the important preventative work that the Women Police Patrols did, Cowlin impressed upon the Street Offences Committee the moral guidance and maternal skills that women could offer to the policing of public spaces. Cowlin proposed that the Women Police Patrols had a central role to play in preventing the corruption of younger members of the community. During the course of her testimony, she talked about the problem of solicitation with direct reference to the issue of youth. She told those present that: 'The great object of the women patrols is to protect young people; we include boys as well as girls, young men as well as young women; and the patrols are specially trained to observe the problem of soliciting'.[59] By discussing these issues together, Cowlin implied that she believed instances of solicitation to be connected to youthful indiscretion. She recalled wartime fears about the sexual interest young women were thought to have shown in soldiers and explained that the patrols were originally established during the war to combat this specific problem. Telling the committee that the patrols had

---

56   Mabel Cowlin and L.D. Potter, Transcript of Evidence, p. 11.
57   Mabel Cowlin and L.D. Potter, Transcript of Evidence, p. 11.
58   Louise Jackson, *Women Police*, pp. 174–5.
59   Mabel Cowlin and L.D. Potter, Transcript of Evidence, p. 11.

'rather kept that [wartime] outlook', Cowlin considered the 'chief danger in the streets at night' to be that faced by the 'young man or girl [who] may fall through the overtures of men or women soliciting. It is for that they are out, very largely'.[60]

Cowlin and the Women Police Patrols' sentiments accorded with the moral anxieties of local religious figures and social purists in the LVA about the sexualization of young people who frequented city spaces. In 1918, the *Liverpool Echo* published an article entitled 'Young Folks' Evil Freedom from Control', giving details of a sermon by the Reverend A. Stanley Parker.[61] The Reverend was said to have told the congregation that, after dark, the moral condition of Lime Street in central Liverpool was 'enough to make the angels weep'. He was terribly concerned by the activities of young people in the area. A particular problem, he reasoned, were the 'high wages which girls and youths were receiving at the present time' which 'had aroused in them a false sense of independence'. Parker tied the idea that social freedom was dangerous to a gendered sense of what was wrong with the area around Lime Street. His fears projected a sense of urban space as potentially polluting the respectability of young women who spent idle time there. Consequently, Parker also propagated the notion that the Women Police Patrols had a role to play in the maintenance of moral order upon Liverpool's streets. Parker suggested that alternative amusements run by volunteers, a police clampdown on solicitation and an increase in the number and authority of women patrols would alleviate the problems in Lime Street.[62]

Just as the Reverend readily equated young men and women's patronization of the area around Lime Street with moral decline, Cowlin reiterated the belief that certain parts of Liverpool threatened the respectability of those who spent time there. Areas which housed the poor or foreigners were regarded as sites of particularly high levels of immorality. Cowlin told the Street Offences Committee about 'one special district in Liverpool', which she described as being 'in the Irish Quarter', where there was a great deal of disorderliness and 'hooliganism' prior to the Women Police Patrols entering the area.[63] Not only did this anecdotal evidence reproduce wider cultural perceptions of the Irish as a group in need of extra moral guidance, it also

---

60   Mabel Cowlin and L.D. Potter, Transcript of Evidence, p. 12.
61   *Liverpool Echo*, 11 March 1918.
62   Revd A. Stanley Parker paraphrased in *Liverpool Echo*, 11 March 1918.
63   Mabel Cowlin and L.D. Potter, Transcript of Evidence, p. 25.

reflected the view that a person could be corrupted simply by spending time on the streets. This latter inference was made more explicit when Cowlin suggested that the patrols would 'centralise on the poor districts where the streets have to be used by the people for their recreation because they have no gardens or outlet otherwise'.[64] In this way, patrolling was an activity steeped in concerns about class and the precarious rectitude of the urban poor.

The Street Offences Committee did not challenge Cowlin's idea that urban spaces presented dangers to the morality of the young. Yet that is not to say that they were content to discuss the issue of solicitation as a purely moral matter. The Street Offences Committee searched Cowlin's testimony for a resolution to their efforts to divorce moral discourses about prostitution from their interrogation of its legality. The committee pursued a deliberate line of questioning with Cowlin intending to draw out to what extent she thought the law could and should be called upon to enforce morality. Macmillan asked Cowlin if she thought it 'undesirable that open solicitation should go on in our streets for immoral purposes'.[65] Questions such as this were loaded in such a way as to give an indication of the chairman's own position on the issue. Despite being given the task of questioning the laws that surrounded it, Macmillan's wording made it clear that he did not want to be seen to be condoning prostitution. His use of the words 'our streets' immediately placed ownership of public spaces in the hands of the supposedly moral and righteous and set these people aside from prostitutes and the men who used them. Nevertheless, there was a sense among the committee members that the issues being discussed were potentially transformative. It was put to Cowlin:

> We have been listening to some evidence which rather surprised some of us, to the effect that solicitation for immoral purposes should be permitted in our streets and the law should take no notice of it unless it reaches the state of actual disorder, breach of the peace.[66]

When asked about her position on this Cowlin responded, 'You are asking a difficult question', leading Macmillan to push, 'It is one of the difficult

64   Mabel Cowlin and L.D. Potter, Transcript of Evidence, p. 27.
65   Mabel Cowlin and L.D. Potter, Transcript of Evidence, p. 13.
66   Macmillan to Cowlin in Mabel Cowlin and L.D. Potter, Transcript of Evidence, p. 13.

questions we have to answer on this side of the table.'[67] The committee were frustrated by Cowlin's reluctance to provide a definitive answer.

Cowlin's reticence to elaborate coherently on her or her organization's legal and moral philosophies reflected a wider conflict in the approach of women police. While some within the women police movement, like Cowlin, were quite willing to promote the potential of a professional women police service by emphasizing what they could offer in terms of moral expertise, others believed that this approach inherently undermined the case for professionalization. Louise Jackson argues that within the Women Police movement there was ambivalence about the extent to which their work should be aligned with welfare work. Some, like Sophia Stanley, who supervised the Met's women police between 1919 and 1922, readily conflated the work of women police with welfare initiatives such as finding accommodation for young women.[68] However, others, such as attested policewoman Lillian Wyles, were critical of this approach, fearing that such efforts undermined women's role within the police service.[69]

In Liverpool, the Women Police Patrols continued to assert that it was only through becoming 'an integral part of the Police Force' that they could 'prove their full value'.[70] Cowlin envisaged roles for women police within the official force which utilized their feminine respectability and morality. However, by conducting themselves in similar ways to moral welfare bodies like the LVA, the Women Police Patrols risked compromising the assertion that women's policing should be official and attested. Moreover, where prostitution was concerned, Cowlin implied that moral welfare initiatives might yield greater success than criminalization in the prevention of prostitution. For Cowlin:

> the whole question of whether [solicitation] should be regarded as a vice that society should deal with through non-legal measures, or whether it should be regarded as a crime which the law should put down, is a very difficult thing … because if you deal with solicitation *per se* as a crime you are laying tremendous responsibility on the people who have to bring that crime to Court, namely on the police.[71]

---

67   Mabel Cowlin and L.D. Potter, Transcript of Evidence, p. 13.
68   Louise Jackson, *Women Police*, pp. 627 and 632.
69   Louise Jackson, *Women Police*, pp. 627 and 632.
70   Liverpool Women Police Patrols, Annual Report 1928, p. 5.
71   Mabel Cowlin and L.D. Potter, Transcript of Evidence, p. 13.

Cowlin explained her own doubts about using the law to deal with solicitation by referring to the practicalities of policing rather than entering into a discussion about the relationship between morality and law. Overall, it was a response that left the committee unsatisfied.

Charged with answering these difficult questions, those present continued to seek clarity from Cowlin on her understanding of the legal and moral status of solicitation. Macmillan asked Cowlin whether the patrols in Liverpool were performing a 'public service' by intervening in instances of solicitation.[72] When she agreed that they were, he continued by asking whether the same efforts should also be applied to instances of smoking in the streets. Cowlin could not agree.[73] The question from the chairman was deliberately intended to distance solicitation from other forms of anti-social behaviour, in order to present solicitation as a moral transgression to which the weight of the law could be applied. Macmillan's personal views on solicitation became apparent when he implied that smoking could not be legislated against while solicitation could because the latter 'is calculated to have unfortunate results upon the people of this country, and because it is in itself an indecent and disorderly thing'.[74] Not only did he present solicitation as a threat to national order, Macmillan believed this threat to be deliberate and conscious. For the chairman, solicitation was both a legal *and* a moral matter. Nevertheless, and despite sharing Macmillan's dislike of solicitation, Cowlin remained uncomfortable with the idea that it should be treated as a legal matter. She replied: 'I think it is almost entirely a matter of conscience. They know they are doing an anti-social thing'.[75] In fact, Cowlin even went as far as to suggest that 'We should do as much [work to combat solicitation] I think', were there no law backing the patrols.[76]

The committee found a similar reluctance to support a legal approach to solicitation in the evidence of Cowlin's colleague, Miss L.D. Potter, the Patrol Leader with the Women Police Patrols in Liverpool. Giving evidence at the same meeting, Potter suggested that the law should only be applied

72   Macmillan to Cowlin in Mabel Cowlin and L.D. Potter, Transcript of Evidence, p. 13.
73   Mabel Cowlin and L.D. Potter, Transcript of Evidence, p. 13.
74   Macmillan to Cowlin in Mabel Cowlin and L.D. Potter, Transcript of Evidence, p. 13.
75   Mabel Cowlin and L.D. Potter, Transcript of Evidence, p. 14.
76   Mabel Cowlin and L.D. Potter, Transcript of Evidence, p. 14.

to instances of solicitation if there was 'annoyance'.[77] She explained that she did not think solicitation should be punished if it was conducted discreetly, leading her to correct an assertion by the committee: 'You were saying a minute ago that it was always an offence against decency and good order; it is usually very quietly done.'[78] Potter elaborated: 'There are different ways of looking at it. You must punish street disorder; therefore disorderly solicitation must be punished; but supposing it is not disorderly, the question is whether you can punish a thing which is in itself a moral offence. No, I do not think I should say so.'[79] In light of this testimony, Potter explained that the patrol work she undertook was 'preventative' in nature and she went on to say that she thought the patrols, and 'to a certain extent' the police, should 'use their discretion to try and stop immorality'.[80] Confused by this position, the committee asked Potter why she would not like greater support from the law.[81] Her response of 'you cannot interfere with private morals' caused Macmillan to interject, 'But aren't you interfering with private morals?'[82] The chairman was correct, insofar as the work conducted by the Women Police Patrols was moral in nature rather than legal.

The Street Offences Committee struggled to make sense of the evidence provided by Cowlin and Potter. The reluctance of these two witnesses to accept that the law's potential to regulate morality was considered to be at odds with their work preventing immoral behaviour on the streets. Both Cowlin and Potter presented the work of the Women Police Patrols as skilled and they argued in favour of the professionalization and formalization of the women police. However, Potter's assertion that they were 'Not really' interfering with private morality did not square with her active role in trying to prevent solicitation.[83] The chairman confessed that he had 'difficulty' understanding 'how the [Women] police patrol, any more than the policeman, should have any right to interfere in a matter of morals between two citizens ... if what they are doing is not an infringement of some legal

77 Mabel Cowlin and L.D. Potter, Transcript of Evidence, p. 16.
78 Mabel Cowlin and L.D. Potter, Transcript of Evidence, p. 16.
79 Mabel Cowlin and L.D. Potter, Transcript of Evidence, p. 16.
80 Mabel Cowlin and L.D. Potter, Transcript of Evidence, p. 17.
81 Wilberforce to Potter in Mabel Cowlin and L.D. Potter, Transcript of Evidence, p. 17.
82 Macmillan and Potter in conversation, in Mabel Cowlin and L.D. Potter, Transcript of Evidence, p. 17.
83 Mabel Cowlin and L.D. Potter, Transcript of Evidence, p. 17.

dictum?'[84] By interrogating the purpose of the Women Police Patrols in this way, the Street Offences Committee were able to draw out the entirely moral character of this work.

What Macmillan failed to appreciate, however, was that neither Cowlin nor Potter considered the moral nature of their work to be contradictory to the idea that this was also professional work. Indeed, from early on in her public service career, Cowlin had understood morality to be an area where women could claim authority and stake a claim for themselves as professionals. In 1917, Cowlin attended a meeting of the Bristol Training School for Women Patrols to discuss her work in Liverpool. She readily incorporated moral concerns about youth and urban lifestyles into her political rhetoric about the need for women police, explaining that 'Guilds' and 'young people's meetings' had failed to tackle the social 'evil' of the 'sex problem' because they had been afraid to deal with it.[85] In their place, Cowlin argued that women police would 'purify' and improve the condition of the streets. For Cowlin, the campaign for women police was not necessarily about getting women to serve on the force in the same capacity as men.[86]

When Macmillan told Cowlin 'we want your view as to whether you could do as good social work and preventive work of the type you are engaged in if you had not behind you the sanction of the law', she said she could not provide an answer.[87] Significantly, she did not challenge or comment on the chairman's understanding of her work as a form of 'social work' rather than policing.[88] Both Cowlin and Potter accepted another committee member's description of their work as 'philanthropic activities'.[89] In fact they readily

84   Macmillan to Potter in Mabel Cowlin and L.D. Potter, Transcript of Evidence, p. 19.

85   *Western Daily Press*, Bristol, 25 May 1917.

86   *Western Daily Press*, Bristol, 25 May 1917.

87   Macmillan to Cowlin, in Mabel Cowlin and L.D. Potter, Transcript of Evidence, pp. 15–16.

88   Mabel Cowlin and L.D. Potter, Transcript of Evidence, pp. 15–16. The description of the Women Police's work as a form of social work was probably unchallenged because it was largely accurate. In her research on the work of the Women Police Patrols in Liverpool, Gaynor Williams has noted that much of the work that the patrollers undertook could be considered 'a form of street centred social work'. Gaynor Diane Williams, 'Women in Public Life', p. 124.

89   E.H. Kelly to Potter, in Mabel Cowlin and L.D. Potter, Transcript of Evidence, p. 27.

adopted this social welfare status as a necessary preliminary step to profes-sionalization, with Cowlin telling those present: 'We do not feel that the country is ready yet for the setting up of what is equivalent to a women's police service'.[90]

The final report of the Street Offences Committee suggested removing the term 'common prostitute' from law and instead introducing more gender-neutral legislation prohibiting anyone, male or female, from solic-iting. The Report also suggested that the evidence of the annoyed passers-by would be necessary for cases to be brought against accused parties.[91] It was recognized at the time that the Report offered 'compromise recom-mendations' from a divided committee.[92] The lack of clear consensus would subsequently undermine the impact of the Report and it was noted in the press that the Street Offences Committee had offered 'No solution … to the vexed problem of securing corroborative evidence in a charge of soliciting or importuning by either sex.'[93] The problem of persuading members of the public to attend court to provide such testimonies remained.[94] For the NVA, the solution to this problem had been simple: they argued that it should be unnecessary to prove annoyance in cases of solicitation. NVA secretary Mr F.A.R. Sempkins told the committee that the law protected non-prostitute women from the immorality of prostitution.[95] At the same time, Sempkins recommended preventative, moral didactic strategies be used alongside the law in an effort to dissuade vulnerable women from succumbing to vice. He urged that women police should be used to improve the condition of the streets, not by giving them powers of arrest but by taking on roles as moral guides in the lives of young women. Certainly, Sempkins wanted to make it clear that he considered the women police to be very distinct from the actual police force, saying, 'I would dress them as women police, and not as men police'.[96]

This notion that women police could be used for specific, non-legal, moral control upon the streets was widespread. The testimony of Cowlin and Potter shows how influential women with close connections to Liverpool's

90   Mabel Cowlin and L.D. Potter, Transcript of Evidence, p. 27.
91   Stefan Slater, 'Lady Astor and the Ladies of the Night', p. 543.
92   *Nottingham Evening Post*, 26 November 1928.
93   *Nottingham Evening Post*, 26 November 1928.
94   *Nottingham Evening Post*, 26 November 1928.
95   *Aberdeen Press and Journal*, 5 March 1928.
96   *Aberdeen Press and Journal*, 5 March 1928.

Women Police Patrols sought to explain their work via notions of social work and philanthropy. In many respects, these women were still more comfortable as moral guides than as law enforcers. These women attempted to pioneer a new professional status for themselves, while at the same time falling back on the traditions of the purity campaigners who patrolled the streets in order to maintain working-class women's morality. As such, Liverpool's Women Police Patrols representatives attempted to offer a solution to the problem of solicitation by suggesting that they could supply professionalized moral surveillance. They did not think that the law should be used to target solicitation or that the official police force should overly concern itself with this offence. Yet they did not think that solicitation should be ignored as a social problem either. Instead, Liverpool's women police proposed their own brand of unofficial and informal street policing whereby they, as respectable women, would watch over and maintain the morality of other women. It was an approach already taken by purity groups around the country and, in the midst of the unrest about the solicitation laws, it was an approach that was to remain prominent throughout the interwar years.

The state remained unable to establish a clear definition of the prostitute's offence. As such, social purists continued to act as an unofficial police force while simultaneously allowing politicians to avoid making any controversial changes to the already controversial solicitation laws. The emphasis that Liverpool's Women Police Patrols placed on prostitution as a moral issue, rather than a social or economic problem, created a sense of urban space as a threat to female respectability. The idea that the prostitute was a transgressive other, from whom innocent women needed to be protected, had clear implications for the moral surveillance of the city's streets. Moreover, it meant that all women's use of public space came under moral scrutiny.

4

Finding Respectable Work for Women in Interwar Liverpool

This chapter examines local social purists' interwar efforts to maintain social and moral order by channelling young, working-class women into traditional forms of employment and jobs which drew upon women's supposedly intrinsic caring and domestic skills. Many of the women encountered by the LVA were travelling to or from positions in domestic service, jobs as ward-maids in hospitals or factory work. In partnership with organizations like the House of Help, the LVA established links between employers in these sectors and the young women who arrived in the city in need of money and security. Though the need to work had encouraged these women to travel and though employment offered women a greater degree of independence, the LVA nonetheless saw working-class female employment as crucial to the containment and reduction of vice in the city.

This chapter argues that local moral issues impacted on the employment prospects of the women who moved through and around the city in search of jobs. While historians have addressed the broad social changes in working-class women's employment trajectories and there has been much written on the changes in young women's interwar lifestyles, the sheer extent to which moral fears continued to impinge upon both women's employment plans and their very presence in urban spaces throughout these decades has not been explored in detail. By providing this local-level analysis of Liverpudlian social purity approaches to women's work and female morality, I want to show that changes in working-class women's lifestyles were counterbalanced by renewed efforts from organizations like the LVA and the House of Help to promote traditional jobs in domestic service, caring roles and mill work. Lucy Delap argues against the idea that domestic service became 'redundant' by the mid-twentieth century. Instead, she suggests that later cleaning and au pair work was genealogically related to earlier twentieth-century domestic service.[1] Understanding social purists' efforts to promote traditionally feminine, domesticated and caring jobs to working-class women during the interwar years partly explains this genealogical relationship. I argue that women's increasing geographic and occupational mobility paradoxically gave the LVA further justification to morally police women's travels through Liverpool and to reassert gender order through traditional forms of employment.

During the interwar years, women's employment maintained and supplemented household incomes. Young, working-class women increasingly moved into areas like retail and clerical work.[2] Though employment could still be precarious, young women's earning power meant that their leisure time could be spent engaging in consumer pursuits like buying clothes, going dancing and going to the cinema.[3] However, these changes did not signal an end to the idea that a woman's ultimate goal should still be to become a wife and a mother. The economic contribution that women made to the family had to be reconciled with domesticated, feminine ideals which continued to situate women in caring roles rather than as providers. Social purists in the LVA, supported by other local philanthropists and welfare workers from the House of Help and even the Women Police Patrols, took a cautious but pragmatic approach to women's employment during these years. Caught between wariness about the employment ambitions of working-class women and a desire to enable them to lead respectable and virtuous lives, these organizations took it upon themselves to place women in *respectable* jobs. Guiding and shaping the often vague and haphazard employment intentions of those who arrived in the city, the LVA regarded certain types of work, domestic service in home and hospital environments in particular, as having an important role to play in keeping women off the streets and diverting them away from the temptation of prostitution.

Social purists' concerns about working-class women's plans for work and travel persisted during the interwar period despite the fact that many

1   Lucy Delap, *Knowing Their Place: Domestic Service in Twentieth-Century Britain* (Oxford: Oxford University Press, 2011).

2   Selina Todd, 'Young Women, Work, and Leisure in Interwar England', *Historical Journal*, 48:3 (2005), p. 793.

3   Claire Langhamer, *Women's Leisure in England, 1920–60* (Manchester: Manchester University Press, 2000), p. 58.

of these women would have been used to holding down different jobs and moving for work. Indeed, the years immediately after the First World War witnessed a culture that, to some extent, encouraged the movement of women for domestic work. Efforts to restore traditional gendered divisions in occupations and to create demographic balance between the numbers of men and women in Britain meant that policies such as the Free Passage Scheme (1919–22) encouraged women to enter domestic service in the colonies.[4] Though the LVA and House of Help did not promote this type of international travel, the frequency with which they encountered women travelling in search of work reflects just how common it was for young, working-class women to move cities for employment. Selina Todd's research has shown that occupational mobility was a fundamental component of working-class women's employment experiences after the Great War.[5] Consequently, the moral anxieties about women's work that are explored in this chapter elucidate the mingling and coexistence of change and continuity during the interwar years.

As much as organizations like the LVA, the House of Help and the Women Police Patrols promoted their own brands of female public service, facilitated the movement of women between places and helped women to find jobs, their activities were nonetheless driven by their moral concern about women's greater occupational and geographical mobility after the war. Anxiety about the effects of urban travel upon female morality saw the LVA in particular regulate and gender public spaces, like the docks, Lime Street station and working-class neighbourhoods, in ways that promoted the moral judgement of working-class women. The activities of these social purists in Liverpool, a key node in the national and international movement of women for work, show that women's geographical mobility fuelled a reactionary narrative which portrayed working-class women's travels through urban spaces as deeply troubling and threatening to the social order of the city.

The employment guidance offered by local social purists saw them use Liverpool's economic situation and insecurities in the local job market in order to push their moral agenda. For many working-class women,

---

4 Lucy Noakes, 'From War Service to Domestic Service: Ex-Servicewomen and the Free Passage Scheme 1919–22', *Twentieth Century British History*, 22:1 (2011), pp. 1–27.

5 Selina Todd, *Young Women, Work, and Family in England 1918–1950*, pp. 114–15.

finding work was essential to their survival. However, interwar economic uncertainty in Liverpool meant that organizations like the LVA could use structural economic conditions in the city in order to discourage women from changing jobs or moving for work unless it was considered to be necessary, either because the work was unreliable and so not a deterrent to prostitution or because the LVA had other moral concerns about the work. In practice, this meant that social purists directed women away from ad hoc jobs in areas of work which might have led to them working late or in lively social settings. The LVA discouraged work in jobs such as waitressing, bar work and the performing arts in favour of placing young women within domestic service positions in respectable, middle-class homes or, failing that, they sent them back to factory work. Indeed, the case studies explored in this chapter indicate that this strategy was adopted despite the fact that many of these young women had travelled to Liverpool in order to get away from the mundanity of work in traditional occupations.

The links that the LVA sought to cultivate with traditional employers reflected the organization's commitment to using work to influence working-class female morality. Case studies from the LVA's annual reports indicate that while social purists supported women's work as a means of under-mining the economic causes of prostitution, the stability and respectability of young women's prospective jobs were paramount concerns for the LVA. Ambition leading to risk-taking in search of social or economic promotion was strongly discouraged by the organization's patrollers. For the LVA, ambition was a trait that required strong moral guidance in order to ensure that it did not corrupt young, working-class women by taking them off on dangerous adventures across towns and cities in pursuit of unlikely or ill-advised employment goals.

Women and the Local Economy

Writing in 1960, H.R. Poole of the Liverpool Council of Social Service offered a bleak recollection of the city's experiences after the First World War. He suggested that Liverpool's 'high hopes' of 'post-war reconstruction' had been 'hampered and distracted by rising unemployment and urgent economic difficulties'.[6] In language that invoked memories of the world wars, Poole claimed that the city's aspirations were 'finally ... blasted and

6   H.R. Poole *The Liverpool Council of Social Service: 1909–1959* (Liverpool: The Liverpool Council of Social Service, 1960), p. 35.

torn when the full weight of the depression hit Merseyside'.[7] He proposed – with regional affection – that while Liverpool's situation was a 'mirror of national events', Liverpool's story cast the difficulties of the time 'in sharp relief', because the city's 'new hopes and ideas were so bold and were fought for so hard, and the economic difficulties were so intense'.[8] Certainly, large sections of the city were seriously affected by the interwar economic downturn. Dock workers were most obviously hit by the depression, which caused economic damage across other employment sectors in the city. Associated businesses in areas such as storage and messenger work were hit, as were small businesses, such as cafés and pubs near the docks.[9]

Differing expectations about the stability or appropriateness of women's work meant that definitions of female unemployment were problematic during the interwar period. Even at the level of the state, the categorization of the unemployed woman was complicated by the fact that she challenged the assumption that women had a guaranteed role working at home for the benefit of their families. Married women were undoubtedly disadvantaged by the state's introduction of the Anomalies Act in July 1931. The Act stated that unemployed married women would not be eligible for benefit in line with other workers and, in Liverpool alone, 3,000 women had been disallowed benefit by November of that year.[10] Yet the lack of recognition afforded to women as workers was out of step with the reality of many women's lives. During times of economic difficulty women found that they had to take on the role of bringing money into the home. High levels of male unemployment in the early 1920s and again in the early 1930s meant that many young women took jobs in domestic service to alleviate economic difficulties caused by their fathers being out of work.[11] With high unemployment in interwar Liverpool, work within domestic service became a necessity for many women.[12] This work was relatively plentiful, even during the economic difficulties of the 1930s, as

7   H.R. Poole, *The Liverpool Council of Social Service*, p. 35.

8   H.R. Poole, *The Liverpool Council of Social Service*, p. 35.

9   Sam Davies, Pete Gill, Linda Grant, Martin Nightingale, Ron Noon and Andy Shallice, *Genuinely Seeking Work: Mass Unemployment on Merseyside in the 1930s* (Birkenhead: Liver Press, 1992), p. 19.

10   Sam Davies et al., *Genuinely Seeking Work*, p. 78.

11   Selina Todd, 'Domestic Service and Class Relations in Britain 1900–1950', *Past and Present*, 203 (2009), p. 186.

12   Sam Davies et al., *Genuinely Seeking Work*, p. 24.

young women took up low-paid positions in lower middle-class and skilled working-class homes with children.[13] As a result, the number of women officially working in Liverpool's personal service sector rose from 31,000 in 1921 to 38,000 in 1931.[14]

Colin Pooley argues that the narrow gap between the social status of service workers and their employers in Liverpool reflects how cheap domestic service was in the city when compared with London.[15] Drawing on Caradog Jones' 1930s survey of Merseyside, Pooley notes that live-in domestic servants earned, on average, 10 to 12 shillings per week, plus board, working 10- to 12-hour days with only half a day off.[16] Todd has argued that this increase in domestic service can be read as evidence of 'downward occupational mobility' for working-class women, who were squeezed out of other, better-paid sectors such as clerical and retail work.[17] Indeed, the opportunities available to women at the time were markedly shaped by their social class.[18] Despite the gap between domestic servants and their employers being narrower than in other parts of the country, a woman's path into domestic service on Merseyside still reflected her social background, with daughters of the 'artisan class' working in private homes, while those of a slightly lower social status worked in institutions.[19] Some women sought to improve their position by moving into other feminized roles, such as nursing. But even in the hospital environment, working-class women still found themselves performing domestic duties. In a bid to improve the status of nursing, one hospital in London created a two-tier system of recruitment, with working-class nurse probationers given more domestic work and asked to work longer hours than those from middle-class backgrounds.[20] When organizations like the LVA and the House of Help assisted women travelling to hospital posts,

13   Colin Pooley, 'Living in Liverpool', p. 205. Adrian Bingham has suggested that nationally there was actually a shortage of domestic servants during the 1920s. See Adrian Bingham, *Gender, Modernity and the Popular Press*, p. 68.

14   Sam Davies et al., *Genuinely Seeking Work*, p. 25.

15   Colin Pooley, 'Living in Liverpool', pp. 205–6.

16   Colin Pooley, 'Living in Liverpool', p. 205.

17   Selina Todd, 'Poverty and Aspiration: Young Women's Entry to Employment in Inter-war England', *Twentieth Century British History*, 15:2 (2004), pp. 131 and 122.

18   Selina Todd, 'Poverty and Aspiration', p. 120.

19   Selina Todd, 'Poverty and Aspiration', p. 127.

20   David Justham, 'A Study of Nursing Practices Used in the Management of Infection in Hospitals, 1929–1948', PhD thesis, University of Manchester, 2014, p. 141.

the working-class status of these women would, therefore, have continued to mark them out.

Though the LVA did not directly campaign on issues to do with Liverpool's economy, the organization was anxious about the impact of local economic fluctuations on the lives of young, working-class women. Aware that unemployment was a problem in the city, the LVA worried about the numbers of young women who were, through necessity if not personal ambition, working outside the home, thereby gaining greater independence from the families that they were, in the immediate term, helping to support. During the interwar years, many young, working-class women from rural areas migrated to towns in order to find work, and it was these mobile women that the purity associations aimed to intercept with their transport station patrols.[21] Further afield, the relationship between economic hardship, travel for work and working-class, female immorality also concerned the LVA's parent organization, the NVA.[22] As the LVA put it in the early 1930s, the NVA had already 'played a leading part in obtaining laws which have put an end to the open activities of traffickers in women', but the task now was to 'prevent the supply of potential victims'.[23] The NVA aimed to do this by assisting 'girls in difficulty or distress at the railway Stations'. From the point of view of both the NVA and the LVA, their patrol work protecting women from traffickers had, in the words of the LVA, 'gradually, and inevitably, become immediately linked with the unemployment problem'.[24]

Fears about Prostitution

The LVA understood that young women needed to travel through and around the city to find jobs, and their patrollers believed that work could offer women a degree of personal economic security and stability. To this end, work could be regarded as a form of moral protection for working-class women. Similarly, Liverpool's Women Police Patrols drew direct links between a woman's employment prospects and the likelihood of her turning to prostitution. They suggested that though they could 'do

21   For more on rural working-class women's work and migration, see Selina Todd, 'Young Women, Work and Family in Inter-War Rural England', *Agricultural History Review*, 52:1 (2004), p. 84.
22   LVA, Annual Report 1932–33, p. 5. Liverpool Record Office, M326 VIG/3.
23   LVA, Annual Report 1932–33, p. 4.
24   LVA, Annual Report 1932–33, p. 4.

little with the professional prostitute', their patrols focused 'on preventing young girls from beginning to earn money on the streets by helping them to get work, keeping in friendly touch with them and taking an interest in their pursuits'.[25] It was not the case, though, that just any work would do for welfare workers looking to direct women away from prostitution. Depending on the type of work sought out by the female traveller, the LVA saw women's employment as a potential means of social improvement or a potential source of moral danger. Their experiences finding reputable employers for women during the First World War had set the tone for the LVA's interwar approach to mediating between employers and women in need of work. The LVA emphasized the high moral stakes they believed surrounded this particular task:

> A moral disaster prevented may not be so sensational as a rescue achieved, but how far-reaching are its beneficial results! In many of the cases with which we have to deal there would, humanly speaking, have been 'one more unfortunate', but we were permitted to stand in the breach and the danger was happily averted.[26]

For the LVA, the main 'danger' faced by women who worked outside the home was the potential for 'moral disaster'. Material and environmental considerations such as low pay or poor working conditions held little interest for the Association. Though the LVA had been set up with the remit of tackling white slavery, the organization attempted to draw links between their concerns about prostitution and the everyday nature of their work meeting boats and trains and securing respectable work for young women. The LVA argued that while rescue work may have produced more 'sensational' stories, the process of investigating the prospective jobs of the women that they met acted as a form of preventative work. The LVA suggested that it was as a direct result of their interventions into discussions between women and potential employers that they 'averted' so many women from falling into disreputable work and, consequently, into immoral lifestyles. Indeed, the suggestion that the LVA's work could prevent a woman from becoming 'one more unfortunate' made it clear that the Association was not focused upon rescue work. Once a woman had begun to work as

25   Women Police Patrols, Annual Report 1935, p. 5. Liverpool Record Office, 365 WOM/18/1–19.
26   LVA, Annual Report 1916, p. 8.

a prostitute the LVA believed there was little they could do to help her. It was for this reason that the LVA continued into the interwar years with their task of vetting women's employment opportunities, regarding this as a legitimate and significant preventative strategy for maintaining working-class women's morality.

After the First World War, the LVA noted that it supported the work of the NVA, through its links with NVA workers in the capital and through their shared understanding of the relationship between the country's economic problems and the moral dangers thought to threaten the respectability of the nation's young women. For the LVA, there was a clear link between prostitution, trafficking in women and economic decline, since unemployment seemed to cause so many women to make sudden and unplanned journeys to new parts of the country in search of work. Though the LVA could place women in domestic service roles in Liverpool, in 1933, the LVA feared that young women were travelling to London for domestic work despite not being 'the class of trained servant' required there.[27] They argued that these women would not have been encouraged to make the journey to the capital in search of work 'were it not for industrial distress'.[28] It is clear, then, that the LVA took a stratified view of domestic service and that they considered the women who they typically encountered to be more suited to the lower-status and lower-paid domestic service jobs of the kind on offer in Liverpool. Working-class women's efforts to step outside of this trajectory of low-paid work worried the LVA. The fear was that once these women realized how difficult it would be for them to find work they would remain in the capital and turn to prostitution as the most likely means of earning money. Representatives from the Women Police Patrols similarly conflated the economic imperatives behind prostitution with questions about the moral fortitude of working-class women. Mabel Cowlin explained to the Street Offences Committee that it was an 'unintelligent class' of woman who turned to prostitution because it provided 'an economically easy way of satisfying many desires which would never be satisfied in her life otherwise'.[29]

It was this sense of material desire and economic ambition that the LVA took steps to manage and, in some instances, curtail. The LVA believed that economic problems did not just encourage an exodus of vulnerable working-class women *from* Liverpool; they supposed that these problems

27   LVA, Annual Report 1932–33.
28   LVA, Annual Report 1932–33.
29   Mabel Cowlin and L.D. Potter, Transcript of Evidence, p. 24.

also fuelled increases in women travelling *to* the port. The LVA argued that many runaways came from large families where the father was unemployed. They suggested that these girls had 'heard there is plenty of well-paid work in Liverpool, Manchester or London'.[30] Indeed, social purists and welfare workers in Liverpool were extremely concerned during the interwar years that the message about Liverpool being a city of unemployment, rather than economic opportunity, was not getting through to some of the women who were travelling there.

In the early 1920s, the LVA's collaborators at the Liverpool House of Help were also worried about the supposedly ill-thought-out nature of so many women's employment ambitions:

> [T]here is a constant flow from foreign lands, from country districts, from Ireland, and from Scotland, of women of all ages who come to the city with no prospect of employment, with little or no money and with only the vaguest notion, or none, of what they are going to do when they get here.[31]

According to the House of Help and the LVA, Liverpool's role as a port meant that the city attracted wanderers with no firm plans to secure their own well-being or prosperity. As unemployment troubled the city in the early 1930s, the LVA suggested that young women travelled to the city full of misguided enthusiasm about their prospects. In 1933, the chairman of the LVA, the Rector of Liverpool, noted that during that year the LVA had dealt with a greater number of young women than average. He explained that this

> may in large part be accounted for by the fact of unemployment. Girls travel about from place to place in search of work, and Liverpool attracts them as a Port of Hope, though so often of hope unrealised. Under such circumstances the timely help of our Society may, and often does, step in and avert disaster.[32]

With this statement the Rector made it clear that the LVA's task where employment was concerned was to manage the unrealistic expectations

---

30   LVA, Annual Report 1932–33, p. 5.
31   House of Help, Annual Report 1922, p. 8.
32   John C.H. How, Rector of Liverpool, in LVA, Annual Report 1932–33, p. 3.

of hopeful young women in order to ensure their overall well-being. The potential 'disaster' that he referred to was moral, rather than economic. Neither the LVA nor the House of Help was politically interested, nor was the LVA a lobbyist group. Members do not appear to have taken a principled or idealistic interest in the material impacts of poverty upon young women's lives, except where material deprivation could be considered a factor in the causes of prostitution. As the LVA saw it, their remit in hard times was to make sure that a downward local economy did not see more girls selling themselves on the streets out of desperation and a lack of alternative prospects.

Employment Guidance

In order to achieve their aims of managing the assumed disparity between so many young women's seemingly unrealistic expectations of work and their economic needs, the LVA devised duel strategies of monitoring women's travel and vetting potential employers. In the first instance, the Landing Stage at the docks and Lime Street train station were focal points for the LVA's practice of informally policing the city's streets. From these entry points the organization could intercept newcomers to Liverpool and investigate their plans before they wandered off alone into the city. Maintaining contact with other vigilance associations (such as the NVA), as well as with employment organizations, the LVA enquired about the situations of young women due to arrive in Liverpool. The Association's workers would also make follow up enquiries about girls previously helped and sent on their way to destinations outside the city. In 1930, the LVA noted its 'sincere appreciation' of the 'various kindred Associations' who co-operated with them in meeting young women and assessing their circumstances.[33] Members of the LVA suggested that they had received help from various regions, including London, Paris, Glasgow, Belfast, Cork, Dublin, Newcastle upon Tyne, Manchester, New York, Australia and Buenos Aires.[34]

In terms of their local connections, the LVA made special mention of the Liverpool House of Help, who temporarily housed women brought there by the LVA, and Nugent House (part of a local philanthropic movement set up by Father James Nugent in the Victorian era in order to help the poor), which also housed women, as well as helping to find employment for

33   LVA, Annual Report 1929–30, p. 7.
34   LVA, Annual Report 1929–30, p. 7.

them.[35] The support of these Houses was important to the LVA's project of protecting the morality of working-class women by making sure that they found suitable work. These refuges provided reputable accommodation where patrollers could temporarily place young women while the LVA set about making employment enquiries on their behalf and, significantly, these institutions were also able to assist the LVA in their employment investigations. During the interwar years, the Matron at the House of Help regularly sought out work for its residents. According to the House of Help this was 'often a very difficult matter, requiring much investigation as well as great tact and discrimination'.[36] Nevertheless, in 1921 alone the House found work for 'no fewer than 200 cases ... which the Committee believe[d] to be a record for the charity'.[37] This figure amounted to 38 per cent of all the women who stayed at the House in that year. In actual fact, 1921 was far from anomalous in this regard: in each year between 1921 and 1929, the House of Help found work for between 32 per cent and 43 per cent of its residents.[38]

With such support to draw upon, it was not surprising that the LVA also had success in facilitating women's employment. The LVA had sown the seeds for their interwar success in this area during the First World War, when the organization had created links with the local Labour Exchange. In one case from the LVA's 1917–18 annual report, a 19-year-old girl was referred to the organization by the Manageress of the Labour Exchange, after the young woman had tried and failed to find work in a munitions factory.[39] On her first visit to the Labour Exchange the girl had met a 'respectable' woman who had given her lodgings. Once the LVA were involved in the girl's case, they were pleased to find that the woman looking after her was 'fully alive to the dangers to which [the girl] was exposed in a large city like Liverpool'. Satisfied that the girl had found an appropriate moral guide to teach her how to navigate the city's urban dangers, the Association proceeded to try to find work for her, while she continued to

35   LVA, Annual Report 1929–30, p. 7. See also Liverpool House of Help Annual Reports 1943–67. Liverpool Record Office, 362/HOU/3.
36   House of Help, Annual Report 1921, p. 8. Liverpool Record Office, 362/HOU/3/30.
37   House of Help, Annual Report 1921, p. 8.
38   House of Help, Annual Reports 1921–29. Liverpool Record Office, 362/HOU/3/30/30–38.
39   LVA, Annual Report 1917–18, pp. 12–13.

make her own enquiries at the Labour Exchange. The girl subsequently found work as a kitchen maid, although when this employment came to an end the LVA placed her in a home and she was eventually 'claim[ed]' and 'given over' to her brother.[40] That the girl was so closely monitored until her brother arrived to take her home was indicative of the LVA's anxieties about women being allowed to travel on their own without a chaperone to protect them. Moreover, the fact that the girl briefly took up work as a kitchen maid shows that the Association considered these types of unskilled domestic duties to be respectable enough for young, working-class female travellers. By doing this type of work, the LVA reasoned that the girl was being kept off the streets. Her job, working in kitchens, was similar to the sort of work that the LVA would regularly promote to young women during the interwar years.

As well as vetting individuals such as the one that this young woman had stayed with while looking for work, the LVA also vetted employment agencies. In 1924, the LVA reported that one of their patrollers had 'observed two young girls aged 17 and 20' talking to a man at a train station.[41] Imbuing the patroller with a sense of moral intuition that served to heighten her expertise in cases such as this, the LVA's report stated that the patroller did not feel 'quite happy' about the man, and 'by diplomacy she got into the conversation'. The girls told her that they had secured work in Yorkshire through the registry office where the man worked. Though it is not clear whether the LVA patroller intervened any further in the girls' journey, she did take the address of the registry office so that the LVA could make enquiries about its reputability. The LVA began communication with the Domestic Servants' Registration Department, who resolved that 'said registry would be watched, and their books carefully supervised'.[42] As this case shows, the LVA was not only willing to intervene in the lives of young women as they passed through the city, the organization also actively pursued enquiries through and about employment agencies in order to ensure that women were not duped into staying with disreputable characters who might lure them into their houses under false pretences of working as domestic servants. Cases such as this also served to add an extra sense of danger to young women's efforts to find work, since they confirmed, in the minds of the LVA staff, that even those young women

40   LVA, Annual Report 1917–18, pp. 12–13.
41   LVA, Annual Report 1923–24, p. 15.
42   LVA, Annual Report 1923–24, p. 15.

who did plan their journeys and who did try to arrange work in advance of setting off for a new town were vulnerable to falling in with dubious people.

Indeed, welfare workers did not consider the path into domestic service to be without its moral dangers. Staff at the House of Help warned that 'domestic service is not as safe and desirable an occupation as some people are apt to think'.[43] Servants who found themselves out of work often found themselves out of a place to stay. These women ended up in lodgings that 'soon exhausted' what little savings they may have had.[44] The House of Help's focus on this aspect of the domestic servant's lot enabled them to emphasize the importance of their work offering reputable shelter for a voluntary contribution. Despite their concerns, the House of Help also continued to find domestic work for young women because so many of those that they encountered were already working in this area. In 1925 alone, the House of Help estimated that almost two-thirds of the women who stayed with them were 'domestic and hotel servants'.[45] By contrast, the House of Help encountered much smaller numbers of women working as 'shop girls' and 'typists'.[46]

Nevertheless, some women who travelled to Liverpool found it difficult to adapt to a life in domestic service. The LVA worried that, even where they had vetted a woman's job, they could not guarantee that her moral safety had been secured. Some women found that they did not like the work once they were in post. In 1920, the LVA helped two girls from Dublin who were travelling to domestic service posts in the north of England.[47] Four days later, the girls again bumped into the LVA patroller at the Landing Stage in Liverpool. They told her that they had not liked the work and were trying to return home. Unable to afford the passage, the LVA secured the girls' fare from the Catholic Aid Society and saw them onto a boat. The LVA later reflected 'Utterly inexperienced and unused to

43   House of Help, Annual Report 1925, p. 7.
44   House of Help, Annual Report 1925, p. 7.
45   The House helped a total of 577 women that year. Of these, 229 were recorded as domestic servants and a further 124 as hotel servants. House of Help, Annual Report 1925, p. 7.
46   The number of shop assistants helped in 1925 was 25 and the number of typists helped was 12. House of Help, Annual Report 1925, p. 7. These figures are a relatively typical representation of the House of Help's clientele throughout the 1920s.
47   LVA, Annual Report 1919–20, p. 10.

travel, one wonders what would have become of them had it not been for the help accorded them.'[48]

Some of the women helped also struggled to keep domestic work due to their own ill-health. In 1924, the LVA helped a Scottish widow who had travelled to Liverpool in search of work but had become stranded.[49] The LVA was able to obtain for her 'a little temporary work', but the woman had initially found it 'very hard to keep in employment, as she was not strong enough for general house work'. Eventually, though, the woman was able to secure longer-term work as 'a nurse to an invalid lady in Cheshire'.[50]

Though it was not always easy to find or keep women in work, the LVA considered themselves well-positioned to locate suitable employment for young women, often defined as some form of domestic service or caring work. The Association kept in contact with organizations such as the Liverpool Domestic Servant's Registry, as well as with 'ladies who are interested in our work'.[51] The LVA proudly declared that it was regularly sought out by people and organizations hoping to benefit from its experience. They said that they received 'a number of appeals by correspondents for … information regarding travel, reliable agencies for seeking employment, for addresses of reliable lodgings, and the bona fides of situations in this country and abroad'.[52] To this end, the LVA was able to establish itself as an organization with a significant degree of expertise, influence and trustworthiness in creating respectable routes into employment for women. Moreover, the LVA considered that their efforts to obtain employment for working-class women had a positive effect on the moral well-being of those helped. In 1924, one young woman left her husband after he 'would not work', and went to stay with her brother.[53] However, the LVA suggested that the woman was 'easily influenced' after she left the 'comfortable home' of her brother to go and live with a man who soon 'tired of her'. When her family declined to help her any further, the woman was helped by the LVA, who promptly took her to a registry office and found work for her as a ward-maid. This caring role was deliberately and consciously intended by the LVA to have a transformative effect on this woman's respectability

---

48 LVA, Annual Report 1919–20, p. 10.
49 LVA, Annual Report 1923–24, pp. 13–14.
50 LVA, Annual Report 1923–24, pp. 13–14.
51 LVA, Annual Report 1923–24, p. 15.
52 LVA, Annual Report 1923–24, p. 13.
53 LVA, Annual Report 1923–24, p. 14.

and moral outlook. They suggested that this role as a hospital ward-maid was one where she 'would have kind influence and control suitable to her weak temperament'.[54] Work as a ward-maid meant that the woman had not only joined a hospital's domestic staff, thereby reacquiring a sense of domesticated respectability, but she would have had to work under the strict guidance and discipline of a matron.[55] For the LVA, this matron and ward-maid relationship had the potential to instil moral discipline in young, working-class women who had previously shown a tendency to waywardness.

Managing Young Women's Ambitions

Women's work was important to the LVA, not least because they believed that it prevented idleness in young single women, supposedly deterring them from engaging in promiscuous behaviour out of boredom. The LVA also believed that working meant that women were less likely to sell themselves into prostitution out of economic necessity. Domestic work was offered to women identified as 'simple' and those who lacked education and qualifications.[56] The LVA, concerned that these women were especially likely to resort to prostitution for lack of alternatives, therefore saw domestic service as offering women in these circumstances a chance at a more respectable lifestyle, though employer prejudice could still be difficult to overcome, even when the LVA intervened. When the LVA failed to find a domestic service position for one Irish runaway, they blamed this failure, in part, on the girl's 'lack of references and of suitable clothing'.[57] Her appearance and lack of experience carried the stigma of low social status. Feeling that they had done all they could for the young woman, the LVA put her on a steamer back to Dublin. Yet, instead of reserving all of their criticism for the employers who had rejected the girl, the LVA portrayed the girl as also carrying some culpability for her poor position. She was described by the Association as 'stupid and stubborn' and they were unimpressed that the girl 'had been unemployed for some

54   LVA, Annual Report 1923–24, p. 14.
55   See Debbie Palmer, *Who Cared for the Carers? A History of the Occupational Health of Nurses, 1880–1948* (Manchester: Manchester University Press, 2014), p. 145.
56   Lucy Delap, *Knowing Their Place*, pp. 42–3.
57   LVA, Annual Report 1930–31, p. 7. Liverpool Record Office, M326 VIG/3.

time and apparently was not at all anxious to find work'.[58] The case typified the LVA's desire to use work to prevent idle women from roaming the streets. Work was intended to be the means by which these women could be steered towards more respectable lifestyles. When it became apparent that no one would employ the Irish girl, the LVA believed that the only other option for protecting her was to send her back to her family, who were found to be 'nice people of good position'. The solution to this girl's 'wandering habits' was, therefore, to see her contained within the domestic sphere, if not through work then through parental influence.[59]

While the LVA might have been disappointed by this particular young woman's inability to improve her position, the organization met other young women whose over-ambitious characters were considered to be equally troubling. With the relationship between work and female morality very much interlinked in the minds of social purists, the LVA was cautious when faced with girls who showed ambition and drive. The LVA did not necessarily regard these traits as inherently dangerous, but they were wary about the potential for these characteristics to lead working-class girls into making poor decisions. The young women whom the LVA encountered were often treated with suspicion when it came to their ability to identify and pursue their own independent goals. This mistrust was not always misplaced, and the organization did encounter women with frivolous plans, but the same limited range of employment opportunities were presented to these girls by the LVA time and time again, regardless of whether the intentions of the girl were realistic or respectable. If the interwar downturn in traditional sectors, such as factory work, had sent these girls off in search of new prospects, it was not always the case that these young women were looking to remain within these fields of employment. Some young women had ambitions to follow more unconventional and glamorous career paths, much to the concern of the LVA. Though the Association did ultimately help these young women by reuniting them with their families, the LVA's discussion about the attitudes and aspirations of the young women actually says much more about the organization's sense of its own importance than the frivolity of the young women in question. These cases provide clear evidence that even young women who were trying very deliberately to resist traditional lifestyles were directed towards jobs in domestic service and factories in order to curtail their unruly behaviour.

58   LVA, Annual Report 1930–31, p. 7.
59   LVA, Annual Report 1930–31, p. 7.

In their 1926–27 annual report, the LVA recounted the story of Hilda, a 16-year-old girl who had been found at the Landing Stage waiting for a boat to take her to 'seek her fortune in Holywood [*sic*]', where she planned to meet with her uncle, Tom Mix (a 'well-known' actor).[60] No doubt sceptical about the girl's story, the LVA worker who dealt with Hilda was immediately concerned about how she had funded her trip thus far. After persuading her to stay in a hostel 'pending … investigations' into her background, the Association found that Hilda had stolen £30 from her father and absconded from the family home. It is significant that the LVA's report noted that this 'sudden lapse' in Hilda's otherwise 'obedient and good' character could be 'put down to the excitement of the cinemas'. The LVA endorsed the assumption that modern consumer culture had had a negative influence on the young. Aspects of popular culture such as the cinema were seen as a destabilizing force on young women's morality, on account of the problematic aspirations they were believed to inspire.

By highlighting Hilda's belief that she could travel to make money in Hollywood, the LVA emphasized her naivety and innocence. The Association was not concerned about the fact that Hilda wanted to better herself, but they wanted to show that this girl could not be trusted to make appropriate decisions about how to organize her own life. Hilda was said to have admitted on her reunion with her father, 'Oh daddy, I wanted to earn a lot of money to help mother and you.' The LVA could therefore rationalize that while Hilda's intentions might have been positive, her decisions were poor. For the LVA, she was a prime example of the sort of naivety that they tried to combat. Prior to her adventure to Liverpool, Hilda had worked in a mill in Lancashire, where she was described as 'excellent at her work'. As part of their intervention into Hilda's life, the LVA made contact with the mill, presumably to negotiate her return to work there. Her employer told the LVA that she earned £1. 10*s.* a week but that her earnings were expected to rise to £2. 5*s.* as a result of her strong work ethic. By turning her back on this stable and, in the LVA's mind, legitimate form of work in preference for a life in Hollywood, Hilda typified the sort of feminine naivety and moral vulnerability that the LVA presented themselves as battling against. The organization used her case to promote the importance of their street patrols in bringing ill-conceived adventures to a halt and guiding young women into more appropriate forms of work.

60   LVA, Annual Report 1926–27, pp. 8–9. Liverpool Record Office, M326 VIG/3.

Hilda's plan to run off to Hollywood was not necessarily representative of the ambitions of most young women who travelled through the port, though she was not the only example of a young, working-class girl falling on hard times after chasing a path to stardom. In 1931, the LVA recalled an encounter with two young women, aged 18 and 19, who came from an unspecified town apparently in the north-west of England.[61] They had arrived in Liverpool one evening, at around 9 p.m. In a move illustrative of the connections that the LVA had created with those working in the local transport sector, it was a taxi driver who took the young women to Lime Street station in order to locate the assistance of the LVA patroller. It transpired that the young women worked in a factory, but they had 'ambitions beyond' this. They had run off in search of careers on the stage and had previously travelled to Manchester and Blackpool where they sought 'dancing engagements' and theatrical work, but with no success. In desperation, the young women had come to Liverpool, though by this point in their travels they were thin and starving. The LVA placed them in a hostel and contacted their 'anxious' parents before sending them home. Unlike Hilda's case, the LVA noted that these young women *did* have a talent for performance and, as such, the Association had been able to 'rouse the kindly interest of the Mayor of the town who got them introduced into an Amateur Theatrical Society, where they could attain a certain amount of their ambition, and could spend some of their spare time in a congenial atmosphere'.[62] But this tactic appears to have had much more to do with corralling and quelling rather than inspiring the ambitions of these young women. Though their aspirations were not completely dismissed by the LVA, the organization was clear that their performing talents needed to be channelled into a hobby rather than a career. It is not clear from the LVA's records whether the young women went back to their factory jobs, but it seems likely, as the organization made no mention of the young women taking on any new form of employment. In allowing the women a 'certain amount of their ambition', the LVA hoped to satiate their acting bug and return them to a more traditional form of employment.

Indeed, the LVA were careful to moderate young women's interest in glamourous employment during the interwar years. They were mistrustful

61   This assumption was based on the fact that the young women were said to have travelled from Manchester to Blackpool and then Liverpool through a combination of hitchhiking and walking. LVA, Annual Report 1930–31, p. 9.
62   LVA, Annual Report 1930–31, p. 9.

of careers in entertainment because they feared that the insecurity of jobs in this sector left young women vulnerable to the temptation of prostitution. For example, in 1932, the LVA reported meeting an 18-year-old 'aerobatic dancer' who had been touring Ireland for three months.[63] The tour was not financially successful, and the company had disbanded, leaving the young woman with just 2*s*. 10½*d*. and no means of getting to her home in the Midlands. The LVA paid her fare and later received a letter from the woman saying that she would now 'accept any employment other than in a theatrical troupe, unless it was under much more reliable management'. Two aspects were significant about the LVA's reporting of this case. First, they made a point of noting that the young woman had approached their patroller after noticing her badge, rather than the worker having to approach the woman. Second, the woman's experiences had changed her attitude to the stage. For the LVA, this was a young woman who was ready to learn the lessons that they were trying to teach. She was not only receptive to their guidance, she actively sought it out, and she had learned to be far more cautious in her work and lifestyle choices.

The LVA's decision to include cases of this sort in their annual reports was intended to reaffirm for their supporters the importance of their preventative work and emphasize the vulnerability of the young women who came to the city. These cases were used as evidence to support the LVA's belief that young women's economic ambitions could, if unchecked, pull them into disreputable trades and misadventures. Not all women possessed such powerful or problematic aspirations as becoming performers, but the literal and metaphorical journey towards finding legitimate and achievable forms of employment could, in the LVA's estimations, be morally treacherous for young women with no family close at hand to advise them. The LVA believed that if this journey were not carefully managed and planned then even those young women with clearer ideas and employment connections could find themselves heading towards disreputable lifestyles as a result of poor decisions, economic desperation or simply eagerness to get ahead.

Certainly, the LVA believed that paid employment could be used to satisfy the material and economic needs of young women, thereby preventing them from ever needing to consider prostitution. Yet, if the ambitions and desires that a young woman possessed were too expansive, then the LVA felt that there was a danger that she would easily be diverted from the path to reputable employment and into more immoral means of earning a

---

63   LVA, Annual Report 1931–32, p. 7. Liverpool Record Office, M326 VIG/3.

living. In the case of Hilda, here was a young woman who, for the LVA, had overstepped her social status. She was a good mill worker and this, they felt, was where she should concentrate on earning her money, if she wanted to achieve her aim of supporting herself and her family. In the case of the theatre performers, their interests were shown to have pulled them away from secure family environments and into the company of strangers. They had used inappropriate tactics to reach their goals by hitching lifts from place to place, with no overall plan and with few respectable contacts. The LVA considered these girls to be open to corruption, not least because their movement through public space might see them make the acquaintance of unscrupulous characters who would manipulate them.

For the LVA, female employment was both a protection from the threat of vice and at the same time a potential path towards vice – if a woman's employment goals proved to be overly ambitious or if they took her away from her family and off on adventures through urban spaces. To this end, the LVA's approach to women's work was less about liberation, social freedom or challenging gender order. Instead, their approach to employment was part of the ongoing legacy of Victorian social purity traditions. The women that the LVA helped were usually defined as being of low social status. As such, social purists regarded these women as being particularly vulnerable to being corrupted by their employment ambitions, as a result of their economic situation, and by their urban wanderings. By guiding women into quintessentially feminine forms of employment, such as domestic service or traditional mill work, the LVA believed that they could stop poor young women from turning to prostitution, without exposing them to lifestyles that might prove to be their moral downfall. Moreover, the LVA was supported in this class-based gendering of women's geographic and occupational mobility by other local organizations such as the House of Help and the Women Police Patrols, who expressed similar beliefs about the need to direct working-class women into domestic and other traditional forms of work in order to deter them from immoral lifestyles. Collectively, these organizations were successful at finding jobs for women, and in a large number of cases their assistance was no doubt appreciated by the women involved. But the work of these organizations perpetuated late nineteenth-century perceptions of working-class women as morally vulnerable and, consequently, their support for women's employment functioned as a tactic for instilling moral discipline in working-class women.

5

White Slavery and
Social Purists' Authority

Though they continued in their co-operation and affiliation with the NVA, in 1921, the LVA decided to follow 'other provincial centres' in setting themselves up as an 'independent society'.[1] In real and practical terms, the greatest change that this brought about was a change in name. Up until this point, the association had officially acted under the title 'National Vigilance Association (Liverpool Branch)'. From 1921, their title changed to 'The Liverpool Society for the Prevention of International White Slave Traffic', though for clarity they are referred to throughout this work under the more commonly known title of the LVA.[2] This choice of moniker indicates that notions of white slavery and trafficking were still a source of moral anxiety during the interwar period. Charting local fears about white slavery during the interwar years, I argue that the LVA used narratives of urban sexual danger to plug themselves into national, and indeed international, conversations about the dangers of female migration.

Though more work is needed on white slavery in Britain, several historians have recently turned their attentions to the way the fight against trafficking formed an important part of the overall social purity movement's agenda in the early twentieth century. White slavery has been approached

1   LVA, Annual Report 1922–23, p. 4. Liverpool Record Office, M326 VIG/3.
2   LVA, Annual Report 1922–23, p. 4. The organization had officially adopted the name 'Liverpool Vigilance Association' by the late 1940s. The similarity between this name and their first title, The National Vigilance Association (Liverpool Branch), means that the Liverpool Vigilance Association is the name most associated with the organization, even during the interwar years.

by these historians as a myth, a moral panic, and a system of class- and gender-based labour relations.[3] Recent research by Simon Jenkins has examined the prevalence of the racial stereotypes that underpinned notions of white slavery in interwar Britain, while Rachael Attwood has argued that the NVA's international efforts to combat white slavery at the turn of the century were undermined by the organization's reliance upon racial profiling.[4] Yet the resilience of white slavery as a discursive tool in the construction and maintenance of gendered codes of urban morality requires further attention, not least because the rhetoric of white slavery continued, through the interwar and even into the post-war years, to be deployed in a nebulous fashion by social purists.

This chapter and the next concentrate on how the LVA appealed to the threat of white slavery in a bid to fashion their work as vital to the maintenance of social order. I want to begin by considering how the fund-raising imperatives of the LVA encouraged them to exploit broad definitions of the term white slavery and show how the LVA used fears about corruption and kidnap to advertise themselves as an organization with special expertise in the protection of women who travelled for work or some other necessity. This argument will be expanded in the next chapter, which uses specific case-studies of suspected 'traffickers' to unpick the LVA's attitudes towards danger and coercion. These case studies show that, although the LVA tended to invoke white slavery to create an impression of young women being kidnapped from public places and sold into prostitution, their records show little evidence of this type of force. That is not to imply that coerced or forced prostitution took place only in the minds of social purists.

3   Rachael Attwood, 'Stopping the Traffic: The National Vigilance Association and the International Fight against the "White Slave" Trade (1899–c.1909)', *Women's History Review*, 24:3 (2014), pp. 325–50; Paula Bartley, *Prostitution*, p. 170; Lucy Bland, *Banishing the Beast*, p. 297; Carol Dyhouse, *Girl Trouble*, pp. 11–41; Julia Laite, 'Between Scylla and Charybdis: Women's Labour Migration and Sex Trafficking in the Early Twentieth Century', *International Review of Social History*, 62:1 (2017), pp. 37–65; Stephanie Limoncelli, *The Politics of Trafficking: The First International Movement to Combat the Sexual Exploitation of Women* (Stanford, Calif.: Stanford University Press, 2011); Stefan Slater, 'Pimps, Police and Filles de Joie', pp. 53–74.

4   Simon Jenkins relates fears about white slavery in Cardiff to the perceived growth in 'amateur prostitution' and ongoing racial stereotypes about black, male sexuality. See Simon Jenkins, 'Aliens and Predators', pp. 575–96 and Rachael Attwood, 'Stopping the Traffic', pp. 325–50.

The unsteady and low-paid status of working-class women's employment complicates the idea of choice in the move between prostitution and other forms of work. The LVA's case files contain plenty of examples of women being convinced to travel to non-existent or improperly advertised jobs. False promises of work left these women vulnerable to those who were ready to suggest prostitution as a means of making ends meet. Yet the LVA's broad application of the term 'white slavery' to these situations needs, first, to be understood from within the context of local social purity ambitions and the city's role as a nexus for migrant women's work.

In her work on trafficking and employment, Julia Laite argues that while concerns about migrant prostitution were bound together with practices of migrant female labour, national policy nevertheless continued to treat these two issues as distinct from one another.[5] Representatives of feminist groups like the Association for Moral and Social Hygiene remained curiously uninterested in the causal links in the career trajectories of low-paid women who moved into prostitution.[6] Laite suggests that the NVA's practice of patrolling ports and train stations meant that they were one of the few organizations to grasp the links between low-paid work like domestic service and prostitution, causing them to shift their focus towards disreputable employment agencies and away from closing down brothels.[7] I want to add to this, though, by noting that, where social purists were cognizant of the association between low-paid work and prostitution, this did not necessarily result in the cultivation of more holistic approaches to female migrant labour and prostitution.

The case of the LVA, and their efforts to control women's travel and their access to work, indicates that we must weigh social purists' interest in challenging exploitative working practices against the restrictive local cultures of female work and travel that they supported. Concern about employment and migration had always been a bigger part of the LVA's work than campaigns against brothel-keeping. Via allusions to white slavery, the LVA infantilized working-class women and subjected them to surveillance that impinged upon, rather than advanced, working-class women's agency. In their efforts to help women, the LVA imbued themselves with the power to define white slavery, to identify what constituted an urban danger and to explain how female immorality could be prevented. In the process of

5   Julia Laite, 'Between Scylla and Charybdis'.
6   Julia Laite, 'Between Scylla and Charybdis', p. 49.
7   Julia Laite, 'Between Scylla and Charybdis', p. 57.

articulating their own fears for the morality of women in Liverpool, the LVA managed to avoid pinning down a clear definition of white slavery while at the same time convincing themselves that white slavery, in whatever form it took, was a significant threat to women. Furthermore, the LVA were able to use fears about white slavery to galvanize support for their efforts to offer young women protection from moral danger.

In arguing that allusions to white slavery continued to underpin the LVA's discussion about why their work mattered well into the post-war years, the study of this organization serves as a useful reminder of divergences within the social purity community during the course of the twentieth century. Even during the early years of the twentieth century, when the wider social purity movement was advocating more straightforwardly repressive policies, such as closing down brothels and arguing for legal forms of moral regulation, the LVA was focused on street patrolling and early intervention to prevent women from turning to prostitution in the first place.[8] Consequently, the LVA's approach had much in common with other preventative organizations such as the Ladies' Associations for the Care of Friendless Girls, who sought to prevent girls from turning to prostitution by providing them with moral guidance.[9] Yet the outcomes of these well-intentioned efforts to prevent young women from turning to prostitution could still be repressive, suggesting that distinctions between prevention and repression are not always entirely helpful. Moreover, I want to show that the vagueness in social purists' use of the term 'white slavery' was one of the factors that created the climate for different approaches within the social purity umbrella to flourish. Evidence presented in the latter part of this chapter shows that, by the 1950s, the NVA was reluctant to see the term white slavery used to push for moral chaperones for young women, but the LVA, who were still sending their patrollers out onto the streets, were still using the threat of white slavery to justify their work. Indeed, one of the things that is so remarkable about the LVA is how consistent the organization remained in terms of their objectives, rhetoric and strategies over the course of almost seven decades of work.

Other local nuances also shaped the way the LVA made sense of the threat of white slavery in terms of women's geographic mobility. Unlike the NVA,

---

8   Trevor Fisher, *Prostitution and the Victorians* (Stroud: Sutton Publishing, 1997), p. xi and Paula Bartley, *Prostitution*, pp. 155–7.

9   See Paula Bartley, *Prostitution*, chap. 3 and Frank Mort, *Dangerous Sexualities*, p. 88.

vigilance workers in Liverpool spent a significant proportion of their time monitoring and interacting with local, British or Irish women rather than with women from further afield. In particular, this contrasts with the NVA's work in London, where their workers concentrated a considerable amount of their attention on East European Jewish migrants.[10] This focus appears to have been an extension of wider anti-Semitic prejudice which also saw the NVA investigate supposed links between prostitution and domestic service in the East End Jewish community.[11] As a port city, transience remained central to the perceived threat of white slavery in Liverpool, with both naive women and their would-be captors believed to be frequenting the streets near the docks and main train station. Consequently, the narrative of white slavery that the LVA constructed was accented by local specificity, with the large numbers of Irish women and women from the north-west of England moving through the port and Lime Street station shaping the character of the work.

Working-class women deemed to be living or embarking upon transient lifestyles came under close examination from the LVA. Young women who crossed geographical borders faced questions about their motives for changing localities and suspicion about their immediate intentions and longer-term ambitions. From the LVA's outset, the reasons why a woman travelled to Liverpool, where she travelled from, and what she hoped to achieve in the city all informed the LVA's assessment of her supposed vulnerability to being caught up in the white slave trade. Moreover, the urgency with which the LVA discussed white slavery indicates that their use of the term was not simply a fund-raising ploy. While the rhetoric of white slavery was certainly used to increase the profile of the organization and elevate the importance of their work, the LVA did consider forms of coerced prostitution to be a genuine problem in the city. Framing this issue of coercion in terms of white slavery had the effect not just of rousing their financial support base but of stoking the LVA's self-belief in the legitimacy of their interventions into women's lives.

Charity and Class

The LVA's parent organization, the NVA, was set up in 1885 in direct response to concerns about child prostitution in London, and in 1899, the NVA played a vital role in the creation of the International Bureau for the

10   Rachael Attwood, 'Stopping the Traffic', pp. 338–9.
11   Julia Laite, 'Between Scylla and Charybdis', pp. 57–8.

Suppression of White Slave Traffic. The anti-trafficking agenda formulated by the NVA was built firmly upon xenophobic principles which closely associated sexual immorality with the 'foreigner'.[12] In her examination of the NVA's trafficking work, Attwood argues that the organization became so blinkered by prejudice against particular social groups that their fractious and racialized approach actually compromised the NVA's efforts to supress sex trafficking. On the international stage, the NVA presumed morality to be an area of British authority and expertise and, at home, the organization's tactics were based upon long-standing class, gender and racial distinctions which effectively stigmatized working-class foreigners, male and female, for their apparent lack of moral fibre.

Of particular concern to the NVA were foreign women, who were considered to be especially morally vulnerable.[13] Bartley suggests that the 'tension between repression and protection was all too evident' during the early twentieth century, as social purists lobbied for restrictions on immigration as a means of protecting young women.[14] This lobbying was fundamental to the organization of international conferences on white slavery. At a 1902 conference in Paris, an International Convention for the Suppression of the White Slave Traffic was set up involving the appointment of officials whose job it was to guard port and railway stations.[15] Hull, Folkestone, Dover and various railway stations in London soon found themselves playing host to a 'social purity network' that helped over 12,000 women between 1903 and 1908.[16] The formation of the LVA had its spiritual roots in this campaign.

Belief in the existence of a white slave trade was significant in the establishment of a local branch of the NVA in Liverpool in 1908. Promoted by and amongst local elites and religious leaders, the LVA found that a significant number of its supporters were women drawn from the middle classes. In this respect the organization closely mirrored its social purity heritage. The social purity movement of the later nineteenth century had a definite class character, with working-class women in particular being subjected to the close scrutiny of middle-class purists.[17] The main figures

12   Rachael Attwood, 'Stopping the Traffic', p. 328.
13   Rachael Attwood, 'Stopping the Traffic', p. 329.
14   Paula Bartley, *Prostitution*, p. 170.
15   Paula Bartley, *Prostitution*, p. 170.
16   Paula Bartley, *Prostitution*, p. 171.
17   Paula Bartley, *Prostitution*, p. 157.

involved in the creation of the LVA were of a higher social status than the women that the organization envisaged protecting. On 5 November 1908, the *Daily Dispatch* ran a notice on a Charity Dinner that was to be held later that evening on behalf of the 'National Vigilance Association, for the suppression of the white slave traffic'.[18] Hosted at Liverpool's prestigious Adelphi Hotel and featuring the Earl of Aberdeen as 'chief guest', the notice emphasized the respectable background of the purity movement's supporters, thereby legitimizing their interest in a topic as scandalous as white slavery. The notice listed six middle-aged, well-off women who would be in attendance at the meeting. Underneath elegant portraits of these women, their names and titles were listed, with three afforded the status of 'Lady': the Lady Mayoress of Liverpool, Lady Petrie and Lady Russell. These women were the very antithesis of white slavery, not simply because of their opposition to the trade but because of their privileged backgrounds. As representatives of white, middle-class respectable femininity they epitomized everything that the potential white slave was not. Unlike vulnerable Lancashire 'mill girls' or the 'failures' found in 'common lodging houses', the women who endorsed the local purity movement had access to money.[19] Their well-maintained, carefully constructed hairstyles and fashionable clothes showed that these women spent considerable time on their public presentation and appearance. While their opposition to white slavery was not entirely motivated by the degree of social cachet to be gained from such philanthropic interests, having their names and pictures publicly associated with the cause offered an opportunity for self-promotion and congratulation.

The prominent role played by local middle-class women as opponents of white slave traffickers was directly informed by class lineages in philanthropic work. Writing about the nineteenth century, Beverley Skeggs has interpreted middle-class efforts to monitor the morals of working-class

18   'Liverpool and the White Slave Traffic', *Daily Dispatch*, 5 November 1908. See LVA, Newspaper cuttings. Liverpool Record Office, M326 VIG/5/1. See also National Vigilance Association, Charity Dinner Pamphlet, November 1908. Liverpool Record Office, M326 VIG/5/1.

19   'Liverpool's Darker Side: How Lancashire Girls are Lured to their Ruin', *Daily Dispatch*, 19 October 1907. See LVA, Newspaper cuttings. Liverpool Record Office, M326 VIG/5/1; Press cutting from unidentified local Catholic newspaper, 17 January 1908. See LVA, Newspaper cuttings. Liverpool Record Office, M326 VIG/5/1.

women as efforts to maintain social stability.[20] Sociologically, concerns about morality were mapped on to fears about the stability of social order, with working-class women cast as the lynchpins that could make or break society. Presumed working-class tendencies towards immorality and disorder were regarded as manageable, so long as working-class mothers could be taught to maintain their own respectability as well as that of their families.[21] The moral sanctity of working-class women was thus seen as a barometer of social order. According to Skeggs, this gendering of morality and class allowed the middle and upper classes to turn class conflict into an issue of respectability, thereby avoiding questions about wider structural inequalities within society.[22] More importantly, Skeggs argues that by teaching working-class women 'to take pleasure from bourgeois domesticity', poorer women were encouraged to accept society's rules 'without direct, obvious control' so as to 'produce themselves as acquiescent, rather than being produced by state regulation'.[23] The ground-level activities of the LVA suggest that this sort of morality-based class politics was an implicit rather than explicit part of their practice. The LVA's work did indeed focus attention onto moral rather than structural issues in gender and class relations, but this was not something that the organization deliberately or even consciously set out to achieve. The LVA did not overtly claim to be interested in helping working-class girls specifically, although the women that they helped tended to be in financial need or seeking some form of working-class employment.

Moreover, there were practical as well as ideological reasons for the LVA to cultivate support amongst the middle and upper classes. The presentation of the 1908 fund-raiser as an occasion for the well-to-do was motivated by the need for the organization to network with individuals who would be willing to make donations to their cause, not least because the LVA made no charge to the women helped.[24] Indeed, money was to be a frequent concern for the LVA's committee. In 1920, G.W. Hockley, Rector of Liverpool, sought to use some of the status of the NVA in order to draw in funds for the local branch. He noted that the work of the NVA had 'long passed beyond the stage of criticism or experiment and [had] won the cordial approval of

20   Beverley Skeggs, *Formations of Class and Gender*, p. 42.
21   Beverley Skeggs, *Formations of Class and Gender*, p. 43.
22   Beverley Skeggs, *Formations of Class and Gender*, p. 43.
23   Beverley Skeggs, *Formations of Class and Gender*, p. 46.
24   LVA, Annual Report 1916, p. 3.

all who have the moral interests of the community at heart'.[25] So it was that Hockley, in his position as chairman of the LVA committee, proclaimed 'We feel that we ought to be able to look with confidence to the public to see that its operations shall not be crippled for lack of funds'.[26] However, further appeals made by the LVA committee suggest that funding continued to be a challenge. In 1928, Hockley's successor as both Rector of Liverpool and chairman of the LVA committee, John C.H. How, made a more urgent appeal for funds. In his preface to the Association's annual report he wrote:

> We badly need more regular subscribers, and I hope that this Report may be given a wide circulation by our present sympathisers, and that many more may be convinced by it, that the work is one that really deserves a much bigger support than it receives at present. I wonder whether it is as widely known as it should be? That is a matter which may help. Please MAKE IT KNOWN.[27]

This statement, particularly How's suggestion that the report be distributed widely, makes explicit that one of the key functions of the organization's annual reports was to promote to subscribers the importance of the LVA's work so that they might secure their financial assistance. As a result, the focus on white slavery evident in the LVA's reports was inevitably tied up with this promotional strategy.

White slavery was presented as a genuine and pressing threat that the LVA battled to overcome. In their 1927–28 annual report, the committee noted that the League of Nations had left 'no doubt whatever of the existence of a terrible amount of traffic in many countries'.[28] However, the report went on to claim that traffickers' 'progress' in Great Britain had been 'impeded and frequently frustrated by the work of this Society and other Vigilance Associations in this country'.[29] The report hoped to win support and financial backing by fostering an image of the LVA as an organization that had a real impact upon the activities of traffickers. Yet, in order to keep funds flowing, the organization's declarations that they were overcoming vice were tempered by their warnings about the resilience of Liverpool's

25   LVA, Annual Report 1919–20, p. 3.
26   LVA, Annual Report 1919–20, p. 3.
27   LVA, Annual Report 1927–28, p. 3 (original emphasis).
28   LVA, Annual Report 1927–28, p. 4.
29   LVA, Annual Report 1927–28, p. 4.

underworld characters. In 1936, David Railton, Rector of Liverpool and chairman of the committee, offered an insidious image of traffickers which carried a warning about the necessity of the LVA's work. He wrote in his preface to that year's report: 'The sharks that make our work so difficult are lurking – more cleverly concealed than ever, close to the surface of our social life, waiting their chance.'[30] Maintaining a sense of hidden danger enabled the LVA to rationalize their appeal for funds to tackle white slavery, despite their work and reporting offering no evidence of this trade.

In a manner similar to the nineteenth-century philanthropists explored by Seth Koven, the LVA's twentieth-century articulation of their white slavery anxieties 'tapped into the unruly passions of the moral imagination and into attempts to reconfigure class and gender relations and sexuality'.[31] However, whereas Koven has written about the 'moral imagination' of philanthropists, it is more apt where the LVA are concerned to analyse their approach in terms of their *urban imagination*. The moral interventions that the organization made into the lives of travelling women and the moral codes that they upheld through their efforts to protect them were fundamentally tied to notions of urban space. Female sexuality, vice and vulnerability were concepts that all informed and were informed by the LVA's understandings of the corrupting nature of Liverpool's street life. The LVA's fears about white slavery crystallized their sense that women needed protecting from urban disorder. Consequently, place and space were absolutely crucial to the LVA's gendered perceptions of risk and immorality. In the urban imagination of social purists, a large port city like Liverpool called to the innocent, the ambitious, the naive and the immoral like a siren. For the LVA, the safety net of their patrol work was essential to identifying vulnerable women and sending them straight back out of the city or furnishing them with the connections and information necessary to negotiate the city with their morality intact.

The LVA's repeated efforts to publicize their desperate need for funds were largely successful during the interwar years. Having convinced their supporters of the threat that white slavery posed locally, the LVA managed to maintain financial stability during the 1920s and 1930s. According to their revenue accounts, the organization's income was the same as its expenditure in the years throughout the interwar period. For example, in the year between 1 May 1922 and 30 April 1923, the organization

30　LVA, Annual Report 1935–36, p. 3. Liverpool Record Office, M326 VIG/3.
31　Seth Koven, *Slumming*, p. 285.

received an income of £812. 12*s*.[32] This income was, in part, made up of £260. 15*s*. in subscriptions and a further £41. 16*s*. 5*d*. in donations. The vast majority of this was used to pay staff salaries (£494. 16*s*. 7*d*. to be precise), but other expenses included rent (£64. 18*s*. 7*d*.), a telephone bill (£16), travelling expenses for workers (£24. 3*s*. 11*d*.), food and travelling expenses for the girls helped (£7. 9*s*.) and an affiliation fee of £1. 1*s*. that was paid to the NVA. A number of the items listed as expenses present a more detailed picture of the character of the LVA's work and how and where it was conducted. The LVA's work at the Landing Stage at the Pier Head was conducted from an office, and, given the early morning nature of their patrols, it is no surprise to find that the organization declared expenditures in 1924 for a gas stove for the office (£3. 1*s*. 4*d*.) and an electric radiator (£1. 13*s*. 8*d*.). In addition to their patrol duties, the LVA also undertook office-based work and, again, their expenses reflect this. A £10 payment for a Remington typewriter was recorded alongside regular disbursements for telephone bills, postage and telegrams, stationery and printing.[33] These costs would have been incurred by the LVA's practices of contacting the prospective employers of young women, tracing runaways and liaising with other Vigilance Associations around the country.[34] Despite receiving middle-class support, then, the LVA had to work to generate enough money to stay open. White slavery was both the organization's greatest fear and its greatest campaign tool where fund-raising was concerned. By repeatedly referencing this one issue, the LVA had found a concise and efficient way to explain, justify and publicize the importance of its work.

Internationalism and Expertise

The expenses listed by the LVA were a clear sign that they did more than simply patrol the streets. Though the organization was not officially sanctioned and had no legal powers to police women's travels, the LVA nonetheless believed their work to be both skilled and vital. During the early 1920s, the committee remarked that even their 'office work' was 'varied and difficult': 'It must be carried on frequently in a foreign language,

---

32   LVA, Annual Report 1923–24, balance sheet.
33   LVA, Annual Report 1923–24, balance sheet.
34   For a discussion of correspondence work conducted by the LVA, see Annual Report 1928–29, p. 10.

and it often involves questions of law and practice.'[35] Very deliberately, the LVA emphasized their credentials and professionalism in dealing with newcomers to Liverpool from around the world and they presented themselves as a leading authority on preventative patrol work. In their effort to define themselves as important players in the prevention of international white slavery, the LVA took every opportunity to assert their international connections and relevance.

In a move that would have bolstered the confidence of LVA supporters, the Reverend Canon Hockley (chairman of the committee) suggested in 1924 that it was 'gratifying to know that our Liverpool Society is to be represented at the important International Congress to be held at Graz, Styria, Austria, in September of this year'.[36] The Congress, on the 'suppression of Traffic in Women and Children' was, according to the LVA, to be attended by 'nearly all countries of the world'.[37] Eager to take advantage of opportunities to discuss the international significance of their work, the LVA was again in attendance at the International Congress when it was held in Warsaw in 1930, when Miss Edith Rose, Secretary of the LVA, travelled there to represent the Liverpool and Irish Committees.[38] These Congresses were organized by The International Bureau for the Suppression of Traffic in Women and Children, an organization that was, in the words of Sheila Jeffreys, the 'sister organisation of the National Vigilance Association'.[39] By remaining in contact with affiliates within the worldwide social purity movement, the LVA joined forces with others who subscribed to the same social and moral anxieties as they did.

The LVA attempted to promote their expert status by arguing that their work had a direct relevance to issues of immigration and international travel. Although the LVA did not make a point of openly criticizing government policies and though they also tended to discuss policy measures without reference to any party-political agendas, the LVA nonetheless suggested that their work was shaped in response to official directives. In 1923, the LVA suggested that the US policy of preventing passengers with poor standards of cleanliness from entering the USA meant that:

35   LVA, Annual Report 1922–23, p. 10.
36   LVA, Annual Report 1923–24, p. 3.
37   LVA, Annual Report 1923–24, p. 5.
38   LVA, Annual Report 1930–31, p. 4.
39   Sheila Jeffreys, *The Idea of Prostitution* (North Melbourne: Spinifex Press, 1997), p. 19.

> [O]ur Workers have very frequently been called in to help and advise unfortunate girls who, having been rejected, have found themselves in great distress, being prevented from embarking on the steamer for which their passage was booked. In some cases the girls had not sufficient money to return to the place from which they came or even to pay their lodgings in Liverpool.[40]

By detailing their efforts to overcome the inadvertent effects of international travel sanctions, the LVA was able to further the idea that their workers had particular skills relevant to the prevention of international trafficking for the purposes of prostitution. In placing their own work in the context of external and formal controls upon international travel, the LVA fashioned themselves as having the capacity to act alongside officials in the policing and monitoring of travel. Just after the First World War, the LVA suggested that 'Perhaps the highest recommendation that we can record of our work is the fact that the Home Office, Naval and Military Authorities permitted us to continue this work at the Boats right through the years of the Great War without hindrance.'[41] Similarly, in 1924, the committee used its annual report to

> record the gratitude it feels to His Majesty's Alien Officers, to the Canadian and American Government Authorities, to the Mersey Dock and Harbour Board, and to all the Shipping Officials with whom the Committee's Workers are in constant touch, and who assist so courteously and cordially in the difficult matters which arise from time to time.[42]

By acting in co-operation with these agencies, the LVA intended to achieve status and legitimacy by proxy. In fact, the LVA had some success in this regard, with officials such as the local police occasionally directing stranded or vulnerable young women towards the care of LVA workers.[43]

The LVA even sought to bring their much-vaunted expertise in

40   G.W. Hockley, Rector of Liverpool and Chairman of the LVA Committee, in LVA, Annual Report 1922–23, p. 4.

41   LVA, Annual Report 1919–20, p. 7.

42   LVA, Annual Report 1923–24, p. 6.

43   LVA, Annual Report 1923–24, p. 13 and LVA, Annual Report 1925–26, p. 13. Liverpool Record Office, M326 VIG/3.

international transience to their localized, everyday patrol work. In 1922, the organization described itself as 'fortunate' to have 'secured the services of Lady Workers whose knowledge of languages comprise French, Italian, Spanish, German, Japanese, Arabic, Yiddish and Russian'.[44] The implication behind this claim was that the LVA had representatives who would be able to engage in dialogue with stranded women from a range of international backgrounds and, as a result, keep larger numbers of women safe from traffickers. However, the real value of these skills does not appear to have been integral to the organization's ability to function. In the same report that lauded the LVA workers' linguistic capabilities, the LVA listed the nationalities of the women helped that year. This itinerary of foreign inter-action was intended to be illustrative of the LVA's internationalism, but the figures themselves actually suggest that the organization had very little need to draw upon their knowledge of foreign languages. Out of the 506 young women that the LVA say they 'dealt with' in the twelve months between 1922 and 1923, just one was French, one was Japanese, and they met no Germans, Italians, Spaniards, Russians and no one from any countries where Yiddish or Arabic was spoken in significant numbers. In fact, 97.4 per cent of the women that they met came from regions where English was spoken as a first or second language (America, Canada, England, Ireland, Scotland and Wales). Yet even this figure presents too varied a view of the nationalities of the women that the LVA assisted during the year 1922–23. The vast majority of their time was actually spent dealing with Irish immigration, with 64.4 per cent of all the women they met being Irish, and a further 22.5 per cent of all the women they met classed as English. Their own figures therefore suggest that the LVA actually had little interaction with non-English speakers.

An analysis of the figures provided by the LVA on the nationalities of the women who were helped between 1916 and 1930 reveals that the LVA's tendency to deal mainly with Irish women was not specific to the year 1922 to 1923. In all years between 1917 and 1937 for which figures are available, the LVA interacted mostly with Irish women and, to a lesser extent, English women. The figure for 1916 only bucks this trend because of an influx of women from the Isle of Man in that year. Moreover, from 1930 onwards the proportion of Irish women dealt with by the LVA rose steadily.[45] This may have reflected an increase in the organization's already considerable interest

44   LVA, Annual Report 1922–23, p. 6.
45   LVA, Annual Reports 1916–37, Liverpool Record Office, M326 VIG/3.

in Irish female immigrants, a point that will be explored in more detail in Chapters 7 and 8.

The LVA's lack of significant interaction with women from a range of international backgrounds suggests that the discourse of internationalism that the organization deployed was, in large part, an exercise in political posturing. By emphasizing their international credentials, the LVA promoted the idea that the city of Liverpool needed their protection from would-be international traffickers. Yet their records provide little evidence of serious organized international trafficking in Liverpool during the interwar period. Instead, the LVA's belief in the threat of trafficking came about as a result of social purists' more fundamental concerns about the dangers of public space and the frailty of female morality.

The Death of White Slavery?

During the Second World War, restrictions on international travel necessarily reduced the LVA's workload, but the patrols meeting boats and trains did not entirely cease.[46] Alongside the smaller numbers of women travellers helped, the LVA channelled their energies into supporting the war effort in whatever small way they could. For example, the LVA pointed out to supporters that they used their office at the Landing Stage to give 'keenly appreciated' cups of tea to 'Soldiers, Sailors, Air Force Recruits, W.A.A.F.S., W.R.E.N.S., A.T.S. and members of the Nursing Service'.[47] These patriotic appeals to helping service personnel were intended to maintain the faith and interest of the organization's supporters while the fight against white slavery was briefly sidelined. The war had temporarily taken away the LVA's capacity to appeal to the international significance of their work, which had been central to their rhetoric of white slavery even if this internationalism was not significantly in evidence in their practice. The LVA issued reminders that trafficking continued to be a problem and that attention would soon turn back to this matter. The work of the International Bureau for the Suppression of White Slave Traffic was described as being 'held in suspense' until the return to 'righteous peace'.[48] Driving home that the fight against white slavery was merely paused, the LVA printed a statement in their

---

46   For more on the decline in the LVA's workload during the Second World War, see Chapter 8.

47   LVA, Annual Report 1941–42, p. 3. Liverpool Record Office, M326 VIG/3.

48   LVA, Annual Report 1940–41, p. 5. Liverpool Record Office, M326 VIG/3.

1941 annual report telling supporters that 'the flame kindled by the establishment of the INTERNATIONAL BUREAU in 1899 will never die out'.[49]

However, changes in women's lifestyles and expectations, many of which were driven by the war, presented a challenge for social purists who had conflated white slavery with ideas of female naivety and a lack of street acumen.[50] In 1952, the *Daily Mirror* reported that the NVA had 'decided to withdraw their corps of women officials who patrol London's main railway stations to protect young girls'.[51] The NVA had conceded that the threat of white slavery was not significant enough to warrant the maintenance of these patrols. According to the paper, Lady Nunburnholme, Chair of the NVA, had explained that 'Young women in this country are quite capable of looking after themselves nowadays.' Apparently, urban living and respectable femininity had found ways to coexist within the capital. The 'Modern Miss', as the *Daily Mirror*'s reporter put it, was 'more than capable of looking after herself', and, according to Lady Nunburnholme, the girls of 1952 were more educated and more independent. Their experiences of wartime had left them more savvy and had shown that they were able to do 'most men's jobs'. As a consequence, Lady Nunburnholme suggested, 'Travelling alone no longer represents a problem to the average girl, who is intelligent enough to deal with an awkward situation.' Instead of concentrating upon these cases, she said that the NVA would be turning its attentions exclusively towards fighting vice on an 'international basis' using their own 'secret' methods.

It was a state of affairs with which purists in Liverpool did not agree, and the LVA made efforts to co-opt the local press into maintaining the fear of white slavery that had sustained the organization since its creation in 1908. In January 1954, the *Evening Express* ran an article with the salacious and deliberately tantalizing headline, 'WHITE SLAVERY IS DEAD – But'.[52]

49   LVA, Annual Report 1940–41, p. 5 (original emphasis).

50   Sonya Rose argues that, unlike the First World War, the Second World War did not halt feminist activism, with women using their war service to argue for equal pay and opportunities. See Sonya Rose, 'Women's Rights, Women's Obligations: Contradictions of Citizenship in World War II Britain', *European Review of History*, 7:2 (2000), pp. 281 and 287.

51   'Girls Don't Need Protecting, Now', *Daily Mirror*, June 1952. LVA, Newspaper cuttings. Liverpool Record Office, M326 VIG/5/2.

52   'WHITE SLAVERY IS DEAD – But', *Evening Express*, 11 January 1954 (original emphasis). LVA, Newspaper cuttings. Liverpool Record Office, M326 VIG/5/2.

At first glance, the headline and accompanying article appeared to signal a move away from interwar exaggerations about the threat of white slavery in Liverpool. According to the article, white slavery had been greatly hindered during the post-war years by official and unofficial forms of street policing, such as those practised by the LVA. Yet this report on the supposed death of white slavery actually repeated Liverpudlian social purists' assertions about the continued danger faced by women when out wandering through the streets. Whereas Lady Nunburnholme seemed to be trying to delineate white slavery in terms of coercion that involved the international movement of women, the LVA were still finding mileage in the more nebulous application of the threat of white slavery to all of the young women in Liverpool who might become prostitutes were it not for their patrollers.

Implicit within the *Evening Express*'s headline and article was the sense that white slavery would surely run rampant on the streets of Liverpool but for the efforts of moral street patrollers in the LVA. Subheaded 'City's Long Battle Against Vice Goes On', the article recounted in detail the work of the LVA, paying close attention to the organization's efforts to meet young women travelling to Liverpool via the Irish boats. The article was made up of examples from the LVA's casebook, suggesting a high degree of co-operation between the LVA and the newspaper. The case studies selected aimed to convince readers of the *Evening Express* of, on the one hand, the innocence and naivety of most young women and, on the other, the morally corrosive effects of women's unchaperoned adventures in urban centres like Liverpool. Not only were the LVA still able to give good copy to the press, their patrollers were referred to by the *Evening Express* as 'officials', indicating that the LVA continued to advertise their authority on these matters and that the tabloid press was still willing to give legitimacy to the LVA's pronouncements about urban immorality.[53]

Both the LVA and the *Evening Express* stood to gain from this effort to sustain white slavery as a modern urban horror story. The sense of urban danger and threat to female respectability implied by stories of trafficking and corruption enabled the LVA to maintain its relevance into the post-war years, while readers of the *Evening Express* were offered a foreboding, gripping, even titillating article about debauchery and scandal. The article framed white slavery around the notion that naive working-class young women were stumbling into prostitution after becoming morally corrupted by urban life. The LVA told the *Evening Express* about two young Irish

53   'WHITE SLAVERY IS DEAD – But', *Evening Express*, 11 January 1954.

women who arrived in Liverpool full of intentions to go on and make lives in London. The LVA fed the girls, made an appointment for them with the local Employment Exchange and found them beds for the night at the Salvation Army women's hostel. However, the young women never arrived at the hostel, leaving the *Evening Express* and the LVA to speculate, ominously, 'At night time, somewhere in the centre of Liverpool, they vanished – vanished, Mrs. Sugden [Secretary of the LVA] is sure, into the life of vice they sought.'[54] The idea that young, working-class women needed to be morally policed and chaperoned was therefore still a key feature of debates about women's presence on Liverpool's streets during the mid-1950s. The mere act of resisting intervention, of striking out on one's own journey without wanting to be helped or indeed monitored by social purists or welfare workers was enough for the LVA to accuse these young women of seeking out a life of prostitution. The *Evening Express* informed its readers matter-of-factly that the LVA could 'help innocent girls' but it could 'do nothing about the good-time girls who come over with fixed ideas of earning easy money from immorality'. There was an implicit warning here for young women to accept the help of the LVA when it was offered, for to turn it down was to be presumed to be a prostitute in the making. White slavery was therefore still being used by the LVA as a discursive tool to justify its continued existence. Mrs Sugden told the paper that while 'White slavery is supposed to have been supressed … common sense tells us that the strange things that happened to these Irish girls suggests that some form of it still exists.'[55] Women who travelled for work, women in need of money and women from Ireland were all still implicated in the LVA's post-war narratives of vice and moral corruptibility.

That the LVA continued to stick to this broad notion of white slavery throughout the interwar years and even after the downturn that the organization faced during the Second World War was in no small part because of the sense of energy and urgency that trafficking gave to their work. In the next chapter, I want to explore in more detail the lack of precision that the LVA displayed in moving between the language of white slavery, trafficking, bad influence and moral corruption. Focusing specifically on the interwar years, before the LVA had to step up their efforts to persuade the public and even other social purists of the threat of white slavery, I examine overlaps between the LVA's broad interpretation of white slavery and similar uses of

54   'WHITE SLAVERY IS DEAD – But', *Evening Express*, 11 January 1954.
55   'WHITE SLAVERY IS DEAD – But', *Evening Express*, 11 January 1954.

the term in the press. I argue that, in amongst the vagueness of what exactly constituted a case of white slavery, certain common features did emerge, and, in Liverpool, one of the most compelling was the idea of the female trafficker. Female traffickers were themselves rather loosely or broadly defined, with 'immoral' or 'prostitute' women being classed as potential traffickers; but, as the next chapter makes clear, this idea of the female trafficker became so important because she seemed to justify moral surveillance on the spurious grounds that 'immoral' women could have a negative influence over 'vulnerable' women.

6

Female 'Traffickers' and Urban Danger*

Despite being set up to tackle white slavery and prostitution, the LVA was mainly concerned with preventative work and with helping women on an individual and opportunistic basis. The annual reports of the LVA show little direct engagement with prostitutes, brothels or suspected pimps and traffickers, with the bulk of their work taking the form of chaperoning young women as they arrived in the city on boats and trains. As the previous chapter argued, the rhetoric of white slavery was politically potent for the LVA; it allowed them to tap into an urban horror story that immediately raised the stakes of their work. During the interwar years, the 'archetypal white slave story' revolved around young white women being abducted by 'secret foreign syndicate[s]', with the help of immoral women acting as 'agents' in the spread of vice.[1] This 'media and popular perception' of a 'helpless innocent victim decoyed by procurers' undoubtedly informed the LVA's emphasis on the vulnerability of naive young women and the threat of immoral agents, but in general the LVA regarded the threat of white slavery in much more subtle terms than

---

* The section of this chapter that deals with ethnic minority men appeared in an earlier form in an article in *Women's History Review* in 2016. See Samantha Caslin, '"One Can Only Guess What Might Have Happened if the Worker Had Not Intervened in Time": The Liverpool Vigilance Association, Moral Vulnerability and Irish Girls in Early to Mid-Twentieth-Century Liverpool', *Women's History Review*, 25:2 (2016), pp. 254–73.

1 Marek Kohn, *Dope Girls: The Birth of the British Drug Underground* (London: Granta Books, 2001 [1992]), pp. 4–5.

this.[2] Evidence of women being taken to foreign lands and 'forced into brothels' was not especially forthcoming in Liverpool and, significantly, myths about girls being drugged with flowers and handkerchiefs were not focused on by the LVA.[3]

In the absence of encounters with kidnapped women, the LVA deployed a broad reading of coercion to justify their work as a battle against the threat of white slavery. As such, the LVA possessed the same 'messier mingling of good intentions and blinkered prejudices' that had been characteristic of many a charitable effort for at least half a century.[4] I argue that, in requiring only the suggestion of coercion to apply the rhetoric of white slavery to their case work, the LVA framed all manner of sexual transactions between young women and men as dangerous and exploitative. Young, working-class women who travelled for work tended to need money, which automatically meant that their engagement in any kind of prostitution, whether amateur or professional, could be deemed coercive. Moreover, the case studies examined in this chapter show that even where poverty was not highlighted by the LVA as the main source of vulnerability, the organization's tendency to see working-class women as morally fragile meant that 'bad girls' could be deemed to be applying pressure to other girls simply by their influence and example.

Before examining how the LVA incorporated the character of the corrupting, female trafficker into their narrative of urban sexual danger, I want first to consider the limits of the LVA's interest in coercion and force. Cases of prostitution where women claimed to be under the control of pimps or madams did, of course, exist in the city. This chapter uses the 1934 case of 'trafficker' Mary McAuley to show that the judiciary and press drew upon a similarly broad rhetoric of white slavery to that of the LVA when seeking to categorize the behaviour of sexually transgressive women. That Mary encouraged prostitution in her home and that she could be cruel to the young women who stayed there is not in question. Instead, I use her case to demonstrate that instances of force

---

2   Lesley Hall, *Sex, Gender and Social Change in Britain since 1800*, p. 87. Sheila Jeffreys writes that '[i]n the popular mind, the traffic was understood to involve force and violence and to be carried out against the victim's will', although she acknowledges that this was not usually the case. Sheila Jeffreys, *The Idea of Prostitution*, p. 8.

3   See Lesley Hall, *Sex, Gender and Social Change*, p. 87.

4   Seth Koven, *Slumming*, p. 3.

and coercion could not be neatly extricated from those of persuasion, economic necessity or, in the LVA's estimations, bad influence. In a market where women struggled with poverty and in a culture where a fallen woman was considered irredeemable, distinctions between coercion and choice were deeply problematic. The LVA did not interact with Mary McAuley or the women who worked as prostitutes in her house. Mary and the women who worked for her were already fallen, and so they remained outside of the LVA's preventative remit. But Mary's case was part of a wider culture that tied white slavery not just to ethnic minority foreign men but to dangerous white British women.

The type of trafficking that the LVA mostly dealt with involved persuasive British women who encouraged girls to travel with them to cities with which they were not familiar. The LVA's nebulous conception of trafficking as persuasion and bad influence rather than kidnap or imprisonment gave women who were believed to be out to corrupt other women special resonance within the organization's overall discourse of sexual immorality. The notion of white slavery that the LVA proliferated eroticized young female travellers in such a way that their innocence and purity were framed as qualities that required urgent guarding.[5] By associating their work with the moral panic about white slavery, the LVA thus presumed that women could be divided into those who were corruptible and those who were corrupting, and that their patrollers had the authority to legitimately distinguish between the two.

Mary McAuley's Mill Street

In early 1934, the racially diverse area of Toxteth, Liverpool, saw three of its residents accused of the sensational crime of participating in white slavery. At 10.45 p.m. on 5 February, police officers raided a house on Mill Street after suspicions were raised that it was being operated as a 'house of ill-fame'.[6] Samuel Joseph McAuley, a 48-year-old black man from the British

5   Similarly, Maria Luddy suggests that in early twentieth-century Ireland 'the appeal of white slavery was its lurid and melodramatic stories of intrigue, crime, seduction and sex. Such tales provided virtually pornographic entertainment to the reading audience'. Maria Luddy, *Prostitution and Irish Society 1800–1940* (Cambridge: Cambridge University Press, 2007), p. 163.

6   *Thomson's Weekly News*, 'Pretty Girls in Coloured Man's Home', 10 March 1934.

Gold Coast colony in Africa, and his 46-year-old white, English wife Mary were arrested, along with their 35-year-old associate Abbas Mohomed. The following month, all three were sent to stand trial at the Manchester Assizes, where they refuted the plethora of alarming accusations made against them. All told, the McAuleys faced over 20 charges, 21 of which related to the 'alleged procuration of four girls'.[7] For his part in the matter, Abbas Mohomed stood accused of seven charges of procuration, and all three defendants were accused of 'feloniously wounding a girl and stealing all her clothing'.[8]

The case was picked up by press around the country and widely reported as an example of white slavery.[9] According to prosecutors, Mary McAuley was responsible for duping young women into staying at 8 Mill Street, while her husband Samuel advertised the couple's services as pimp and madam to potential male clients. In fact, the prosecution argued, Mary's role in this transaction was key. It was claimed that she sought out young, attractive, white girls, often with backgrounds in low-paid positions such as domestic service.[10] Mary would invite these girls back to the house at Mill Street, where they would be given alcohol, introduced to 'coloured men' and encouraged to socialize, cavort and even sleep with them. During the trial, some of the women explained that they had felt compelled to stay on at the house after these illicit interactions out of shame, too embarrassed to return to their families. Others suggested that they genuinely feared they would be physically harmed should they attempt to leave.[11]

In court, the couple's victims elaborated on the specifics of Mary's manipulative tactics and the levels of coercion that she would use on her prey. While giving evidence, a 20-year-old woman told the court that she had innocently accepted Mary's invitation to have a cup of tea at the house before events quickly spiralled out of control.[12] The young woman said

---

7   *Thomson's Weekly News*, 'Pretty Girls in Coloured Man's Home', 10 March 1934.

8   *Thomson's Weekly News*, 'Pretty Girls in Coloured Man's Home', 10 March 1934.

9   'Five Year Sentence on Woman', *Hull Daily Mail*, 26 March 1934; 'Penal Servitude for White Slavers', *Liverpool Echo*, 26 March 1934; 'Coloured Men and White Girls', *Nottingham Evening Post*, 2 March 1934; 'White Slave Traffic Allegations', *Sheffield Independent*, 6 March 1934; 'White Slave Traffickers Sent to Prison', *Thomson's Weekly News*, 31 March 1934.

10   *Thomson's Weekly News*, 'Pretty Girls in Coloured Man's Home', 10 March 1934.

11   *Thomson's Weekly News*, 'Pretty Girls in Coloured Man's Home', 10 March 1934.

12   *Thomson's Weekly News*, 'Pretty Girls in Coloured Man's Home', 10 March 1934.

that Mary had remarked on her tired clothing and offered to introduce her to 'a coloured man who would keep you and dress you so well that you would be able to walk past your own home and let your mother see what you can do for yourself'.[13] The young woman said that she was then introduced to a West African man, Coffee Johnson, and that she stayed at the house with him for two weeks before returning 'home to her mother', apparently full of shame. Two months later, while working as a hospital maid, the young woman coincidentally ran into Mary McAuley when the elder woman was a patient at the hospital. Upon her discharge from the hospital, McAuley persuaded the young woman to accompany her back to Mill Street and the two celebrated Mary's return to health by drinking together. The young woman explained that she was so embarrassed about her behaviour that, the next morning, she accepted Mary's invitation to stay on at the house while occasionally taking money back to her mother under the pretence that she was still working at the hospital.[14] That the young woman was able to come and go from the property while in receipt of money should not necessarily be taken to mean that she was lying about Mary McAuley's influence over her; after all, as madam of the house, Mary had plenty of blackmail ammunition to use against young women who feared bringing shame to their respectable, working-class families.

However, the case that was built against Mary McAuley did not focus on questions of kidnap or the women's agency. Instead, Mary was interrogated for her contravention of gendered and racialized tropes about sexuality and domesticity. In drawing vulnerable women away from apparently legitimate forms of women's work in domestic service and nursing and away from the positive influence of their respectable, working-class families, Mary was constructed as a perverse mother-figure who ruled Mill Street with an iron fist, sharing her surrogate daughters with local black men and hordes of visiting sailors. In true matriarchal style, it was claimed that Mary encouraged one young woman to take the same surname as her.[15] The fact that this was a name Mary had herself gained through patriarchal convention upon her marriage to Samuel appeared not to matter to the case being weaved against her, nor did the fact that Samuel had a previous conviction for 'aggravated assault on his wife'.[16] This was 'Mary Mac's

13   *Thomson's Weekly News*, 'Pretty Girls in Coloured Man's Home', 10 March 1934.
14   *Thomson's Weekly News*, 'Pretty Girls in Coloured Man's Home', 10 March 1934.
15   *Thomson's Weekly News*, 'Pretty Girls in Coloured Man's Home', 10 March 1934.
16   *Illustrated Police News*, 5 April 1934.

Shanty' and for almost two years it had catered to the sexual proclivities of 'seamen of all nationalities'.[17]

As a white woman and as a mother, Mary defied social expectations about the caring and sexually demure instincts that were believed to define white, British womanhood. She made manifest all the moral uncertainties about modern matrimony, female power and the sexualization of domestic relations between husbands and wives. During the interwar years, the domestic realm was renegotiated. There was increasing public acknowledgement of the importance of sexual as well as social compatibility to the health of the modern marriage.[18] But marriage was still governed by a largely segregated vision of the domestic sphere: the male breadwinner may now have shown more care and consideration for his wife's sexual and social needs, but housework was still women's work and female autonomy was still viewed with suspicion. In the return to peacetime conditions after the First World War, Victorian and Edwardian forms of social and moral order based upon gender and class distinctions were reworked, and working-class women were chastised for having become drunk upon their wartime freedom. Young women were criticized for the climate of sexual liberalization, for not relinquishing their employment in *masculine* industries and for resisting the call of the domestic sphere.[19]

As the codes of modern marriage were being redrawn, women like Mary inadvertently offered themselves up as stark warnings about the dangers of female power. Mary's criminal entrepreneurialism was conflated with her sexual interest in black men and the power she held within her own sexually charged marriage. Mary was reported to have told a girl of 15 not to trust a black man who had promised to marry her, claiming 'Coloured men can always bluff white women, but they can't bluff me.'[20] As such, Mary's shanty had wider ramifications beyond the threat that she posed to local women. Her case played upon the idea that working-class women needed watching

17   *Thomson's Weekly News*, 'White Slave Traffickers Sent to Prison', 31 March 1934.
18   See Lesley Hall's analysis of men's correspondence with Marie Stopes after the First World War. Lesley Hall, 'Impotent Ghosts from No Man's Land, Flappers' Boyfriends, or Crypto-Patriarchs? Men, Sex and Social Change in 1920s Britain', *Social History*, 21:1 (1996), pp. 54–70.
19   Lucy Noakes, 'Demobilising the Military Woman: Constructions of Class and Gender in Britain after the First World War', *Gender & History*, 19:9 (2007), p. 145.
20   *Illustrated Police News*, 15 March 1934.

in case the poverty that surrounded them led to their moral corruption. Though the prosecutor made a point of noting in court that the police 'had no reason to suspect that there were other establishments of this kind in Liverpool', he still told the judge that Mill Street was situated in a 'somewhat rough district, and one in which there were a lot of coloured men living'.[21] Relationships between black men and white women were therefore used by the prosecution as a supposed sign of the area's moral poverty. Moreover, that Mary lived in a poor part of town and that she recruited poorly paid women into her fiefdom was indicative of the gap between domestic ideals and some of the realities of working-class life. During the economic problems of the 1930s, poorer women saw their health decline due to the laborious task of maintaining homes with no hot water while having no access to health care.[22] Mary McAuley's case was a reminder that the image of middle-class suburban domesticity was not available to everyone.

Mary had previous convictions for various offences, including larceny, disorderly conduct and running a disorderly house, criminal traits that were supposedly exacerbated when her marriage to Samuel McAuley caused her to become 'more violent'.[23] Indeed, Samuel's ethnicity was tightly woven into Mary's criminal biography of domestic breakdown. The 1919 race riots that tore through Liverpool were said by *Thomson's Weekly News* to have had a very personal impact upon the McAuleys, especially Mary:

> The summer of 1919 made an upheaval of her domestic life. It brought the memorable coloured riots which caused a great deal of trouble in the city and forced her husband to go to sea as a fireman.[24]

While separated from her husband during the early 1920s, Mary showed a propensity to engage in interracial and extra-marital relationships by embarking upon a relationship with another black man.[25] Mary's apparent

---

21   'Penal Servitude for White Slavers', *Liverpool Echo*, 26 March 1934.

22   Selina Todd, *The People: The Rise and Fall of the Working Class* (London: John Murray, 2015), p. 88.

23   *Thomson's Weekly News*, 'White Slave Traffickers Sent to Prison', 31 March 1934.

24   *Thomson's Weekly News*, 'White Slave Traffickers Sent to Prison', 31 March 1934.

25   *Thomson's Weekly News*, 'White Slave Traffickers Sent to Prison', 31 March 1934.

disregard for her marital vows and the maintenance of a stable family unit was further emphasized by the report's suggestion that she had moved to Montreal for six years, until Samuel McAuley had found her and reported her to the authorities. She was then sent back to England along with her children.[26]

By combining an account of Liverpool's race-rioting with a history of Mary's marriage, this newspaper report was indicative of the widespread interwar discursive intersections between miscegenation and prostitution, particularly in port cities.[27] In contravening gender codes and crossing racial lines, Mary and Samuel's marriage was presented as part of a social problem. Chris Waters has proposed that during the interwar period British national identity became more feminized, as domesticity was emphasized over the public sphere.[28] This had important implications for cultural understandings of interracial sexual relationships because fears about black men engaging in sexual activity with white women generated anxieties about the health of the nation itself. Tensions rose during the 1920s and 1930s and opposition to interracial relationships became a significant issue in a number of port towns.[29] Waters' findings that, in the 1950s, women who formed relationships with black men were often regarded as transgressive and deviant can also be applied to interwar Liverpool.[30] John Belchem notes that, in Liverpool, the 1919 race riots were directly linked by those with authority and influence to the fraternization between black men and white women. The city's Head Constable blamed the disturbances on the supposed sense of entitlement and swagger amongst local West Indian men and the sexual confidence of the local white women who stepped out with them, buoyed by their wartime sexual adventures.[31] Michael Rowe's analysis of local and

---

26   *Thomson's Weekly News*, 'White Slave Traffickers Sent to Prison', 31 March 1934.

27   Simon Jenkins' history of race and prostitution in Cardiff shows that in that city, too, British sexual morality was defined in opposition to '"foreign" desires and sexual practices'. See Simon Jenkins, 'Aliens and Predators', pp. 575–96.

28   Chris Waters, '"Dark Strangers" in Our Midst: Discourses of Race and Nation in Britain, 1947–1963', *Journal of British Studies*, 36:2 (1997), p. 212.

29   Chris Waters, '"Dark Strangers" in Our Midst', p. 212.

30   Chris Waters, '"Dark Strangers" in Our Midst', pp. 228–9.

31   John Belchem, *Before the Windrush: Race Relations in 20th-Century Liverpool* (Liverpool: Liverpool University Press, 2014), p. 43. Charlotte Wildman has also suggested that concerns about unemployment and miscegenation fuelled these

national press reporting shows that newspapers proliferated the notion that the riots had been started by tensions about sexual relationships between white women and black men, with articles stoking fears about miscegenation.[32]

The threat of white slavery carried a significant degree of cultural currency for those who sought to moralize about sexual relations in the city. The sexual practices of black men had long been pathologized in Britain, with eugenic theories of racial difference still evident in interwar sexual politics. In 1930, the *Report on an Investigation into the Colour Problem in Liverpool and other Ports* (also known as the Fletcher Report) was published. The report claimed to be scientific but its appeals to science were a cover for its racism. It claimed that black seamen spread venereal disease, were cruel to their white wives and girlfriends, and that 'half-caste' children were more likely to lead immoral lives.[33] In 1932, social investigator Nancie Sharpe claimed that black men in London and Cardiff were 'hot-blooded' because they originally came from warmer parts of the globe, causing them to mature more quickly than men from cooler climates.[34] As a result, Sharpe believed that black men were more sexually motivated than their white English counterparts, and she believed that their stronger sexual urges caused them to form relationships with white women who were either very young or overly sexualized 'semi-prostitutes'.[35] Indeed, interwar concerns about miscegenation frequently resorted to the tropes of the sexually passive woman as a victim and the sexually active woman as morally corrosive.[36]

In Liverpool, the association between miscegenation and problematic forms of womanhood was so strong that white working-class women who formed relationships with black men were considered to be morally and

riots, with Liverpool witnessing 'the worst of the violence and with murderous results' when black sailor Charles Wooton drowned at the docks having jumped or been pushed into the water while a crowd looked on. Charlotte Wildman, 'Urban Transformation in Liverpool and Manchester, 1918–1939', *Historical Journal*, 55:1 (2012), p. 122.

32   Michael Rowe, 'Sex, "Race" and Riot in Liverpool, 1919', *Immigrants & Minorities* 19:2 (2000), pp. 57–60.

33   John Belchem, *Before the Windrush*, pp. 62–3.

34   Simon Jenkins, 'Aliens and Predators', p. 564.

35   Simon Jenkins, 'Aliens and Predators', p. 564.

36   Lucy Bland, 'White Women and Men of Colour: Miscegenation Fears in Britain after the Great War', *Gender & History*, 17:1 (2005), p. 33.

socially lacking.[37] Throughout the interwar years, the moral street patrollers in the LVA and Women Police Patrols read interracial mixing as a sign of immorality. In 1924, the LVA reported on the case of a girl who was apparently given a venereal disease by a 'coloured man', and in 1927, the Women Police Patrol's Hostel in Knotty Ash reported their difficulties in reforming a 19-year-old Irish woman who had come to England to work in service 'but had afterwards gone on to live with a coloured man'.[38] The young woman was described as 'weak-willed', only leaving the man after they 'quarrelled' and a Woman Police Patroller brought her to the Hostel to make arrangements for her to return to Ireland.[39] In a similar case from 1929, the LVA described a young woman who had taken up with 'coloured acquaintances' as 'hardened and difficult to influence from her loose mode of living'. Her stepfather reportedly told the organization 'that it was absolutely impossible to induce her to live at home'.[40] Also in 1929, the LVA described meeting a girl who took up the 'undesirable company of coloured acquaintances', and in 1933, the LVA worked with the Newcastle Vigilance Association to prevent two Northern Irish girls travelling to Newcastle to meet the foreign fiancé of one of the girls.[41] This intervention was apparently justified on the grounds that the man was living in 'undesirable surroundings' with a group of Egyptians.[42]

It was from within this racialized and gendered context that the McAuleys were presented to the public as 'white slavers'.[43] This term could be relied upon to cultivate fear that interracial relationships could be harmful to the wider community. The association between the brothel that the McAuleys ran and white slavery was based largely upon the racial dynamics of the white prostitutes and black customers at Mill Street. In interwar Liverpool, accusations that the city's black men were running white slave rackets were indicative of racialized moral panics about sexual corruption rather

---

37   Laura Tabili, 'Women "of a very low type": Crossing Racial Boundaries in Late Imperial Britain', in Laura Levine Frader and Sonya O. Rose (eds), *Gender and Class in Modern Europe* (Ithaca, NY: Cornell University Press, 1996), p. 176.
38   LVA, Annual Report 1923–24, p. 14; Hostel for Girls, Knotty Ash: Liverpool Women Police Patrols and Training Centre, Annual Report 1927, p. 6. Liverpool Record Office, H364/5 WOM.
39   Hostel for Girls, Knotty Ash, Annual Report 1927, p. 6.
40   LVA, Annual Report 1928–29, p. 7.
41   LVA, Annual Report 1928–29, p. 7; LVA, Annual Report 1932–33, p. 8.
42   LVA, Annual Report 1932–33, p. 8.
43   'Penal Servitude for White Slavers', *Liverpool Echo*, 26 March 1934.

than any widespread issue with trafficking. Forced prostitution did exist within the city; in 1918, the Home Office identified a number of Liverpool children's homes which it believed were operating as brothels.[44] But the notion that there existed racially segregated groups of traffickers taking women from the streets appears to have been more myth than reality. In fact, both the local police and the Home Office failed to find evidence of trafficking gangs in the city.[45]

The house run by the McAuley's was not part of a wider criminal enterprise, but it represented the supposed corruption of young womanhood in the city. In their examination of the case, the papers and the judge focused upon Mary. It was only upon news of her sentencing that Mary was imbued with a traditionally feminine characteristic, when the press noted that she fainted in the dock. Newspapers from around the country reported that she implored the judge, 'Have mercy for the sake of my dying child. I will never sin again.'[46] Mary was a fallen woman, though, and she had caused other women to fall, meaning that she was afforded no leniency. When finding the three defendants guilty, the Judge rounded on Mary. He told her, 'You used the two men, who are standing by you in the dock, for the purpose of carrying on your horrible trade.'[47] The judge identified Mary as the 'dominating mind behind the wicked business' and sentenced her to five years' penal servitude, the harshest sentence of the three.[48]

Mary's harsher sentence reflects the fact that she had transgressed not just the law but also the gender role that society proscribed for her. Moreover, unlike the male trafficker, the female trafficker embodied the vulnerability supposedly inherent to womanhood. Women like Mary were

44   Pamela Cox, *Bad Girls in Britain: Gender, Justice and Welfare, 1900–1950* (Basingstoke: Palgrave Macmillan, 2013), p. 39.

45   John Belchem, *Before the Windrush*, p. 56.

46   The reporting of the case in areas unconnected with the crimes committed speaks to the extent to which tales of white slavery captured popular attention. See 'Woman's Appeal for Mercy', *Illustrated Police News*, 5 April, 1934; 'Five Year Sentence on Woman', *Hull Daily Mail*, 26 March 1934; 'Woman's "Mercy" Cry', *Western Gazette*, 30 March 1934.

47   'Penal Servitude for White Slavers', *Liverpool Echo*, 26 March 1934.

48   'White Slave Traffickers Sent to Prison', *Thomson's Weekly News*, 31 March 1934. The McAuleys were found guilty of most of the charges against them, including procuring girls, keeping a disorderly house and living on immoral earnings. They were found not guilty of procuring one of the four girls identified in the case; nor were they found guilty of larceny.

severed up as examples of what transience and sexual indiscretion could do to women. Due to the weight of racist stereotypes about sexuality, black and Asian men like Samuel McAuley and Abbas Mohamad were readily imagined as traffickers, but they did not inspire the same introspection about the corrupting potential of urban life in 'rough' areas because their actions were erroneously presumed to a product of their race. It is telling that when the press relayed information about the sentencing of the two men, their races were highlighted and Abbas Mohamad was described in particularly derisive terms: Samuel, described as Mary's 'coloured husband', received three years' penal servitude, and Abbas Mohamad, described in the press as 'a Bengalese seaman', a 'Hindoo' and a 'loathsome creature', was sentenced to 12 months' imprisonment with hard labour.[49] But the female trafficker could inspire greater moral outrage than her male counterpart, because she made manifest the idea that immorality worked like a contagion. The press, members of the judiciary and social purists feared that once these women were infected with licentiousness, criminality and debauchery, they would move though the city like a virus looking for fresh young women to blight.

Social Purity and the Female Trafficker

The LVA's work in Liverpool was intended to act as a deterrent to women like Mary McAuley, but their patrollers showed little interest in wandering the streets of areas like Toxteth. Instead, they focused their attentions on trying to prevent young women from being taken in by the likes of Mary by intercepting them before they left the city centre. However, as with the case of Mary McAuley, the LVA's notion of a female trafficker was nebulous. The following case studies from the LVA's reports show that LVA-identified traffickers tended to operate in an ad hoc fashion and often as lone wolves rather than as part of highly organized vice rings. Many of the suspected traffickers apparently thwarted by the LVA were women, and their cases were used to warn about the effects of disreputable womanhood upon the gullible and immature. In practice, though, this meant that the LVA frequently intervened in the lives of women with no obvious connections to prostitution of any kind. Women were scrutinized as *potential* traffickers or *potential* prostitutes, as predators or as victims.

49   *Thomson's Weekly News*, 31 March 1934 and *Western Gazette*, 30 March 1934. 'Penal Servitude for White Slavers', *Liverpool Echo*, 26 March 1934.

Figure 2   'Stranded': National Vigilance Association Charity Dinner
Pamphlet, November 1908
(Liverpool Record Office, Liverpool Libraries)

From their earliest days, the LVA drew upon the figure of the female trafficker as an example of the danger that public space held for respectable womanhood. Ahead of the 1908 charity dinner set up to establish their work in the city, the NVA issued a pamphlet advertising the event. An illustration on the back of the pamphlet depicted a young, naive, female traveller caught between the caring gaze of a patrol worker, identifiable by her badge and warm expression, and the stare of a suspicious-looking woman who lurked around the corner with her male companion (Figure 2). The sketch presents the LVA patroller as the very antithesis of the couple on the left. The patroller's clothes are feminine but also simple and practical; her hat, gloves and scarf are less an indication of an interest in fashion than a symbol of the early-morning, outdoor nature of the work that she performed. By contrast, the man's tailored overcoat and trousers are complemented by a detailed waistcoat and smart hat. The woman next to him is even more flamboyantly turned out. Her travelling coat, with its large, ruffled sleeves, hangs open to reveal a frilled blouse, and the brim of her large hat is covered with decorative flowers. These garments were a sign that the couple had access to money, though their surreptitious positioning just out of the young woman's sight implied that there was something secretive and threatening about the character of these individuals. The accompanying caption, 'A perilous moment!!', left no doubt that the couple had dangerous intentions towards the young woman. The image also gives considerable agency to the female trafficker in this scene. The woman does not hold on to the man's arm in a passive fashion; instead, she pulls him back to warn him of the LVA patroller's presence. In this sense, the woman in the picture is endowed with a knowing and active role in the targeting of young women. She is presented as being equally as dangerous as her male counterpart.

This image of the finely dressed but highly dangerous older woman remained part of the LVA's anti-white slavery discourse well into the interwar years. In 1933, the LVA argued that it was 'not only men' who presented a 'danger to young girls travelling alone'.[50] They suggested that 'a well-dressed woman' could 'also exercise an amount of confidence with inexperienced girls coming to Liverpool for the first time'.[51] It was feared that these women could, by virtue of their appearance alone, persuade young women to trust or admire them. In a case from the year 1933–34, a 'flashily dressed much older woman' was said to have made the

50   LVA, Annual Report 1932–33, p. 9.
51   LVA, Annual Report 1932–33, p. 9.

acquaintance of a young Irish girl travelling to a destination in London by offering her 'refreshments' while aboard a boat to Liverpool.[52] The one similarity that the LVA could countenance between their patrollers and female traffickers was the suggestion that the LVA were equally adept at winning the trust of vulnerable young women. The Irish girl opted to leave the scene with the LVA patrol worker, explaining that her sister had been helped by the LVA 'some months previously' and had told the girl 'to look out for the lady wearing the badge and be advised by her'.[53] After making enquiries at the railway station, the LVA reported that the woman who had approached the girl had been drinking and that 'her attitude and behaviour had been altogether undesirable'. Once again, details about the precise nature of the woman's behaviour were lacking, but such was the LVA patroller's level of concern about the intentions of this woman that the patroller arranged for an NVA representative to meet the girl in London to ensure that she completed her journey safely.[54]

It was not uncommon for the LVA patrol workers to go to considerable lengths to monitor interactions between suspicious women and girls. In addition to monitoring vulnerable girls, the LVA's surveillance techniques involved following potential traffickers until they were satisfied that they did not present a moral danger to others. In one encounter, an LVA patroller was drawn towards a 'pretty, but poorly dressed' 16-year-old who had travelled to Liverpool from Ireland.[55] While the LVA patroller spoke to the girl, a 'well-dressed woman' approached and claimed that she knew the girl and would 'see her to her destination'.[56] Her suspicions roused, the LVA patroller took the same bus as the pair and found that the woman was taking her young companion to Lime Street train station. Knowing that the girl could not get to her destination by train, the patroller again approached the pair at the station and enquired where they were going. The woman claimed to be simply leaving her luggage at Lime Street station for collection later that day, but the LVA representative insisted that she would see the girl to her destination. Though the woman had been 'invited' by the patroller to accompany them, she 'quietly slipped away without a word'.[57] The LVA's

---

52   LVA, Annual Report 1933–34, p. 6. Liverpool Record Office, M326 VIG/3.
53   LVA, Annual Report 1933–34, p. 6.
54   LVA, Annual Report 1933–34, p. 6.
55   LVA, Annual Report 1930–31, p. 6.
56   LVA, Annual Report 1930–31, p. 7.
57   LVA, Annual Report 1930–31, p. 7.

report suggested that the woman had been lying to both the patroller and the girl. It transpired that the woman did not know the girl but had met her on the boat. The girl, not knowing Liverpool, had accepted the woman's acquaintance because she had been 'glad to find someone to help her'. Keen to rectify the girl's naivety, the LVA worker left her at her destination with a 'warning' about 'the danger of too easily making friends with strangers, especially, when travelling'.[58]

However, it should be noted that the LVA did not always portray female 'traffickers' as being older than the woman that they preyed upon. In their bid to distinguish between women as victims and predators, a woman's age could be twisted to fit either character. In 1926, the LVA stated that it had been closely involved in a case that had resulted in the authorities preventing a 'young girl' suspected of 'trafficking' from remaining in the country.[59] The practice of infantilizing problem women, a characteristic of the Victorian Ladies Associations, was very much in evidence in the LVA's assessment of this interwar case.[60] The 'young girl' in question was actually 25 years old.[61] Rather than exonerating her from any wrongdoing, the LVA created a youthful impression of the woman to project a sense of her poor moral judgement and decision-making. The woman had entered Liverpool from the USA, whereupon she was investigated by the Authorities and the LVA. The woman explained that she had been 'persuaded' to travel to England by an Englishman who 'lived a double life'.[62] Having brought her to England, the man had offered to marry her when her entry to the country was halted on 'medical grounds'.[63] Though this aspect of her story was not challenged or doubted by the LVA, the organization did not appear at all concerned that, far from having encountered a trafficker, the woman herself appeared to fit their own definition of a trafficked woman. That she had, at the very least, been manipulated by her male companion did not afford her any great sympathy. Instead, the LVA proceeded to present the woman as a trafficker herself and her case was used by the organization to indicate how a woman could pass beyond the threshold of redemption to become irretrievably fallen.

58   LVA, Annual Report 1930–31, p. 7.
59   LVA, Annual Report 1925–26, p. 8.
60   Paula Bartley, *Prostitution*, p. 75.
61   LVA, Annual Report 1925–26, p. 8.
62   LVA, Annual Report 1925–26, p. 8.
63   LVA, Annual Report 1925–26, p. 8.

In narrating her story, the LVA emphasized the woman's perceived moral frailty. They noted that she was the mother of a nine-year-old son, whom she had left in the USA, that she had been married at 15 and that she was believed to be 'suffering from drug taking'.[64] Marriage, motherhood and domestic stability were all presented as anathema to this woman. According to the LVA, the woman had arrived in the city with dubious ambitions to find work 'dancing in a Night Club', a detail that spoke directly to LVA's assessment of this woman as sexually impure.[65] Though they presented no evidence to support this, the LVA argued that there was 'very little question left in our mind that she was coming with a purpose of "trafficking" girls'.[66] In being designated a 'trafficker', she was not someone that the organization was particularly interested in saving; such women were considered beyond their help. Instead, the LVA concentrated upon using this woman as a symbol of urban danger. The LVA reported that the woman had told them that there 'was nothing in the "Underworld" she did not know and had not been through in the United States'.[67] The woman's American background thus heightened the LVA's sense of danger surrounding the case. Andrew Davies' work has shown that there were concerns during the 1920s and 30s about the influence tales of the American 'underworld' might be having upon young British men. He argues that although America was held in stark contrast to the more 'peaceable' Britain, fears abounded that disreputable forms of Americanization might spread through British cities like a 'contagion'.[68] It was against this backdrop that the LVA intercepted this woman and closed down the potential for her to spread the vices of the American underworld to British girls and women.

The LVA also dealt with a number of cases that involved young women being persuaded to travel to new or unknown places by younger women of potentially immoral character. In 1933, the LVA suggested that 19-year-old Mary had 'induced another to come to Liverpool, promising to take her to a famous seaside resort, where she would secure well-paid employment during the summer season'.[69] Upon arrival in the city, the young woman

64   LVA, Annual Report 1925–26, p. 8.
65   LVA, Annual Report 1925–26, p. 8.
66   LVA, Annual Report 1925–26, p. 8.
67   LVA, Annual Report 1925–26, p. 8.
68   Andrew Davies, 'The Scottish Chicago? From "Hooligans" to "Gangsters" in Inter-War Glasgow', *Cultural and Social History*, 4:4 (2007), p. 515.
69   LVA, Annual Report 1933–34, p. 6.

was said to have 'found to her horror that Mary was well known in the city as a bad girl'.[70] Indeed, this was not the LVA's only interaction with Mary that year; as a result of this case, the organization was able to prevent her from bringing another 'young girl' to Liverpool 'under false pretences'.[71] Though Mary was not labelled a trafficker, the threat that she was believed to present to other young women was nonetheless framed, for the LVA, by the same concerns about the potential for immoral women to encourage others into vice and promiscuity. Ideas about women being taken literally and figuratively across borders, about women being encouraged to move to new and unknown areas by other women fuelled the LVA's belief in the corrupting influence of disreputable women. For the LVA, the threat posed by these women had to be countered by the organization's own surveillance strategies and by the positive example of respectable womanhood that the organization represented.

It cannot be denied that the LVA's watchfulness in cases of this kind prevented many young women from being manipulated by dubious and potentially criminal characters. However, the way the LVA understood the help that they offered formed part of a gendered urban imagination that presented public spaces as morally corrosive to womanhood due to the presence of fallen women upon the city's streets. This urban imagination was not simply a construction of the LVA. As the case of Mary McAuley shows, women involved in vice and immorality were singled out for criticism by both the press and the judiciary because they unsettled conventional gender roles. The LVA took wider cultural attitudes towards urban womanhood and white slavery and used them to justify strategies of surveillance and social control. The LVA believed urban spaces held moral dangers for all women and they argued that working-class and young women needed special protection and surveillance in order to maintain their moral integrity. The LVA's belief in the widespread existence of white slavery was a product of their overall sense of the fragility of female respectability in urban settings.

In much the same way that Mary McAuley had come to be labelled not just a brothel keeper but a white slaver, the LVA's rhetoric of white slavery oversimplified, combined and conflated the relationships between criminality, prostitution, promiscuity, bad influence and working-class women's transience. However, the LVA went even further than the case against Mary McAuley had done. Notions of disreputability and trafficking were

70   LVA, Annual Report 1933–34, p. 6.
71   LVA, Annual Report 1933–34, p. 7.

blurred by the LVA, with women's boisterous behaviour in public and a prolonged presence in public spaces like railway stations attracting the attention of LVA patrollers. At the same time, gaudy clothes were taken as a sign of an exaggerated or even grotesque form of womanhood. Far from being respectable, overdressed women who loitered in public were perceived as having been corrupted by their lifestyles. By attempting to stop these women from gaining influence over other women, the LVA set out its preventative and protective agenda. They used cases of female traffickers, defined in broad terms, as examples of the sort of dangerous and disreputable womanhood that they aimed to prevent. They also made clear that they thought young women needed the LVA's moral protection lest they follow the same path as the female traffickers, madams, prostitutes and promiscuous women found on the streets.

As the mix of cases explored in this chapter indicates, there was often considerable overlap between these different types of women in the LVA's moral discourse. While Bartley has suggested that, in the early twentieth century, 'social purists were more repressive than protective in their efforts to curb prostitution', for purists in the LVA at least, prevention remained paramount over and above dealing directly with women already working as prostitutes.[72] Yet these preventative polices could still have repressive results for women. The LVA saw trafficking as one example of a broad range of urban dangers that they believed all women faced. By concentrating upon the threat of female traffickers and presenting them as manipulative and persuasive, the LVA made it much easier to relate their fears about trafficking to their work helping women to avoid vice and immorality in general. To this extent, it is accurate to suggest, as Sheila Jeffreys does, that white slavery was 'about more than the traffic itself'. She has suggested that 'For Feminists, campaigning against the White Slave Traffic was a way of gaining ground in their struggle against prostitution in general.'[73] However, I would argue that, for women social purists in Liverpool, the campaign against white slavery was a way of gaining ground in their effort to influence the morals of women in general and working-class women in particular.

The image of the female trafficker represented the sort of sexual and moral corruption that the LVA believed threatened *all* young women travelling in and around Liverpool. Since working-class women were thought to be the group of women most likely to need to travel alone for work, or to spend

72 Paula Bartley, *Prostitution*, p. 173.
73 Sheila Jeffreys, *The Idea of Prostitution*, p. 8.

more time socializing on the streets, they were perceived to be at most risk of falling under the influence of the female trafficker. Thus, the female trafficker added extra potency to the LVA's belief that their efforts to protect young, working-class women in public spaces were of paramount importance to social morality.

7

Irish Girls in Liverpool (1)

Interwar Moral Concerns*

It was a 'typical case [that] occurred early one morning' between 1932 and 1933; an LVA patroller was at her usual position at Liverpool's Landing Stage, quietly observing passengers as they disembarked from the latest boat into port.[1] Her eyes scanned the people as they passed by, assessing their age, their state of dress, the amount of luggage they carried, and she listened to catch snippets of conversations, to flourishes of English and Irish accents; this was one of the regular boats that sailed between Liverpool and Ireland. Amongst the scene, the LVA patroller found her attention 'attracted by two young Irish girls'. It was a familiar sight for the LVA patroller, who was used to monitoring the area looking for vulnerable girls arriving in Liverpool. The Irish girls who piqued her interest that particular morning seemed to have already made the acquaintance of a suspicious character. The girls were 'in the company of a well-dressed, middle aged woman, about whom [the LVA patroller] did not feel quite happy'.[2] Propelled by her intuition, the LVA patroller strode over to the trio and enquired about their journey and their relationship to one another. At this inquisition, the older woman insisted that she was looking after the girls; then she turned to her

* Parts of this chapter appeared in an article in *Women's History Review* in 2016. See Samantha Caslin, '"One Can Only Guess What Might Have Happened if the Worker Had Not Intervened in Time": The Liverpool Vigilance Association, Moral Vulnerability and Irish Girls in Early to Mid-Twentieth-Century Liverpool', *Women's History Review*, 25:2 (2016), pp. 254–73.
1   LVA, Annual Report 1932–33, p. 9.
2   LVA, Annual Report 1932–33, p. 9.

young acquaintances and 'strongly advised them to have nothing to do with our [the LVA] Worker'.[3]

The LVA could not apprehend people on the grounds of their suspicions. Yet what the LVA worker lacked in official powers she made up for in resourcefulness, as she quickly sought the help of a nearby 'official', probably a member of the ferry company's staff.[4] Faced with further questioning, this time from someone with more authority, the well-dressed woman refused to answer any more questions and she walked away from the party and climbed into a taxi. The girls then confessed that they had in fact only just met the woman. She had offered to take care of them after one had felt ill on the boat. The LVA representative considered her suspicions about the woman to be validated when it transpired that the woman had lied to the girls, telling them their eventual destinations were close to hers and suggesting that they should share a cab. With no geographical knowledge about where they needed to go the girls had trusted the woman.

To the LVA patroller's relief, the girls assured her that they were making their way to a hospital where they had acquired jobs as nurse probationers.[5] The patroller supposed that the girls' employment was appropriate even if their understanding of the dangers presented by apparently well-meaning strangers was not. Indeed, the LVA's report on the incident exclaimed, 'One can only guess what might have happened if the Worker had not intervened in time'.[6] For members of the LVA, it was easy to guess at all manner of physical and moral threats to these girls. The Association was deeply concerned about the well-being of young women who found themselves unchaperoned in large cities like Liverpool, especially when they came from Ireland, since their patrollers supposed that these young women would have little or no knowledge of the city. It was a concern that the LVA put to the matron at the hospital when they contacted her to ensure that the girls had completed their journey safely. The matron agreed wholeheartedly and gratefully

3   LVA, Annual Report 1932–33, p. 9.
4   LVA, Annual Report 1932–33, p. 9.
5   This role had much in common with domestic service, with nurse probationers taking considerable responsibility for ward cleanliness, from cleaning behind beds to flower arranging. See David Justham, 'A Study of Nursing Practices Used in the Management of Infection in Hospitals, 1929–1948', pp. 127–8.
6   LVA, Annual Report 1932–33, p. 9.

requested that the LVA meet other Irish would-be nurses en route to her hospital in future.[7]

Cases such as this were not unusual for the LVA. As this chapter and the next will show, throughout the interwar and post-war periods the LVA regularly encountered Irish women entering Liverpool by boat and attempted to intervene in their journeys and lives. Not all the women that the LVA engaged with were Irish and, in principle at least, the organization did not exist to help Irish women specifically, but the nature of Liverpool's port life meant that most women helped by the LVA *were* Irish. The research presented in this chapter and the next will therefore consider how concerns about vice were constructed in response to local patterns and fluctuations in travel and immigration. In this regard, the history of social purity in Liverpool makes for a particularly interesting comparison with London-focused histories of vice and immorality, where the figure of the Irish woman is notably missing.[8] For example, Stefan Slater's work productively draws out the considerable attention that was devoted to immigrant prostitutes in interwar London; yet Irish women do not feature in Slater's picture of the capital at all.[9] This is especially striking when one considers that London was 'a prominent destination for second-wave Irish migration following the partition of Ireland in 1922'.[10] It seems, then, that other immigrants to the capital received more sensationalist attention than the Irish, a proposition that underlines the need for historians to consider how fears about vice, immorality and urban danger were regionally nuanced.

This is not to argue that the gendered perceptions of the Irish in interwar Liverpool existed in a vacuum or only in that locality. Jennifer Redmond's work brings attention to the gendered view of emigration taken by the state

7   LVA, Annual Report 1932–33, p. 9.
8   See, for example, Seth Koven, *Slumming*; Julia Laite, 'Taking Nellie Johnson's Fingerprints'; Frank Mort, 'Striptease: The Erotic Female Body and Live Sexual Entertainment in Mid-Twentieth-Century London', *Social History*, 32:1 (2007), pp. 27–53; Stefan Slater, 'Pimps, Police and Filles de Joie'; Judith Walkowitz, *City of Dreadful Delight*.
9   Stefan Slater, 'Pimps, Police and Filles de Joie'.
10   Colin G. Pooley, 'Getting to Know the City: The Construction of Spatial Knowledge in London in the 1930s', *Urban History*, 31:2 (2004), p. 216. Pooley notes that young Irish women were 'especially attracted to work in London in the mid 1930s' because of the employment opportunities on offer in the region. Moreover, he proposes that the majority of these girls came from the south rather than the north (also on p. 216).

and the Catholic Church in Ireland, with these institutions showing far more concern with the sexual purity of expatriate women than men.[11] Moreover, research in the area of Irish gender history has begun to cast light on the connections between white slavery panics and prostitution in Ireland, while Bronwyn Walter has produced an analysis of the way perceptions of Irish women as pure and virtuous have become part of Irish national identity and femininity.[12] The work of Maria Luddy and Lindsey Earner-Byrne has highlighted the close relationship between Irish feminine ideals and moral purity, while Mo Moulton's recent work on the Irish in interwar England brings together broader understandings of Irish immigration with experiences in cities like Liverpool.[13] For example, Moulton notes fears amongst the LVA and other organizations in England about young Irish women engaging in immoral, sexual behaviour.[14]

However, I want to propose that the treatment of these Irish women, in Liverpool at least, can tell us a lot about the gendered moral surveillance of the streets more generally during the interwar years. Though aspects of Irish national identity were central to the LVA's rhetoric of vulnerability, it would be a mistake to think that the LVA homed in on young Irish female

11   Jennifer Redmond, '"Sinful Singleness?" Exploring the Discourses on Irish Single Women's Emigration to England, 1922–1948', *Women's History Review*, 17:3 (2008), pp. 455–76.

12   See Maria Luddy, *Prostitution and Irish Society*; James M. Smith, *Ireland's Magdalen Laundries and the Nation's Architecture of Containment* (Manchester: Manchester University Press, 2007); Bronwen Walter, *Outsiders Inside: Whiteness, Place and Irish Women* (London: Routledge, 2001).

13   Lindsey Earner-Byrne, *Mother and Child: Maternity and Child Welfare in Dublin, 1922–60* (Manchester: Manchester University Press, 2007); Maria Luddy, *Prostitution and Irish Society*; Mo Moulton, *Ireland and the Irish in Interwar England* (Cambridge: Cambridge University Press, 2014). For more on the social history of the Irish in Liverpool, see John Belchem, *Irish Catholic and Scouse: The History of the Liverpool Irish, 1800–1939* (Liverpool: Liverpool University Press, 2007); Frank Neal, *Sectarian Violence: The Liverpool Experience, 1819–1914: An Aspect of Anglo-Irish History* (Manchester: Manchester University Press, 1987). For more on the history of the Irish in Liverpool prior to the twentieth century, see Ryan Dye, 'Catholic Protectionism or Irish Nationalism? Religion and Politics in Liverpool, 1829–1845', *Journal of British Studies*, 40:3 (2001), pp. 357–90; Colin G. Pooley, 'The Residential Segregation of Migrant Communities in Mid-Victorian Liverpool', *Transactions of the Institute of British Geographers*, New Series, 2:3 (1977), pp. 364–82.

14   Mo Moulton, *Ireland and the Irish in Interwar England*, p. 283.

immigrants simply because they were Irish or simply because they were outsiders. This chapter argues that, of all the players in the LVA's urban imagination, the organization cast the immigrant Irish girl in a leading role because she was most likely to embody some or all the risk factors that the LVA looked for when assessing moral vulnerability: she was away from the surveillance of her family, she may show signs of ambition or be over-eager for independence, she may well have grown up rurally and be unaccustomed to city life and, most importantly, she was likely to be working class.

Consequently, this work focuses on social purists' impressions of Irish female immigrants rather than on the experiences of the immigrants themselves, though this chapter does draw upon archived oral histories to build up a contextual picture of how the Irish settled in England. It is telling that the voice of the Irish female immigrant is either missing or heavily mediated in the LVA archive. For the LVA, help meant keeping a maternal eye on these young women rather than engaging in an open dialogue about the material, economic or emotional needs of this community. The LVA routinely used Irish women to develop and justify their networks of moral surveillance in and around the city, yet they did not keep detailed records of the way Irish women reacted to their patrollers and they did not keep letters received from women helped by the organization. Nevertheless, the annual reports of the LVA, and records kept by their affiliated organizations such as the Women Police Patrols and the House of Help, provide clear evidence of the way Irish female immigration reinforced local social purists' concerns about poor women. As a result, Irish young women were incorporated into the moral surveillance of a local charitable network that made as many judgements about young working-class women as it did offers of help to this community.

Irish Immigration and Social Status

Throughout the twentieth century, Irish immigration was the subject of debate and concern in both Britain and Ireland. Irish women represented the 'largest migrant group to come to Britain in the past 150 years', with more women than men leaving Ireland 'in most decades since 1871 when reliable statistics were first recorded'.[15] For many women, emigration

---

15   Mary J. Hickman and Bronwen Walter, 'Deconstructing Whiteness: Irish Women in Britain', *Feminist Review*, 50 (1995), p. 6; Bronwen Walter, *Outsiders Inside*, p. 15.

offered an opportunity to earn money that could be sent back home to their families.[16] For others, the economic factors behind emigration were more about individual subsistence. Walter argues that the partition of Ireland in 1922 had differing and gendered effects on employment in the north and south of the country, with the north-east's industrial economy, particularly around Belfast, providing more employment for women in this area. As such, women living there had less economic need to emigrate than women in the southern Free State.[17] Certainly, women migrating from Dublin and the rest of the South featured more in the LVA's dealings with Irish immigrants than those from the north, although in many cases the organization's records did not distinguish between women from Northern Ireland and those from independent Ireland. Nor did the organization distinguish between Protestant and Catholic Irish girls, with the LVA associating themselves broadly with various Christian leaders in Liverpool and even individuals representing non-Christian faiths, such as Judaism. To this end, the LVA, publicly at least, avoided sectarian politics. For many years, the LVA's roster of vice presidents simultaneously included the Roman Catholic Archbishop of Liverpool, the Anglican Lord Bishop of Liverpool, senior Jewish Minister Reverend S. Frampton and the President of the Free Church Council.[18]

That English purity organizations were regularly coming into contact with large numbers of Irish immigrant women was not unnoticed in Ireland. Earner-Byrne has argued that 'Independence not only led to a greater level of moral and cultural introspection, it also highlighted the trail of unmarried mothers to Britain.'[19] She suggests that this was politically embarrassing, since the washing of 'Ireland's moral linen' in Britain 'was anathema to the aspirations of the new state'.[20] In England, sections of the press claimed that the large numbers leaving Ireland provided 'conclusive evidence of the failure

16   Sharon Lambert, 'From "Irish Women's Emigration to England 1922–1960: The Lengthening of Family Ties"', in Alan Hayes and Diane Urquhart (eds), *The Irish Women's History Reader* (London: Routledge, 2001), p. 183.

17   Bronwen Walter, *Outsiders Inside*, p. 17. This argument is supported by Pooley's research on the Irish in London. He suggests that of the 39,229 Irish women in London in 1931, just 12.4 per cent were from Northern Ireland. See Colin Pooley, 'Getting to Know the City', p. 216.

18   See, for example, LVA, Annual Reports for the years 1923–24, 1925–26, 1926–27, 1927–28.

19   Earner-Byrne, *Mother and Child*, p. 173.

20   Earner-Byrne, *Mother and Child*, p. 192.

of Home Rule to fulfil the promise of providing a home for men and women of Irish birth', with articles expressing concern about the 'menace' of Irish immigration in large urban centres like Liverpool.[21] The appropriate response to all of this, according to one English newspaper during the interwar years, was to consider the merits of 'restrictive legislation' on Irish immigration.[22] In Liverpool, public perception aligned uncertainties surrounding the city's economic prosperity with the so-called Irish problem, as local councillors complained that the Irish could not be repatriated if they became a burden on the public purse nor prevented from swelling the pool of local labour during periods of intense competition for employment.[23]

At the same time, questions were asked about the local economic impact of caring for unwed Irish mothers. Women in Ireland were caught between the potential stigma of becoming an unmarried mother and bans on contraception.[24] In her research on the migration of Irish women to England between 1922 and 1960, Lambert proposes that sexual activities were considered so taboo and sinful within Irish society that pregnancy outside of marriage often precipitated the migration of Irish girls to England, as many left to hide their pregnancies.[25] Luddy notes that these women had a better chance of keeping their babies in England than they did at home.[26] As a result, charities in England became concerned about the number of unmarried mothers coming into the country. In 1924, the Liverpool and County Catholic Aid Society suggested that there had been a 'notable increase in the numbers of pregnant Irish girls looking for assistance from English charities'.[27] Indeed, Luddy argues that the Catholic Church had

21   *Western Morning News and Gazette*, 'Irish Problem for Britain', 11 January 1937. British Newspaper Archive.

22   *Western Morning News and Gazette*, 'Irish Problem for Britain', 11 January 1937.

23   John Belchem, *Before the Windrush*, pp. 69–70.

24   Bronwen Walter, *Outsiders Inside*, p. 21.

25   Sharon Lambert, 'Irish Women's Emigration to England', p. 183. See also Mark Finnane, 'The Carrigan Committee of 1930–31 and the "Moral Condition of the Saorstát"', *Irish Historical Studies*, 32:128 (2001), p. 524; James M. Smith, *Ireland's Magdalen Laundries*, p. 2; James M. Smith, 'The Politics of Sexual Knowledge: The Origins of Ireland's Containment Culture and the Carrigan Report', *Journal of the History of Sexuality*, 13:2 (2004), pp. 208–33.

26   Maria Luddy, 'Moral Rescue and Unmarried Mothers in Ireland in the 1920s', *Women's Studies: An Interdisciplinary Journal*, 30:6 (2001), p. 808.

27   Maria Luddy, 'Moral Rescue and Unmarried Mothers', p. 808.

become so concerned about this problem by the 1930s that it produced pamphlets and pastoral letters warning immigrant women about moral dangers.[28] Yet most of the Irish girls that the LVA helped were not pregnant, or if they were they kept it secret from the LVA. As in the case of the two Irish girls described at the start of this chapter, the LVA was full of pride at apparently being able to maintain the moral integrity of Irish young women who were not already pregnant. This enabled the LVA to claim to their supporters that preventative patrolling was successful and that the monitoring of young women's wandering through public space was justified.

The LVA's aim was not to expand the parameters of female travel and employment, rather their efforts were focused on managing and protecting the innocence of those women who could not or would not be dissuaded from travelling. Within the LVA's philosophy, preventative patrol work was therefore part of a self-fulfilling prophecy of moral danger, whereby patrollers sought to maintain young women's innocence while at the same time fearing that that very innocence made them morally vulnerable. The Association's perception of Irish young women shows that the organization struggled to find a balance between promoting feminine virtue and inadvertently cultivating the type of innocence that could be exploited by supposed white slavers.[29]

Although the naivety of Irish young women worried the LVA, they also felt that it was important to protect the innocence of these young women. In 1928, the LVA reported that two girls had travelled from Ireland to Liverpool by boat, where they were approached by an 'elderly' woman.[30] As the girls explained, the woman tried 'to persuade them to go with her to her lodging house, where she had a lot of men lodgers, and they would be sure of a good time'. Intent upon travelling to a local convent, one of the girls 'wisely' (in the words of the LVA's report) informed the woman of their plans and they declined to go with her. Although the woman persisted with her interest in the girls and offered to accompany them on their way, she eventually left the two alone when an LVA patroller, 'not liking her attitude', approached the three of them.[31] These convent girls were representative of an idealized Irish femininity. For the LVA, their religious affiliations conveyed a sense of moral uprightness and their wariness of the suspicious woman suggested

28   Maria Luddy, 'Moral Rescue and Unmarried Mothers', p. 809.
29   See Chapters 5 and 6.
30   LVA, Annual Report 1927–28, p. 6.
31   LVA, Annual Report 1927–28, p. 6.

that they had an adequate awareness of the dangers of urban life. Virtuous, devout and repelled by immorality, these girls represented the vision of Irish femininity that the LVA sought to uphold.

However, alongside this virtuous, idealized Irish feminine identity, sat another, more unpleasant characterization of Irish women in England. Derogatory, moralizing discourses about the Irish, about the type of work that they should take up, about their intelligence and their economic prospects, meant that the Irish in England often suffered from low social status.[32] From the mid-nineteenth century onwards Irish women in England tended to take menial roles in the service positions that had been vacated by local women as they moved into more profitable jobs.[33] During the interwar years, even second- and third-generation Irish young women found their class status bound together with their Irish heritage, to the detriment of their prospects. As she grew up, Margaret Butler, a working-class woman born in Bury in the north-west of England in 1920, continued to identify with her Irish Catholic roots owing to the influence of her grandmother, who had moved to England from Mayo.[34] She recalled 'none of us could look forward to a good job, they weren't for the Irish, you know'. Class, poverty and heritage were intrinsically linked in these communities. Margaret noted that 'the English people who lived among us were the same, they were treated in the same way because they were poor', before adding 'but the Irish people, some of them were highly intelligent, but they were poor as well'.[35]

Just as middle-class discourses of class and respectability defined English working-class women according to whether they were redeemable or irredeemable, Irish immigrants found their identities categorized in polemic terms.[36] The irredeemable Irish were stereotyped as 'dirty', an image that had much to do with the stereotype of Irish men working outdoors as labourers.[37] Through being affiliated with the supposedly

32   Wendy Webster, '"Race", Ethnicity and National Identity', in Ina Zweiniger-Bargielowska (ed.), *Women in Twentieth-Century Britain* (Harlow: Pearson Education, 2001), p. 293.

33   Bronwen Walter, *Outsiders Inside*, p. 1.

34   Margaret Butler, oral history interview, 2005.0395 Box 98, North West Sound Archive, Lancashire Record Office.

35   Margaret Butler, oral history interview.

36   For more on the importance of the dichotomy between the redeemable and irredeemable to definitions of respectability, see Beverley Skeggs, *Formations of Class and Gender*, p. 47.

37   Bronwen Walter, *Outsiders Inside*, pp. 23 and 88.

unclean Irish man, the Irish woman's feminine domesticity was called into question.[38] John Belchem's work on the Liverpool Irish shows that, in the early twentieth century, Irish women's ability to take care of their family money was questioned.[39] Both Bronwen Walter and Penny Summerfield have suggested that this view of Irish women as dirty endured well into the twentieth century.[40] Even by the 1950s, in cities like Liverpool and London, the Irish working class were still closely associated with dirt and overcrowding.[41]

Interwar Networks of Moral Surveillance

It was against this backdrop of prejudice that the LVA brought their preventative approach to vice and immorality to bear upon Irish immigrant women who were fresh off the boat. Where the LVA spent time helping or investigating female Irish immigrants, it was generally because they saw them as women not yet corrupted by their travels across the water and through the urban landscape. These newcomers were not yet living destitute or supposedly 'dirty' lifestyles. The LVA's approach to immigrant Irish women was therefore part of a tradition whereby middle-class women would attempt to educate working-class women so that they would be 'moral regenerators of the nation'.[42] The LVA's local partners in maintaining social order through female morality, the Women Police Patrols and the House of Help, also showed concern about the moral well-being of Irish women in Liverpool. However, when compared with the work of the LVA, the Women Police Patrols' interactions with the Irish community were more implicit than explicit. The Women Police Patrols monitored a greater geographical area, so their workload was much more varied that that of the LVA, who were much more dependent upon Irish female immigration to justify their

38   Bronwen Walter, *Outsiders Inside*, p. 88.
39   John Belchem, *Irish, Catholic and Scouse*, p. 32.
40   Walter cites Penny Summerfield's 1984 research showing that welfare managers during the Second World War still thought of Irish workers in terms of the stereotypes of drunkenness and dirt. See Bronwen Walter, *Outsiders Inside*, pp. 88–9.
41   Bronwen Walter, *Outsiders Inside*, p. 209. For more on the earlier stigmatization of Irish migrants, particularly in Liverpool, see John Belchem, 'Comment: Whiteness and the Liverpool Irish', *Journal of British Studies*, 44:1 (2005), pp. 146–52.
42   Beverley Skeggs, *Formations of Class and Gender*, p. 47.

work.[43] Still, the Women Police Patrols did make a point of patrolling the Scotland Road area of the city, which was closely associated with the Irish working-class community.[44] Additionally, Irish women were featured in the annual reports of the Women Police Patrols' hostel as typical examples of their casework.[45] The House of Help, too, noted that 'many' of their 'applicants' came from 'distant towns, from Scotland and from Ireland'.[46] Despite this mention of Scottish girls, this community did not attract the same degree of moral concern as Irish girls. The attention devoted to Irish young women was, in part at least, escalated by the notion that these women were especially innocent and unsuspecting, an image proliferated in Liverpool by the LVA.

In the absence of official controls on Irish immigration, the surveillance of Irish young women came to be seen by the LVA as both necessary and acceptable, with the LVA more than willing to liaise with employers and carers to arrange to escort young Irish women to or from the boats.[47] The LVA also suggested that women wrote to them to ask for advice about 'reliable agencies' of employment, with the organization concerned about the propensity for those who did not make such preparations to come chasing unverified adverts in newspapers.[48] As part of their office-based work, the LVA considered it within their remit to investigate job opportunities in

43   See Chapter 5 on the limits of the LVA's 'internationalism' and Chapter 8 on the downturn in the LVA's work with the difficulties in Irish travel during the Second World War.

44   Women Police Patrols, Annual Report 1928, p. 7.

45   See, for example, the 1925 case of a 17-year-old Irish girl who got the wrong train on her trip back to Ireland to see her sick mother, and the 1927 case of the 19-year-old 'weak-willed' Irish girl sent back to Ireland after going to live with 'a coloured man' with whom she had 'quarrelled'. Hostel for Girls, Knotty Ash: Liverpool Women Police Patrols and Training Centre, Annual Report 1925, p. 3 and Annual Report 1927, p. 6.

46   House of Help, Annual Report 1927, p. 7.

47   For example, in a case from 1923/24, a woman from Kent wrote to the LVA asking if they could locate a hospital place in Kildare for an Irish girl who was convalescing in Kent. The LVA obliged and met the girl in Liverpool to see her on her way. See LVA, Annual Report 1923–24, p. 14. Also, see the case mentioned at the start of this chapter, which resulted in the LVA liaising with a hospital to monitor the travel arrangements of Irish nurses. LVA, Annual Report 1932–33, p. 9.

48   LVA, Annual Report 1922–23, p. 10; Notes on Irish immigrants, LVA papers, 326 VIG/9.

order to prevent unnecessary travel.[49] The LVA's presumptions about the moral vulnerability of Irish young women and about the need for moral surveillance consequently brought them into contact with employers who had little else to do with the work of the LVA. Moreover, as part of their efforts to monitor the movements of young women, the LVA would also liaise with the NVA, sending them 'weekly lists of the Irish girls who come to this country, with information of their names and future addresses, which they [the NVA] forward to organisations in their particular districts, who help the girls after their arrival'.[50] This meant that the monitoring of Irish young women could be networked in such a way that their movements could be tracked across the country.

During the interwar years, purists in Liverpool and Ireland were aware of each other's activities in their respective local settings. Fears about the threat of prostitution were also shared by purity associations in Ireland. In many ways, the moral fears of Irish purists about the corrupting effects of urban life upon respectable femininity were similar to those of the LVA in Liverpool. However, in Ireland, close discursive associations between femininity, purity, Catholicism and the rural idyll were used in constructing Ireland's national identity.[51] For Walter, the Catholic Church's veneration of the Virgin Mary as a model of ideal womanhood after the famine meant that 'restrictive and limited roles for women became Catholic religious ideals'. Gender-defined qualities such as devotion to the family, a caring function and asexuality became important components of Irish women's identities.[52] Significantly, then, the LVA's perception of Irish women as sexually and socially naive was a cultural identity that was as prevalent in Ireland as much as it was ascribed to Irish female immigrants once they reached England.

Indeed, organizations in Ireland and England would sometimes communicate with one another to protect Irish women's morality. Garrett has suggested that the Child Protection and Rescue Society of Ireland worked with English vigilance associations to repatriate unmarried Irish mothers.[53]

49   LVA, Annual Report 1922–23, p. 10.
50   LVA, Annual Report 1938–39, p. 5.
51   Maria Luddy, *Prostitution and Irish Society*, pp. 1–2 and James M. Smith, *Ireland's Magdalen Laundries*, p. 6.
52   Bronwen Walter, *Outsiders Inside*, p. 18.
53   Paul Michael Garrett, 'The Abnormal Flight: The Migration and Repatriation of Irish Unmarried Mothers', *Social History*, 25:3 (2000), p. 331.

He argues that despite the 'impetus for repatriation' coming from English societies, Irish agencies co-operated in this process. One possible reason for this was a concern in Ireland about Catholic children being brought up outside the faith if they remained in England.[54] Whether it was by design or a confluence of interests, then, Irish and Liverpudlian social purists formed an interwar network for monitoring the movements of Irish women. The LVA proudly declared their links with Ireland in their 1938–39 annual report, noting that the Association maintained 'close co-operation and mutual help' with 'all the Vigilance Associations in Britain and Ireland'.[55]

The LVA relied upon this network of moral surveillance to counteract what the organization regarded as the immaturity of many Irish girls, who were often suspected of arriving in Liverpool with no real clue as to what they were going to do next or with little awareness of how difficult journeys further afield could be. For many Irish women, docking in Liverpool was only one stage in their overall journey to a life outside Ireland, and in these circumstances the LVA could be very useful. For example, Irish women with health problems could find themselves stranded in Liverpool when doctors would not permit their travel to the USA. In one such case from 1923, an Irish girl with 'throat trouble' attempted to circumvent the medical rejection by considering marriage to 'an elderly man in America (who was a friend of the girl's sister)'.[56] The LVA managed to convince the girl that she should not 'compromise herself to a man she did not know' and the girl returned to Ireland, determined to travel again when she was well. Though there is little doubt that the LVA offered good advice to this particular girl, the discussion of her case in their annual report as an example of their work for that year was part of the LVA's overall effort create a sense of young, female travellers as a volatile and dangerously impulsive group. In a case from the following year, another Irish girl was 'rejected in the Embarkation Examination room' from travelling to America because she was illiterate.[57] At this news, the girl began to 'talk wildly about committing suicide'. The LVA could not send her back

54   Paul Michael Garrett, 'The Abnormal Flight', p. 331.
55   LVA, Annual Report 1938–39, p. 5. The LVA also made a similar point of highlighting its connections with other agencies, including those in Dublin, Belfast and Cork. LVA, Annual Report 1939–40, p. 5. Liverpool Record Office, M326 VIG/3.
56   LVA, Annual Report 1922–23, p. 7.
57   LVA, Annual Report 1923–24, p. 9.

to Ireland, as would have been their usual practice, since her family had already moved to America. Instead, the LVA entrusted the girl to the care of a Convent, where the Mother Superior taught her to read and write so that she could travel and be reunited with her family later in the year.[58]

Even where Irish young women intended to stay within England, their transience still piqued the fears of social purists. Cities were imagined as sites of potential white slavery and moral degradation. Moulton notes that organizations like the LVA thought Irish girls were naive to the dangers of urban life, though she is sceptical about the organization's belief in the actual threat of white slavery.[59] Certainly, the LVA does not appear to have uncovered evidence of organized traffickers seeking to kidnap unsuspecting Irish girls.[60] However, the LVA conflated concerns about white slavery with their general concerns about prostitution and more broadly defined notions of sexual coercion. For the LVA, it did not matter that their patrollers failed to uncover any scandalous trafficking rings: their work was not about trying to uncover a criminal enterprise, and, in any case, the organization promoted the idea that their work was vital in making sure that traffickers could not get a foothold in the city. In one report, the LVA suggested that there was a 'terrible amount of traffic in many countries' and that trafficking in Britain was 'impeded and frequently frustrated by the work of this Society'.[61] The protection of Irish women within England and within Liverpool was therefore framed as part of the organization's overall fight against white slavery.

Abroad in a new city and away from their families, the LVA became anxious that Irish girls were ideal prey for those seeking to traffic them or induct them into immoral lifestyles. The LVA argued that surveillance was necessary because of the 'risks' that travelling posed to these supposedly innocent girls:

> From time to time the criticism is made that these girls should not be encouraged to come to England, we do know that a great deal has been done in Ireland to prevent them running risks, but there are so many of them who are genuinely anxious to 'better themselves'. But their ignorance of distance is appalling, and often when asked where

---

58   LVA, Annual Report 1923–24, p. 9.
59   Mo Moulton, *Ireland and the Irish in Interwar England*, p. 87.
60   For more on this, see Chapters 5 and 6.
61   LVA, Annual Report 1927–28, p. 4.

they are going to, the reply is Yorkshire or Lancashire, and they do not realise the difference of name between a County or town.[62]

Notions of ignorance and naivety were central to the LVA's perception of the risks that Irish young women took by travelling for work. The organization was convinced that the naivety of these girls was borne out of more than simply being a newcomer to an area; the LVA promoted the idea that Irish women were ignorant of the very concepts of urban space and distance.

In presenting Irish young women as lacking sufficient knowledge of urban space, it was assumed that many who arrived in Liverpool came from rural backgrounds.[63] Unable to appreciate the size of the locations to which they travelled, the quotation above suggests that it was the transience of Irish women that was particularly alarming. The LVA did not take for granted that Irish girls were able fully to comprehend what was meant by a city in terms of the sheer scale and design of this type of settlement. Fears of this kind infantilized Irish women's knowledge about travel and underestimated their ability to adapt to new locations. These fears were likely to have been overstated by the LVA. While many Irish young women who emigrated did come from rural backgrounds, they often had links to communities in England and, where Irish immigrants intended to settle in places like Lancashire, it was not always a simple matter of having swapped a rural lifestyle for an urban adventure. Born to Irish parents in Haslingden in 1932, John Mulderigg recalled his mother's sense of 'resentment' at having been brought to England with her family in the early twentieth century when she was eleven.[64] On one level, the 'physical nature' of the move had been profound for his mother, who felt 'deprived of' the 'flat and open and wide vista with water birds and curlews' that she had experienced in Mayo, but her new life was not in a large city. Instead, she resented the feeling that 'she'd been brought here to help with the domestic chores, including taking

---

62   LVA, Annual Report 1932–33, p. 5.

63   This assumption was probably reasonable in many cases. Brown has suggested that 'The twenty-six counties of independent Ireland were indeed strikingly rural in the 1920s. In 1926, as the census recorded, 61 per cent of the population lived outside towns or villages'. Terrence Brown, *Ireland: A Social and Cultural History* (London: Harper Perennial, 2004), p. 9.

64   John Mulderigg, oral history interview, 2005.0393 Box 98, North West Sound Archive, Lancashire Record Office.

[her] older brothers their meals as they worked the land on top of an ice age hill in Helmshore'.[65]

Nevertheless, the LVA remained concerned that even if Irish girls intended to settle in smaller towns, the journey through a city as large as Liverpool could prove morally treacherous. This anxiety on the part of the Association was compounded by their belief that Irish young women were likely to be too shy or timid to seek out reputable help if and when they got lost. In 1924, one Irish girl, who was approached by an LVA worker patrolling Liverpool's Exchange Station, was said to be 'particularly nervous'.[66] She had applied for a position in domestic service in a north Lancashire town following an advert in an Irish newspaper. Unsure of which train she needed to take, the young woman was 'too frightened' to seek assistance. The LVA explained: 'It was the first time that she had been away from her country home in Ireland, and she felt very strange.'[67] It was significant that the LVA noted that this young woman's home was in the countryside. This detail spoke to the notion that these young women were particularly innocent and uncorrupted by city living and it implied that Irish girls were worryingly out of touch with the modern world. After putting the girl in this case onto the correct train, the LVA noted: 'It seems incredible in these days to realise that a girl of her age should be so helpless and nervous on a journey'.[68] In this instance, the naivety and innocence displayed by the girl was so extreme as thoroughly to alarm the LVA. Though the organization worked to defend moral purity amongst women, their patrollers recognized that it was not beneficial or practical for young women to be completely ignorant of how to negotiate urban space.

While the LVA patrols were certainly helpful on a practical level for Irish women who became lost and stranded in the city, the rhetoric that surrounded this type of work was still full of moral judgement about the dangers of city life for respectable womanhood. No doubt, some of the women who travelled had made inadequate preparations or encountered unexpected complications along the way. However, the way the LVA presented these cases as typical in their annual reporting speaks to the degree to which the LVA depended for support upon concern about Irish female immigration. Irish women were useful to the LVA because they

65   John Mulderigg, oral history interview.
66   LVA, Annual Report 1923–24, p. 12.
67   LVA, Annual Report 1923–24, p. 12.
68   LVA, Annual Report 1923–24, p. 12.

represented moral vulnerability in two distinct ways. First, in England, Irishness was frequently associated with being working class during the early and mid-twentieth century. Consequently, Irish young women were subjected to the same type of moral guidance and instruction as local working-class young women. Secondly, the class identity that was ascribed to the Irish was supplemented by a female moral identity that prioritized purity and innocence. Significantly, the LVA did not create this image of the vulnerable Irish 'girl' in order to justify their interventions into her travels. The LVA imported social purity ideas about femininity and Irishness from Ireland and repurposed them in service to their preventative patrol work agenda.

As such, the disproportionate attention that the LVA paid to Irish women should not be interpreted simply as well-intentioned, though largely misguided or offensive, stereotyping. The LVA found their idealized impression of the Irish woman replicated by their associates in Irish purity organizations. This meant that the figure of the morally pure Irish young woman was appropriated, rather than completely manufactured, by the LVA as a particularly compelling character in their campaign to prevent moral decline in Liverpool. As the next chapter will show, so important were concerns about Irish female immigration to the work of the LVA, that a drop in the numbers of women coming to Liverpool during the Second World War negatively impacted the work of the organization, and, as a result, the LVA tried hard to raise concern about Irish women as levels of travel returned to normal during the post-war years. As such, Irish women travelling through Liverpool would prove to be important characters in the LVA's ongoing effort to justify, sustain and galvanize support for their preventative moral patrols.

8

Irish Girls in Liverpool (2)

The Second World War and the Post-War Years*

This chapter examines concerns about the alleged moral frailty of Irish immigrant women in Liverpool between start of the Second World War and the early years of the 1960s. I argue that, although the Second World War presented challenges to the work of the LVA, by the 1950s, the organization had revived its earlier tactics and discourses of moral frailty. The war did offer new working opportunities and status for women.[1] However, as a number of historians of women and the war have already pointed out, assessment of these opportunities must take account of the extent to which women were already working outside the home before the war and the significant wartime moral push-back against perceived increases in women's social freedoms. Penny Summerfield and Corinna Peniston-Bird argue that the 'Second World War was one of the most contradictory periods in British history for the boundary between male and female roles'.[2] During the early years of war, resistance to women workers was maintained by employers,

---

* Parts of this chapter appeared in an article in *Women's History Review* in 2016. See Samantha Caslin, '"One Can Only Guess What Might Have Happened if the Worker Had Not Intervened in Time": The Liverpool Vigilance Association, Moral Vulnerability and Irish Girls in Early to Mid-Twentieth-Century Liverpool', *Women's History Review*, 25:2 (2016), pp. 254–73.

1　See, for example, Robert Hart, 'Women Doing Men's Work and Women Doing Women's Work: Female Work and Pay in British Wartime Engineering', *Explorations in Economic History*, 44:1 (2007), pp. 114–30.

2　Penny Summerfield and Corinna Peniston-Bird, 'Women in the Firing Line: The Home Guard and the Defence of Gender Boundaries in Britain in the Second World War', *Women's History Review*, 9:2 (2000), p. 232.

and it was not until 1941 that single women and childless widows were conscripted into war work out of necessity.[3] Alison Twells argues that women's experiences of work during the war 'could be both liberating and oppressive', as their behaviour was scrutinized for signs of impropriety.[4] Concerns about the moral impact of the war were articulated at local and national levels in reference to the belief that war work was moving women into spaces that threatened their respectability. Government reticence about the moral implications of asking women to work in support of the war effort were evident in the state's support for austere, women-only hostels located near armament factories, a policy aimed at reducing the amount of time women workers spent travelling between work and home.[5]

Where Irish women were concerned, the situation was further complicated by the political relationship between Britain and Ireland and by the way Irish women continued to be used by social purists to magnify their fears that young, working-class and immigrant women required moral surveillance. Focusing on the LVA's interest in Irish women during the Second World War and after, this chapter emphasizes lingering continuities in local social purity concerns about this community. The chapter begins by examining the LVA's efforts to stay relevant during the Second World War, amid travel regulations, blitzes and renewed debate about the role of women in society. The LVA's patrolling was reduced during the war and travel between Britain and Ireland became more complicated. Moreover, I acknowledge the disjuncture between the LVA's perceptions of urban space as a site of moral corruption and young women's perceptions of urban space as a site of opportunity. The diaries kept by a young Irish woman, Mary Eileen Rodgers, demonstrate that young women's wartime lives were much more complex than the impression created by the LVA; Mary spent significant amounts of her leisure time during these years socializing and shopping in Liverpool and the Wirral. Yet the LVA opted to maintain their focus on the moral vulnerability of female travellers and Irish women because they anticipated a return to business as usual once the conflict was over.

---

3   Sandra Trudgen Dawson, 'Busy and Bored: The Politics of Work and Leisure for Women Workers in Second World War British Government Hostels', *Twentieth Century British History*, 21:1 (2010), pp. 29–30; Juliet Gardiner, *Wartime Britain 1939–1945* (London: Headline, 2004), pp. 504, 515.
4   Alison Twells, '"Went into Raptures": Reading Emotion in the Ordinary Wartime Diary, 1941–1946', *Women's History Review*, 25:1 (2016), p. 150.
5   Sandra Trudgen Dawson, 'Busy and Bored', pp. 29–30.

In terms of immigration statistics, the LVA's expectations were realized. After the war, a combination of economic necessity and personal ambition meant that many young women continued to move for work. By the 1950s, almost half a million Irish people came to work in Britain, 'the peak of emigration from twentieth-century Ireland'.[6] Enda Delaney's valuable recent work on post-war Irish immigration details the overcrowded and tiring conditions on the seven-hour boat journey from Dublin and suggests that a city like Liverpool would have seemed large and unfamiliar to those who had only known rural Ireland.[7] Delaney suggests that a 'minority' would have 'run into difficulties' and, in this regard, he briefly mentions that help that the LVA could offer to stranded Irish travellers.[8] The LVA did offer practical advice and assistance to women who found themselves stranded after connecting trains were missed, job opportunities fell through or they simply ran out of money, but I want to show that the LVA's work had much wider significance than this.

The LVA's archive of news cuttings indicates that the organization was concerned with the economic and social aspects of Irish immigration, particularly after the move from Free State to Republic.[9] This is unexpected, as their annual reports tended to avoid making statements about British and Irish political relations. Furthermore, the LVA's often patronizing and overbearing attitude towards Irish young women was part of a gendering of city life, whereby young, working-class women's presence on the streets was problematized by social purists, philanthropists, journalists and even policy-makers who linked it with prostitution, promiscuity and moral ignorance. The LVA welcomed opportunities to tell the local and national press about their work, each time emphasizing the idea that respectable femininity was threatened by urban conditions. A number of the post-war newspaper reports about Irish immigration explored in this chapter were collected and saved in an LVA collection of news-cuttings. Although this

6   Enda Delaney, 'Transnationalism, Networks and Emigration from Post-War Ireland', *Immigrants & Minorities*, 23:2–3 (2005), p. 426.

7   Enda Delaney, *The Irish in Post-War Britain* (Oxford: Oxford University Press, 2007), p. 50, 52.

8   Enda Delaney, *The Irish in Post-War Britain*, p. 53.

9   Ireland's relationship with Britain underwent a significant period of transformation during the twentieth century. From 1922, the country existed as the Irish Free State, before becoming Eire in 1937 and then the Republic of Ireland in 1948.

means that these sources have been mediated, insofar as they have been compiled by the LVA, the existence of this collection of cuttings and the reporting itself illustrates the close relationship between local social purists and the press during this period. The two worked together to disseminate the idea that Irish young women were a problem group. Guided by social purity, the local and national press courted their readership with sensationalist stories about Irish women, prostitution and promiscuity. These articles continued, therefore, to cultivate support for the unofficial surveillance of marginalized groups of women well into the post-war years.

Travel, Morality and the War

In her influential work on women's citizenship during the Second World War, Sonya Rose situates wartime concerns about female morality within a series of 'episodes in a relatively continuous public discourse about sexuality and especially about appropriate norms of female sexuality'.[10] Her argument that times of significant national tension magnified ongoing concerns with female morality has significant implications for the LVA's local work. Wartime conditions should have enabled the LVA to expand their work and gain greater influence. In 1943, the LVA's annual report reprinted a statement by the NVA; it stated that although there had been 'throughout the year a steady decrease in professional Prostitution and Solicitation ... the problem remains most serious and is aggravated by war conditions increasing sexual promiscuity amongst young people on an amateur as contrasted with a professional basis'.[11] Other moral welfare organizations in Liverpool found that the war had actually increased their workload. In 1940, the House of Help reported that it had 'been used more than ever by people passing through Liverpool', although still with fewer 'night-cases'. In fact, the House suggested that their numbers had 'almost doubled' since the previous year, with the number of women referred to them by the Women Police Patrols alone going up from 32 in 1939 to 76 in 1940.[12] Part of this increase might be attributed to the increased reliance of the Women Police upon the House of Help following the temporary

10   Sonya O. Rose, 'Sex, Citizenship, and the Nation in World War II Britain', *American Historical Review*, 103:4 (1998), p. 1148.
11   LVA, Annual Report 1942–43, p. 4.
12   House of Help, Annual Report 1940, p. 4. Liverpool Record Office, 362/ HOU/3/49.

closure of their own hostel when it was 'blitzed', as the House of Help suggested that the number of referrals from the Women Police Patrol's went into retreat upon the opening of their new hostel.[13] Nevertheless, the buoyant impression of their workload created by these organizations was not matched by the LVA. That the LVA was not able to capitalize upon the notion that the Second World War was threatening to moral order was, in no small part, due to the organization's dependency upon a steady flow of Irish women into the city.

Throughout the interwar years, Irish female immigration was central to the LVA's justification of their patrol work and their monitoring of women as they arrived in the city. However, during the Second World War, the numbers of Irish women travelling to Liverpool decreased. The Anglo-Irish Treaty of 1921 had meant that Irish people could still travel freely to Britain after the establishment of the Irish Free State in 1922. During the Second World War, greater controls were placed on this border between Britain and neutral Ireland. From June 1940, those leaving Ireland for Britain were required to obtain a British employment visa and have an Irish travel identity card.[14] These policies remained in place until 1947, in the case of the need for a British employment visa, and 1952, in the case of the Irish identity cards.[15] Indeed, Jennifer Redmond's work highlights that many of the Irish already living in Liverpool started to leave the city when the war broke out.[16] So although the war heightened concerns about women's morality and changes in women's social status, the decrease in Irish young women coming to Liverpool meant that the LVA's work was undermined by the conflict.

Indicating just how dependent the LVA was upon the issue of Irish female immigration, the wartime reduction in Irish travel led to a reduction in the organization's staff: by 1943, the LVA was run almost entirely by two women, the LVA Secretary, Edith Rose, and part-time patroller Mrs Blyth, save for the LVA's figurehead committee members.[17] When the war broke

13   House of Help, Annual Report 1941, pp. 3–4. Liverpool Record Office, 362/ HOU/3/50.

14   Enda Delaney, *The Irish in Post-War Britain*, p. 72.

15   Enda Delaney, *The Irish in Post-War Britain*, p. 72.

16   Jennifer Redmond, 'Immigrants, Aliens, Evacuees: Exploring the History of Irish Children in Britain During the Second World War', *Journal of the History of Childhood and Youth*, 9:2 (2016), pp. 295–308.

17   LVA, Annual Report 1942–43, p. 2.

out, the LVA quickly recognized that changes in travel would challenge their remit, so the LVA emphasized the overarching nature of the work, claiming in 1940:

> whilst some aspects of the work have changed, the number of girls helped at the Boats and Trains has exceeded previous years, and the figures do not include the hundreds helped with directions and advice during their transport through this great Port, as we only record those upon whom we have to spend a good deal of time.[18]

The supposed bravery of the LVA's work was given an extra degree of potency when one of the 'Blitzes' left the organization's offices 'a sorry sight', with 'Miss Rose [having] emerged alive from the shelter' as the work of the organization continued from 'the one room that survived'.[19] Similarly, in 1940, David Railton, Chairman of the LVA and Rector of Liverpool, optimistically allied the work of the Association with his anticipation of Britain's victory over Germany: 'Gradually … victory over Nazidom is dawning, and the morale – soul-strength to that end – comes in part by the fellowship in dire need given by our Society to the women and children of the Empire and indeed of all people in distress [*sic*].[20]

Despite the difficulties of travel during the war, the LVA and social purists in Ireland remained concerned about the moral vulnerability of Irish women. Leanne McCormick notes that even in Northern Ireland, where religious and political division complicated responses to the war, the presence of large numbers of American troops galvanized the interests of religious leaders and social purists in women's behaviour, reinforcing the dichotomous images of women as both bastions of moral guardianship and sources of immoral contamination.[21] The reassertion of a sexually pure, ideal type femininity, from both Protestant and Catholic communities, was in large part a response to the greater freedom that women had obtained through the expansion of their employment opportunities. Massive increases in the number of women working in sectors such as

---

18   LVA, Annual Report 1939–40, p. 4.
19   LVA, Annual Report 1940–41, p. 3.
20   LVA, Annual Report 1939–40, p. 3.
21   Leanne McCormick, '"One Yank and They're Off": Interaction between US Troops and Northern Irish Women, 1942–1945', *Journal of the History of Sexuality*, 15:2 (2006), pp. 228–9.

engineering facilitated geographical mobility, as Northern Irish women left rural areas in search of work in towns.[22]

Figures contained within the LVA's records suggest that Northern Irish women were still travelling to Liverpool during the war, although in smaller numbers than they had in peacetime. The organization's Chairman noted in 1940 that it was 'true that the Southern Ireland calls have ceased', but out of the 967 women that the LVA helped in that year, 900 were still listed as 'Irish'.[23] The Association also maintained its links with social purists in Dublin and Belfast, as well as with organizations in various UK cities.[24] The difficulty surrounding international travel was more apparent by 1941, however, when the overall number of women helped that year dropped to 379, although again the vast majority of these, 337, were 'Irish'.[25] A degree of Irish female travel was also noted by the LVA's affiliated refuge, the House of Help, who explained during the early 1940s that a number of Irish women had travelled to Liverpool on compassionate leave to visit their husbands stationed in the military.[26] Consequently, even when women's travel had been made more difficult by the war and the number of Irish women passing though Liverpool was greatly diminished, organizations like the LVA and the House of Help were still frequently reporting on the status of Irish women in the city due to the continued degree of moral concern surrounding these women.

The Irish Girl and Wartime City Life

Despite the resilience of social purists' interest in Irish women, the young women of Liverpool's Irish community did not necessarily view their own experiences of city life in such morally uncertain terms. The diaries of Mary Eileen Rodgers, a young Northern Irish woman who had moved to Wallasey, Wirral, with her family in 1919, when she was just a year old, suggest that local young, Irish, working-class women did not regard

22   McCormick notes that the number of women working in engineering rose from just 300 before the war to 12,300 in 1943. Leanne McCormick, '"One Yank and They're Off"', p. 234.

23   LVA, Annual Report 1939–40, pp. 3–4.

24   LVA, Annual Report 1939–40, p. 5.

25   LVA, Annual Report 1940–41, p. 4.

26   House of Help Annual Report 1942, p. 1. Liverpool Record Office, 362/ HOU/3/51. See also House of Help Annual Report 1943, p. 3. Liverpool Record Office, 362/HOU/3/52.

decorum and respectability to be incompatible with a busy lifestyle filled with work, consumerism, dating, dancing, walking through town and trips to the cinema.[27] Mary's diaries show that, despite moving to Merseyside at such a young age, she actively identified with the local Irish community, socialized with Irish immigrants and made trips to Ireland.

As well as illuminating her sense of her own respectability, Mary's diaries also draw out the spatial components to her work and leisure activities. During the early years of the Second World War, Mary regularly attended dances with male and female friends, and her shopping excursions to Liverpool were part of her socializing habits. Indeed, she articulated her friendships and romantic relationships through her descriptions of her consumer pursuits in Liverpool. On 13 February 1939, just a few months before the outbreak of war, Mary noted that she had had 'a great laugh all day buying Valentines bought 3 in Liverpool and sold one [*sic*]'.[28] Mary's fondness for new clothes was also closely tied to the courtship rituals of her friends. Though she had to work on St Patrick's Day in 1939, Mary still found the time to go to St George's Hall, dressed in 'my new yellow blouse and green skirt', where she danced with Jack Roche, who was 'full of protestations of love and wanting me to go out with him'.[29]

Mary's diaries are illustrative of the coexistence of change and continuity in the psyches of young women at the start of the Second World War. She worked hard in a telephone manager's office, with her diary entries frequently containing the note 'working late'. As an Irish woman who had left Ireland when she was only a child, Mary used her social excursions and even her work, where the opportunity presented itself, to maintain links with other members of the Irish community. On 3 October 1939, Mary bumped into a friend who told her that a young Irish woman had started working in her office, and the very next day Mary paid her a visit. Though the two young women socialized together that evening, Mary displayed a degree of caution about her new friend. In her diary, Mary wrote that the young woman was a 'wild looking piece of goods'.[30] That Mary was nevertheless prepared to accompany the woman on an evening out suggests that friendship with other women of Irish heritage was important to her.

27   Diaries of Mary Eileen Rodgers, Liverpool Record Office, M920 ROD.
28   Diaries of Mary Eileen Rodgers, 13 February 1939.
29   Diaries of Mary Eileen Rodgers, 17 March 1939.
30   Diaries of Mary Eileen Rodgers, 3 and 4 October 1939.

Working enabled Mary to go out with her friends, to visit the cinema and to buy the new clothes that she was keen to show off at dances. However, Mary did not cast herself as rebellious or disrespectful of social decorum. Prior to and during the war, Mary considered herself always on the respectable side of social boundaries. When, on 18 January 1939, Mary wrote in her diary 'John O'Brien kept holding my hand in the middle of Liverpool', she implied a sense of nervousness, as well as excitement, about her excursions with young men. Though she did not object to John holding her hand in this most public of settings, Mary's admission that this happened 'in the middle of Liverpool' added a playful flirtation with the idea of moral boundary crossing, but no more. In fact, Mary observed religious conventions such as attending mass and confession, and, while she would hold hands and dance with the boys she knew, Mary distanced herself from overtly promiscuous behaviour. On 2 February 1939, she 'Dressed up' and went to the Caledonia Society with her friend Dorothy, where they encountered 'a fellow called Maurice', who, Mary noted somewhat scandalously, had 'been out with Glenys all day' despite his being 'apparently married and separated from his wife'.[31] Once the war had begun, Mary maintained her negative attitude towards suggestions of promiscuity. In December 1939, Mary appeared to disapprove of an acquaintance's pursuit of soldiers, when she wrote that she was 'glad we didn't start off for their do because they went to the soldiers [*sic*] camp'.[32] To this end, Mary was able to enjoy a degree of social freedom, much of it facilitated by her financial independence owing to her work, without considering herself to breach the boundaries of respectability.

Certainly, the start of the war altered Mary's relationship with city spaces; on 6 September 1939, she wrote of a 'Dreadful war scene'.[33] Planes over Liverpool were 'fired on' and some people went to the local air-raid shelter. In October 1939, she wrote about embarking upon a week's holiday to the town of Larne in Northern Ireland and explained in her diary that she had been delayed because she 'Had to pass through immigration officers', who were being extra diligent.[34] However, unlike the quiet, nervous Irish girls depicted in the LVA's reports, Mary appears to have been relaxed about the delay and confident about her trip: 'Travelled about 10.15', she

31   Diaries of Mary Eileen Rodgers, 2 February 1939.
32   Diaries of Mary Eileen Rodgers, 28 December 1939.
33   Diaries of Mary Eileen Rodgers, 6 September 1939.
34   Diaries of Mary Eileen Rodgers, 7 October 1939.

continued, 'and went over with a girl – protestant from Larne – a civil servant in London.'[35] Even during the early days of the war, then, when there was extra uncertainty about the dangers of travel, Mary negotiated her way around. Indeed, the acquaintance that she made of the young woman on the boat shows that friendships struck up between young women while travelling could be useful rather than, as the LVA feared, a precursor to immoral women winning the confidence of naive travellers.[36]

As the war drew on, Mary continued to frame her social life and dating habits around places. On Friday, 24 November 1939, she met up with three of her friends and wrote, 'We had a very good night dancing with all and sundry. Home with the little red haired fellow from Rock Ferry.'[37] It is not clear who the 'red haired fellow' was or whether he was a serious boyfriend, but it is apparent from Mary's diaries that she did date. On 10 December 1941, she 'Went out for a walk with Eddie O'Reilly – to arrowe park [*sic*]'.[38] This romance with Eddie was on the wane, though; she responded to his questioning about whether she was 'bored with him' by being 'casual'; 'must just wait for this affair to slide out naturally', she surmised.[39]

It does not appear that Mary came into contact with the LVA when travelling back to visit Northern Ireland, nor does she appear to have come into contact with them via the Irish women she knew. The LVA did not, as a rule, draw upon this sense of community among Irish women in and around Liverpool when helping Irish women to settle in the city. Indeed, it is plausible that, in the LVA's estimations, despite being a hardworking young woman, Mary would not have been considered an appropriate contact or friend for a young Irish woman fresh off the boat simply because of her active social life and urban adventures. In any case, fostering a sense of Irish community and trying to facilitate contact between newcomers and young women like Mary were not parts of the LVA's brief. Instead, the LVA kept themselves busy during the Second World War by maintaining the sense that female travel was a precursor to prostitution and that Irish girls were particularly naive and vulnerable to corruption. Though the war

35   Diaries of Mary Eileen Rodgers, 7 October 1939.

36   See section on 'Social Purity and the Female Trafficker', in Chapter 6.

37   Diaries of Mary Eileen Rodgers, 24 November 1939.

38   Diaries of Mary Eileen Rodgers, 10 December 1941.

39   Mary did not marry any of these men. She did not get married until 1965, when she wed John Rogers, a former ships' engineer from the Wirral. See accompanying archive notes for the Diaries of Mary Eileen Rogers.

meant that the LVA had fewer Irish case studies to draw upon, they kept their focus on Irish girls as part of their long-term strategy. For the LVA, the war years were anomalous in terms of their impact on international travel. Though their own wartime workload was considerably lightened during the Second World War, the LVA was motivated to maintain their influence and connections so that, after the war, 'we may be ready to protect the interests of women and children travelling through the port and city, once such travel becomes general again'.[40]

In another move which displayed how keen the LVA were to continue to assert links between their concerns about prostitution, urban immorality and the migration of women, the LVA's annual meeting in 1943 saw the organization host as Guest Speaker Madame Wanda Grabinska, 'the first woman lawyer and Judge in Juvenile Court in Poland'.[41] Grabinska, who received a standing ovation for her words at the meeting, gave weight to the idea that the LVA must weather the reduced workload of the war years in anticipation of the peacetime workload ahead. She was said to have declared that 'owing to weakened morals there would be need for a spiritual as well as a material revival when the war was over', with the work of organizations like the LVA expected to rise in significance. According to Grabinska, the LVA would be well placed to 'circumvent the criminal activities of those women and children amid the confusion inseparable from the post-war travel conditions'.[42]

Peacetime and Irish Immigration

In 1945, the LVA confidently declared, 'Now that hostilities have ceased we expect to see a rapid extension of our work.'[43] Their expectations proved correct. As Irish female travel resumed, the LVA picked up where it had left off before the war. The organization continued to show concern about the ability of Irish women to navigate their way through the urban landscape

40   LVA, Annual Report 1942–43, p. 2.
41   LVA, Annual Report 1943–44, p. 4. Liverpool Record Office, M326 VIG/3. Madame Wanda Grabinska was also involved with the International Bureau for the Suppression of Traffic in Women and Children and she was part of a campaign to the Home Office calling for internationally co-ordinated efforts to help trafficked women and children in enemy-occupied states. See LVA, Annual Report 1944–45, p. 6. Liverpool Record Office, M326 VIG/3.
42   LVA, Annual Report 1943–44, p. 4.
43   LVA, Annual Report 1944–45, p. 3.

and, once again, rather than being manufactured by local social purists, the image of the naive Irish girl that the LVA promoted continued to draw upon Irish influences. In 1950, the LVA suggested that there were 'several bodies doing work among girls in Dublin' who 'frequently' used the LVA's 'services'.[44] At times, the Irish influence was felt even closer to home. Between 1948 and 1949, LVA patroller Mrs Blyth was joined in her work by another, Mrs Saville, who declared 'Being Irish myself, I can appreciate some of the feelings of the girls starting out on their first job away from the influence of their own people.'[45] Mrs Saville described patrolling as a 'wonderful experience' and an 'opportunity' to see 'life in the raw'; she readily gave credibility to the LVA's fears about the innocence of Irish girls, writing 'The majority are very **ignorant of the ways of the world, and are liable to believe anything** they are told.'[46] The LVA report emboldened these words, emphasizing that even a fellow Irish woman took a negative view of her compatriots' ability to spot moral danger.

Though Mrs Saville only remained with the LVA for one year, the organization maintained links with Irish purity organizations and continued to show particular interest in Irish female travel, so much so that, by the 1950s, there was a popular perception that the LVA existed in the main to deal with Irish young women. In 1954, Mrs Sugden, responsible for the running of the office as Secretary of the LVA, noted: 'So often I am confronted with the remark "Why do you only help Irish Girls?"' To this, she answered: 'We help all in need whoever they are, but being the main port for Ireland the greatest need for our work lies among these very young Irish immigrants who arrive with practically no knowledge of the geography or conditions of this country.'[47] The LVA's attitude towards Irish female immigrants had therefore not changed from before the Second World War. The LVA still viewed these women as naive, rural maidens in danger of being corrupted by their urban adventures in search of work in England.

44   LVA, Annual Report 1949–50, p. 5. Liverpool Record Office, M326 VIG/3.
45   Mrs Saville's Report, in LVA, Annual Report 1948–49. Liverpool Record Office, M326 VIG/3.
46   Mrs Saville's Report, in LVA, Annual Report 1948–49 (original emphasis).
47   Mrs Sugden's Report, LVA, Annual Report 1954. Liverpool Record Office, M326 VIG/3. See also the statement 'Our total of 1,627 [girls and children helped] is comprised mainly of Irish immigrants together with a sprinkling of other nationalities as well as English schoolchildren, the aged, the infirm and the blind'. From 'General Report' within LVA, Annual Report 1955, Liverpool Record Office, M326 VIG/3.

Mrs Sugden worked closely with the British Vigilance Association (BVA; formerly the National Vigilance Association) during the 1950s to devise and implement strategies for monitoring Irish female travel.[48] Mrs Sugden, representing the LVA at a meeting of the BVA Executive Committee in 1953, suggested that there 'should be legal measures to prevent girls coming over' without reliable work, and raised the possibility of lobbying the Home Office.[49] The BVA went so far as to set up an 'Irish Girls' Sub-Committee' to investigate Irish female immigration as an ongoing and serious moral issue.[50] This subcommittee was noted by the BVA to be 'principally linked to the work of Mrs. Sugden and the Liverpool Vigilance Association'.[51] Working in conjunction with Mrs Sugden, the BVA explored official avenues for curtailing the movement of Irish women. At a meeting of the Irish Girls' Sub-Committee in 1956, Mrs Sugden 'spoke about the close collaboration which existed in Liverpool between her organisation and the Police, and she said that the information they had collected there had been particularly useful in tracing missing girls'.[52] In addition, the Irish Girls' Sub-Committee was keen to influence the Irish Embassy by, for example, writing to them to ask them to review welfare provision for Irish women.[53] The minutes of the subcommittee also record that Mrs Sugden regularly wrote to employers and Labour Exchanges to try to obtain more information about the numbers of Irish women travelling for

48   For more on the change from the NVA to the BVA, see Chapter 9.

49   Minutes of the Meeting of the Executive Committee of the British Vigilance Association and the National Committee for the Suppression of Traffic in Persons held on 26 March 1953. Women's Library, 4BVA/E/5 (Box FL349).

50   See Irish-Girls and Related Problems Sub-Committee, 29 October 1954–4 February 1957. Women's Library, 4NVA/1/7 (Box FL198). It should be noted that from July 1955 the Sub-Committee opted to expand its remit to cover 'Irish Girls and Related Problems', which seems to have been a tactic designed to allow greater discussion of other nationalities. However, Irish girls continued to be the main focus of the subcommittee. See British Vigilance Association, Minutes of Irish Girls' Sub-Committee, 4 July 1955. Women's Library, 4NVA/1/7 (Box FL198).

51   British Vigilance Association, Minutes of the Meeting of the Irish Girls and Related Problems Sub-Committee, Wednesday, 11 January 1956. Women's Library, 4NVA/1/7 (Box FL198).

52   British Vigilance Association, Minutes of the Meeting of the Irish Girls and Related Problems Sub-Committee, 27 April 1956. Women's Library, 4NVA/1/7 (Box FL198).

53   British Vigilance Association, Minutes of Irish Girls' Sub-Committee, 4 July 1955.

work. One such contact resulted in the manager of the Blackpool Labour Exchange reporting back that the area did see a 'seasonal influx of domestic servants from Eire', but he did not share Mrs Sugden's worry for these girls, suggesting that 'in his view the situation did not call for any special action'.[54] Mrs Sugden was not especially mollified by this reassurance. In 1955, the LVA noted that they shared with the BVA the expense of printing leaflets containing Vigilance Association addresses and that they then sent these leaflets to 'Irish agencies and welfare bodies'.[55]

In her work with the BVA, Mrs Sudgen showed herself to be savvy at engaging the press. The BVA Irish Girls' Sub-Committee wanted to advertise in the press to warn Irish girls not to come to England unless they were sure that the employment agencies they were using were legitimate. Mrs Sugden pointed out that 'advertising charges were very high'; instead, she 'hoped to gain some editorial co-operation'.[56] Mrs Sugden established a reciprocal relationship with the press whereby she could offer sensational stories which would grab the attention of editors and readers while at the same time publicizing the work of social purity agencies like the LVA and BVA. During the 1950s, and even into the early 1960s, the local and national press gave space to social purity accounts of the supposed potential for Irish female immigrants to turn to prostitution. One of the LVA's press-cuttings from a 1961 edition of *The Times* made the point explicitly: it suggested that if 'it were not for organizations such as the British Vigilance Association [female Irish immigrants] would mostly drift into prostitution'.[57] When, in 1962, the *Liverpool Echo and Evening Express* went so far as to argue that 'no teenage girl ought to be able to enter the Liffey dock who cannot show that she is on her way to an assured job, and has the money to get to it', the paper acted as a mouthpiece for the LVA.[58] Though the LVA was in serious decline by the 1960s, struggling to maintain their relevance in an increasingly consumer-focused, post-war

54   British Vigilance Association, Minutes of Irish Girls' Sub-Committee, 29 October 1954. Women's Library, 4NVA/1/7 (Box FL198).

55   LVA, Annual Report 1955.

56   British Vigilance Association, Minutes of Irish Girls' Sub-Committee, 29 October 1954.

57   *The Times*, 'Irish Immigrants who Enter UK without Jobs or Prospects', 13 November 1961. LVA, Newspaper cuttings. Liverpool Record Office, M326 VIG/5/2.

58   *Liverpool Echo and Evening Express*, 'A Thousand Miss O'Whittingtons', 30 January 1962. LVA, Newspaper cuttings. Liverpool Record Office, M326 VIG/5/2.

urban culture, these newspaper articles indicate that editors would give a voice to social purists because the stories they told were so sensational. During the 1960s, the LVA was not especially well known outside of the city, or even by the people of Liverpool, but the organization knew that their work fed into broader debates about morality, promiscuity, vice and even political relations between Britain and Ireland.

Despite economic and moral concerns about the Irish in Liverpool, controls on Irish immigration were not implemented and women continued to leave Ireland for many reasons during the post-war period. The LVA's decision to archive press reports on Irish immigration indicates that the organization did in fact take an interest in the politics of Irish immigration and that they favoured restrictions. One of the reports archived, a *Daily Mail* article entitled 'The Pretty Girl in the Irish Packet', published on 16 November 1961, considered Liverpool's status as a gateway for young Irish women entering the country with hopes of obtaining work.[59] The *Daily Mail* sought to bring to light the naivety of these 'girls' and their lack of skills appropriate to the English workforce. Some immigrants were said to be 'almost illiterate', while others 'had no craft or skill by minimal British standards'. Ireland itself was presented as an underdeveloped 'rural' region while Britain was portrayed as a modern, technically proficient and heavily industrialized country. The urban environment was therefore a focal point for anxieties about the ability of Irish women to cope with the transition from an idealized rural life to mechanized, masculinized modernity. It was suggested by the *Daily Mail* that some Irish immigrants knew 'nothing of the complexities and perils of an industrial city'. To substantiate this, the paper published examples offered to them by the LVA. This included the case of a 'pretty 19-year-old brunette' who arrived in Liverpool with very little money and a confused story about having children in Birmingham and a husband in London.[60] Helped by Mrs Blyth, the 'motherly' LVA patroller, the woman's 'pretty' femininity was associated with a child-like vulnerability. Indeed, the 'pretty girl' mentioned in the article's title stood as a figurehead for the youthful ignorance attached by local and national press and by organizations such as the LVA to women entering Britain from Ireland. According to the LVA and the press, femininity and Irishness were synonymous with naivety, imprudence and danger.

59   *Daily Mail*, 'The Pretty Girl in the Irish Packet', 16 November 1961. LVA, Newspaper cuttings. Liverpool Record Office, M326 VIG/5/2.
60   *Daily Mail*, 'The Pretty Girl in the Irish Packet', 16 November 1961.

Writing about teenage girls and boys, the *Daily Mail*'s article perfectly mimicked the LVA with the contention that these young people all too often left Ireland with little money, assuming that this would not matter once they reached England: 'they think it admits them to paradise'.[61] Where proposed restrictions on immigration were discussed, the *Daily Mail* article referred only to female travellers with no mention of their male counterparts. Rather than this being a sign of more progressive attitudes towards Irish men, this focus on women was probably due to the LVA being the main source of the *Daily Mail*'s information. It was suggested that '[s]ocial workers in Liverpool [agreed] there ought to be a stricter check in Eire to prevent Irish girls arriving without jobs or references'. The LVA and the Catholic Social Service Bureau in Liverpool were also said to support the proposal.[62] In this way, calls to restrict Irish female travel reflected anxieties about the vulnerability of women within urban spaces. Supposedly unable to traverse the dangers of British cities, the low social status of Irish women within Britain facilitated this public pronouncement in the *Daily Mail* that their movements should be watched and authorized or curtailed accordingly.

Despite the city's considerable Irish heritage, the local press in Liverpool similarly reinforced associations between Irish female immigration and the potential for urban life to corrupt those singled out as morally vulnerable. *The Liverpool Echo and Evening Express* speculated favourably upon the logistics of any potential surveillance of Irish women's travel to Liverpool:

a much greater effort should be made in the republic of Ireland – particularly in the remote country districts where life is strikingly different from that in the most pastoral part of England – to instruct young girls that much more is needed as a passport to prosperity than a ticket to Princes Dock East.[63]

Once again, assumed rural origins and youth were perceived as making Irish women under-qualified to cope with Britain's urban landscape, while the idea that these women came in search of 'prosperity' played on contemporary cultural associations between affluence and the city. In chasing the

---

61 *Daily Mail*, 'The Pretty Girl in the Irish Packet', 16 November 1961.
62 *Daily Mail*, 'The Pretty Girl in the Irish Packet', 16 November 1961.
63 *Liverpool Echo and Evening Express*, 'A Thousand Miss O'Whittingtons', 30 January 1962.

consumer society these women were understood to be seeking greater social and personal freedom and, as a result, entering into a morally dubious urban existence.

The Irish Girl in the Affluent Society

For the post-war LVA, paid employment continued to be understood as a means of keeping young Irish women off the streets and, paradoxically, out of the so-called 'affluent society' of the 1950s.[64] The philosophy of the LVA supposed that obtaining work for young, single, childless women would ensure their financial stability and thereby make them less likely to fall into disreputable habits. In 1958, the *Daily Mirror* reported on LVA patrol workers' dealings with female Irish immigrants.[65] The newspaper suggested that '[some] of the Irish girls looking for work in Britain are greener than the Emerald Isle itself'. The report reflected the concern that if respectable work was not found for these women they would succumb to the mores of the affluent society: 'Within a week they can change from a sweet simple country girl into a dolled-up street girl.' The *Daily Mirror* prodded the anxieties of its readers but referred in unspecific terms to one young Irish woman who arrived in the city 'unspoilt', with 'no make-up or jewellery'. Her transformation into an immoral character was said to have taken place after only a short time in Liverpool, at which point she gave off the air of 'an older, harder girl' due to her new taste for 'heavy make-up', extensive jewellery and 'jewelled combs in her hair'.[66] Emphasizing the embodied nature of disreputability through the extravagances of her attire, this woman symbolized the notion that young Irish women needed to be morally guided by the LVA. Her sexualizing and ostentatious accessories implied that she actively participated in consumer affluence and that her ability to pay for these goods may have come through immoral means and associations.

64   This term is typically associated with John Kenneth Galbraith's work on America, *The Affluent Society* (Boston: Houghton Mifflin, 1958), though it has been used to analyse British experiences of class and economic progress. See, for example, Laurence Black and Hugh Pemberton (eds), *An Affluent Society? Britain's Post-War 'Golden Age' Revisited* (London: Routledge, 2004).
65   *Daily Mirror*, 'Vigil on the Waterfront', 8 May 1958. LVA, Newspaper cuttings. Liverpool Record Office, M326 VIG/5/2.
66   *Daily Mirror*, 'Vigil on the Waterfront', 8 May 1958.

In an effort to further their network of surveillance beyond the purity movement, the LVA continued to involve employers and employment agencies in the organization's moral discourses of naive young women, respectable work and supervision. Where immigrant women were concerned, the LVA argued that there was much work to be done in ensuring that unofficial Irish employment services were reputable in their dealings with women seeking work. The 1955, LVA's annual report worried about the existence of 'double agencies' in Ireland.[67] Believed to be a recent 'phenomenon', they recruited young women for domestic work in England through a Dublin office. The women were then sent to the English offices of the agency with instructions to collect their employer's details from there. The LVA argued that this left Irish women in an especially vulnerable position:

> We feel this is a most unsatisfactory procedure as these girls arrive without employer's address, conditions of work or salaries offered, probably with insufficient money to return home if dissatisfied with their terms of employment.[68]

Rather than framing this issue in terms of bad practice on the part of these agencies, the LVA's description of them as 'double agencies' strayed into hyperbole, since it was far from clear that these employment offices routinely colluded to traffic Irish young women. The LVA even had some success in challenging this way of recruiting when they convinced one agency to discontinue the practice.[69] The LVA's interventions into the structures of female employment did, therefore, yield some genuinely helpful results, though the language surrounding the campaigns continued to reinforce the image of Irish immigrant women as naive and incapable.

Where the work of the LVA was even more problematic was in their efforts to encourage employers to join them in the surveillance of young Irish women. The *Liverpool Echo and Evening Express* argued for extensive communications between British employers, the LVA and recruitment agencies in Ireland.[70] The newspaper recommended the surveillance of young women's departures and arrivals between Ireland and Britain: 'There

67   LVA, Annual Report 1955.
68   LVA, Annual Report 1955.
69   LVA, Annual Report 1955.
70   *The Liverpool Echo and Evening Express*, 'A Thousand Miss O'Whittingtons', 30 January 1962.

are reputable agencies in the Republic through which girls who want to work in homes over here can get jobs. It would help if the [LVA] was told when such girls were expected. Firms here accepting Irish girl applicants could also assist in this direction.' Along with the LVA, the *Liverpool Echo and Evening Express* ascribed to local employers moral responsibility for the Irish women they hired. The movement of Irish women away from their homes and families therefore gave rise to structures of moral and social control in Liverpool that were designed to mimic the domestic codes which these women were thought to have abandoned. The paternalistic authority that employers were encouraged to assume over Irish women employees was a direct complement to the maternal social surveillance of the LVA patrollers.

With the LVA and local employers construed as acting *in loco parentis*, Irish young women were constructed as childlike and inexperienced. The LVA expressed concern about the 'extreme youth' of the 'Irish girls' that they helped.[71] They asked, 'What happens to these young girls away from the restraining influence of home life? What becomes of the young girls who arrive with no work at all? … imagine the dangers that can beset these young girls.'[72] The Association even went so far as to elevate their own responsibility for these young women by calling into question the decisions made by their actual parents. The LVA argued: 'Another great cause for anxiety is the number of girls who accept work in response to press advertisements. No enquiries are made either by the girls or their parents as to the desirability of the work or the place.'[73]

Despite drawing links between the economic vulnerability of women who travelled for work and the potential for these women to fall into prostitution, the LVA was not concerned about politically or socially challenging the economic subordination of women within British society. Instead, their frequent references to the economic causes of prostitution were merely illustrative of the associations they believed to exist between immorality and poverty. Although Irish women may have possessed a potent symbolic value within the debates about employment and respectability, they were often discursively conflated with working-class women in general. Perceived to be of the same social standing as working-class local women, Irish women were

<hr>

71   Untitled LVA notes on Irish female immigrants, undated (*c.*1954). Liverpool Record Office, 326 VIG/9.

72   Untitled LVA notes on Irish female immigrants, undated (*c.*1954).

73   Untitled LVA notes on Irish female immigrants, undated (*c.*1954).

singled out because it was feared that they added to the numbers of impoverished women already living in Britain. In 1955, the LVA drew a clear link between Irish women, poverty and unemployment when it suggested that there was 'little need to look for the motive that sends overseas a girl with seven brothers and four sisters, of whom only the father and one brother are employed, and the eldest sister, with four children, has an unemployed husband.'[74] The Irish woman in Liverpool was thus symbolic of the moral dangers presented by the presence of all working-class women upon the city's streets.

Moreover, it is too simplistic to view the LVA's perception of Irish women as the product of straightforward racism, or as founded on an image of femininity that the organization cultivated to suit their own preventative agenda. Rather, it was the case that the LVA accepted the idealized, homespun image of Irish women because it was easily accommodated in their overall views about women's moral vulnerability in urban settings. In order to understand how social purists in Liverpool situated themselves within national networks of moral surveillance and how they justified their existence, we must recognize the role of the Irish young women in the LVA's discourse of moral vulnerability. Social purists' perceptions of young Irish women were formed through their dialogues with Irish purity associations, meaning that Irish experiences in Britain were not simply shaped by stereotypes that cast them as part of an underclass.

Virtuous Irish femininity was central to the LVA's philosophy of using preventative patrol work as a means for combating immorality on the streets of Liverpool. For the LVA, Irish girls were the embodiment of innocent yet vulnerable femininity, and so were presented as ideal candidates for the organization's moral guidance and support. Though the Second World War seemed to offer a challenge to the work of the LVA, the war did not dampen the potency of the Irish girl as a figure of moral anxiety. During the conflict, the LVA's practices were merely on hiatus. That they were able regularly to feed their work into sensationalized national and local newspaper articles about post-war urban life speaks to the extent to which the ideas of social purists could still gain traction in the post-war years. Overall, the work of the LVA changed little across the course of the interwar and post-war years. Irish women continued make up the bulk of the women helped by the LVA and they continued to be viewed by the organization as prime examples of working-class female vulnerability. Certainly, the LVA can be seen to

74 LVA, Annual Report 1955.

have engaged in a form of profiling, with Irish ethnicity emerging as one of the key factors that the Association considered when deciding whether to intervene in the lives of young women arriving in the city. But, ultimately, the LVA was intent upon upholding an anti-prostitution, anti-promiscuity moral code that monitored *all* women regardless of ethnicity. Protecting the considerable number of Irish women within the city was, in the LVA's mind, one distinctive way of achieving that goal.

9

A Changing of the Guard

Moral Order, Gender and Urban Space in the Post-War Years

In this chapter, I examine social purity's post-war decline in Liverpool in terms of broader, national challenges to the work of organizations like the LVA. While Liverpool's Women Police Patrols had joined with the city's main police force in 1948, and the House of Help had closed their doors by the end of the 1960s, the LVA's survival until 1976 requires closer attention.[1] I want to show that in order to understand the eventual decline of the LVA, we need to examine the state's involvement in the control of prostitution from the 1950s onwards. My analysis of the slow decline of the LVA over these decades draws upon research into associational life and citizenship in the post-war years. Historians have increasingly begun to question the extent to which the post-war welfare state rendered voluntarism and philanthropy obsolete. James Hinton notes that the 'ongoing professionalization of social work in the welfare state placed a question mark over the continuing relevance of the kind of voluntary work traditionally undertaken by middle-class housewives'.[2] Yet Hinton also identifies the 1960s as a period of growth for the voluntary sector, with new campaigning organizations like Child Poverty Action Group (1965) and Shelter (1966) emerging.[3] More recently, Anna Bocking-Welch has pointed to the ways

---

1 For details on the incorporation of the women police into the main police force, see Gaynor Diane Williams, 'Women in Public Life', p. 119.

2 James Hinton, *Women, Social Leadership, and the Second World War: Continuities of Class* (Oxford: Oxford University Press, 2002), p. 157.

3 James Hinton, *Women, Social Leadership, and the Second World War*, pp. 235–6.

post-war volunteering was increasingly promoted towards young people as a form of citizenship, while Pat Thane has emphasized the long coexistence of public and private welfare initiatives.[4] Moreover, Chris Moores' work on the rise of Neighbourhood Watch in the 1980s shows that there was still an appetite for late-Victorian-inspired 'voyeurism' in terms of the social control of urban spaces even after groups like the LVA and the BVA (formerly the NVA) had ceased to patrol.[5]

This raises questions about why the specific forms of moral patrolling practised by the likes of the LVA and the BVA faded from public life during the post-war years and why, despite there still being space for charitable and philanthropic organizations to exist alongside the post-war welfare state, the LVA and BVA closed. In response to this, I argue that we cannot ignore that the state had increasingly begun to supervise and intervene in prostitution prevention and control by the end of the 1950s in a way that closed out social purists. This chapter addresses both the Wolfenden Committee (1954–57) and the 1959 Street Offences Act and argues that these developments had much in common with earlier social purity approaches to vice. However, the state wanted to avoid accusations of moral interventionism and could not, therefore, appear too close to groups like the LVA and the BVA. Women police could and did undertake what was essentially moral patrol work to intervene in the social lives of young people in large cities like Manchester.[6] However, the work of non-professionalized organizations like the LVA could not be repackaged under the veneer of professionalized services.

Nor did organizations like the LVA and the BVA manage to reposition themselves as lobbying groups. While the BVA did try promoting themselves as experts with the ability to critique aspects of the Street Offences Act 1959, their criticism was not enough to reinvent the organization. At the

4   Anna Bocking-Welch, 'Youth against Hunger: Service, Activism and the Mobilisation of Young Humanitarians in 1960s Britain', *European Review of History*, 23:1–2 (2016), pp.154–70; Pat Thane, 'The Ben Pimlott Memorial Lecture 2011: The "Big Society" and the "Big State": Creative Tension or Crowding Out?', *Twentieth Century British History*, 23:3 (2012), pp. 408–29.
5   Chris Moores, 'Thatcher's Troops? Neighbourhood Watch Schemes and the Search for "Ordinary" Thatcherism in 1980s Britain', *Contemporary British History*, 31:2 (2017), p. 244.
6   Louise Jackson, '"The Coffee Club Menace": Policing Youth, Leisure and Sexuality in Post-War Manchester', *Cultural & Social History*, 5:3 (2008), pp. 289–308.

same time, the moral didacticism of the LVA was built upon a heritage of telling working-class women how to behave, rather than critiquing structural inequalities in women's social and geographic mobility. This meant that they could not rebrand themselves as one of the new pressure groups. Newer organizations like the Child Poverty Action Group and Shelter could situate themselves as campaigning groups aimed at challenging social structures, and, later, Neighbourhood Watch schemes could be incorporated into a 1980s neo-liberal politics of crime prevention that aimed to merge active citizenship with a local sense of community.[7] However, in the interim, the preventative patrol work of the LVA and the BVA's pedigree of moral guardianship appeared to be increasingly out of step with the state's dubious insistence that the solicitation laws were not about intervening in private morality.

As such, I begin my analysis of the fatal decline of the LVA by addressing social purists' loss of ground to official efforts to prevent prostitution during the 1950s. Drawing on debate between social purists about the future of preventative patrol work and examining discussions between members of the Wolfenden Committee and the Chief Constable of Liverpool, I argue that the idea that social order was dependent on maintaining female sexual morality remained crucial in the post-war years. However, these discourses began to carry less weight when coming from the mouths of social purity patrol workers. It was not the case that concerns about prostitution as a form of moral contagion had been rendered out of date. Though the politics of the social and sexual regulation of women had begun to change after the Second World War, these changes were often subtle, and they did not represent a total break with earlier forms of regulation.[8]

Sex outside of marriage continued to provoke moral outrage, even during the supposedly more permissive 1960s. Though the number of unmarried teenage mothers increased in the 60s following the post-war baby boom, attitudes towards lone mothers remained critical.[9] Moreover, changes in women's fashions and ambitions did not mean that they were no longer subjected to infantilization and moral judgement when wandering

---

7   Chris Moores, 'Thatcher's Troops?', p. 246.

8   In this respect my work builds on the cautious approach to the scale of post-war moral change advocated by Jeffrey Weeks and Frank Mort. See Jeffrey Weeks, *Sex, Politics and Society*, p. 254; Frank Mort, *Capital Affairs*, p. 4.

9   Pat Thane and Tanya Evans, *Sinners? Scroungers? Saints? Unmarried Motherhood in Twentieth-Century England* (Oxford: Oxford University Press, 2012), pp. 132–3.

through urban spaces.[10] The idea that prostitution posed a threat to the health of the nation was revitalized by the 1963 scandal that surrounded the affair between Christine Keeler, a young woman from a working-class background, and John Profumo, Secretary of State for War. Keeler blurred the boundaries between prostitution and promiscuity by explaining her sexual escapades in terms of her own fun and entertainment.[11] Mort argues that the unresolved national moral reflection generated by the case 'testified to the long reach of the nineteenth century into the 1960s'.[12]

The post-war legal and moral regulation of prostitution was still predicated upon the sense that legitimate female sexuality was supposed to be passive and demure.[13] During the 1960s, the notion that women were capable of sexual desire on their own terms became more widely accepted, but even then this notion was appropriated and distorted by pornographers and it failed to translate into the decline of the chaste and sexually pure woman as an ideal type.[14] The visibility of female sexual agency still proved problematic for British society in the 1960s, and beyond. While female sexuality was increasingly made passive in the male gaze of pornographic consumption, negative attitudes towards women who sold sex by soliciting on the street continued to reflect the broader attitude that female sexuality should be hidden. Legal challenges to the prostitute's use of the streets and the determination of some social purists to continue their patrol work during the 1950s and 60s meant that women were still required to behave in ways that were sexually reticent if they wanted to

10   Carol Dyhouse notes the infantile style of much of the 1960s fashion aimed at young women, as they embraced the pre-pubescent stylings of icons like Twiggy. See Carol Dyhouse, *Glamour: Women, History, Feminism* (London: Zed Books, 2010), pp. 146–7.

11   Frank Mort, 'The Ben Pimlott Memorial Lecture 2010: The Permissive Society Revisited', *Twentieth Century British History*, 22:2 (2011), p. 288.

12   Frank Mort, 'Ben Pimlott Memorial Lecture 2010', p. 292.

13   Carol Smart has criticized legal approaches and attitudes towards prostitution in the post-war years, arguing that prostitutes were vilified in order to reinforce the gender and sexual politics which limited women to the private sphere. See Carol Smart, 'Law and the Control of Women's Sexuality: The Case of the 1950s', in Bridget Hutter and Gillian Williams (eds), *Controlling Women: The Normal and the Deviant* (London: Croom Helm, 1981), pp. 40–60.

14   Marcus Collins, 'The Pornography of Permissiveness: Men's Sexuality and Women's Emancipation in Mid-Twentieth-Century Britain', *History Workshop Journal*, 47 (1999), pp. 99–120.

be considered respectable. As a result, I argue that nationally significant discussions about prostitution and the boundaries between public and private were intertwined with local-level moral policing, with real implications for women as they worked in and travelled through a city like Liverpool.

This changing of the guard of moral order from the unofficial to the official precipitated the eventual closure of the LVA. The strengthening of the solicitation laws after Wolfenden exposed the LVA for what it had always been, an unofficial body advocating moral surveillance. Consequently, this chapter warns against using the health of the social purity movement as a barometer of how permissive society was during the 1950s and 60s. Even as organizations like the LVA and the BVA went into decline during the years of the so-called permissive society, women were still being judged on a spectrum that ran from the sexually pure but naive and morally vulnerable girl to the disreputable 'street-girl'.[15] Women's presence in urban space was still regarded as hugely problematic; policymakers still fretted about young women becoming sexually corrupted by wandering through the streets, as evidenced by the law's attitude towards prostitution. Though the LVA did well to weather the cultural changes of the 1960s, the organization struggled to justify their unique purpose during this decade. The greater independence displayed by women as they travelled though the city combined with the law's more explicit role in the moral policing of prostitution so that, by the time the organization dragged itself into the 1970s, the LVA's patrol work had become decidedly low-key and their authority with young women irrevocably damaged.

Policy and Purity in the 1950s

In 1953, at the LVA's annual meeting in Liverpool's Town Hall, Lady Maxwell Fyfe, wife of Conservative Home Secretary and 'traditional moralist' Sir David Maxwell Fyfe, underlined the importance of patrol work to Britain's towns and cities.[16] She told those present that 'women and girls still needed – in many cases consciously in all others unconsciously – the smile of a friend and the help of somebody who knew the way things should

15   'Liverpool – A Street-Girl's Paradise?' *Liverpool Weekly News*, April 1965. LVA, Newspaper cuttings. Liverpool Record Office, M326 VIG/5/2.
16   Frank Mort, *Capital Affairs*, p. 140; LVA, Annual Report 1953, p. 4. Liverpool Record Office, M326 VIG/3.

be done'.[17] Her close connection to a central government figure put Lady Maxwell Fyfe in a position of being able to address social purists' concerns about their work being taken over by officials. She reassured the LVA that 'A funny sort of remote Central authority will never take the place of friendly help and a friendly smile.'[18] However, not all social purity organizations were so easily reassured.

By the early 1950s, the National Vigilance Association had begun to reassess their sphere of influence and their ability to engage policymakers. At an 'Emergency Meeting' of the NVA Executive Committee, on 6 May 1952, it was noted that Lady Nunburnholme, Chair of the NVA, had instigated discussion between the NVA and the Home office, including David Maxwell Fyfe. The NVA wanted the Home Office's 'opinion as to whether the National Vigilance Association and Travellers' Aid Society had real value from the Government point of view'.[19] They also wanted to explore whether the Home Office might be of any help in terms of revenue raising, though any hopes of a Treasury Grant were unfulfilled when it was explained that there had been cuts to 'other voluntary societies'.[20] Following these none too reassuring noises by the Home Office, and concerned about the future of their work, the NVA convened a Working Party to consider their remit. When the Working Party met in July 1952, it was decided that the NVA should move away from 'meetings of travellers' and, instead, redefine as an organization focused on tackling the international traffic in persons.[21] As a result of these changes, the NVA became the British Vigilance Association and National Committee for the Suppression of Traffic in Persons (BVA).[22]

17   Lady Maxwell Fyfe paraphrased in LVA, Annual Report 1953, p. 4.

18   Lady Maxwell Fyfe quoted in LVA, Annual Report 1953, p. 4.

19   Minutes of the Emergency Meeting of the Executive Committee of the National Vigilance Association and Travellers' Aid Society, held on Tuesday, 6 May 1952, at 12 Old Pye Street, Westminster, SW1 at 11 a.m. Women's Library, 4BVA/E/5 Box FL349.

20   Minutes of the Emergency Meeting of the Executive Committee of the National Vigilance Association and Travellers' Aid Society, held on Tuesday, 6 May 1952.

21   'Notes of Meeting of Working Part[y] to Consider Future Policy of National Vigilance Assocn. 31 July 1952'. Women's Library, 4BVA/E/5 Box FL349.

22   The British Vigilance Association and the National Committee for the Suppression of Traffic in Persons Constitution, 12 February 1953. Women's Library, 4BVA/E/5 Box FL349.

When Lady Numburnholme gave a speech at the same LVA meeting as Lady Maxwell Fyfe in 1953, she spoke about the 'International aspects of Vigilance work'.[23] Numburnholme remained convinced that it was this particular aspect of vigilance work that would enable social purists to prove their worth. Her sense that moral street patrolling was no longer the best way for social purists to tackle prostitution and immorality was a pragmatic response to the NVA/BVA's concerns that official bodies were increasingly encroaching upon their turf and undermining their authority. For Numburnholme, the fight against international trafficking was the arena were vigilance workers could make a unique contribution to the maintenance of moral order. As such, the BVA withdrew their practice of patrolling stations in London in 1952.[24] Ethel Sugden, secretary of the LVA, publicly disagreed with Lady Nunburnholme's move away from patrolling. Sugden told the press that the young women her organization encountered 'DO need looking after … we are continually separating them from men who have picked them up.'[25] Though she admitted that there was 'no proof' of 'an organisation behind the men', Sugden remained 'convinced that to withdraw the patrols in London would be to hang out a "welcome" sign to such creatures'.[26]

Although relations between the LVA and the NVA were not strained by the diverging views of Sugden and Numburnholme, their disagreement was indicative of rising anxiety within the social purity movement about their public role in post-war society. Despite nodding towards internationalism throughout their existence by pointing out some of the linguistic abilities of their workers, the LVA had always been more focused upon thwarting the supply of potential prostitutes on the streets of Liverpool.[27] Sugden complained in an LVA report in 1952, 'So many people think that nowadays the Welfare state covers all needed charitable work but this is not the case.'[28]

23   LVA, Annual Report 1953, p. 4.

24   'Notes of Meeting of Working Part[y] to Consider Future Policy of National Vigilance Assocn. 31 July 1952'.

25   'HELP GIRLS' PATROLS MAY GO ON – UNPAID', *Daily Mirror*, June 1952. LVA, Newspaper cuttings. Liverpool Record Office, M326 VIG/5/2.

26   'HELP GIRLS' PATROLS MAY GO ON – UNPAID', *Daily Mirror*, June 1952.

27   See Chapter 5 for more on LVA's international veneer.

28   LVA, Annual Report 1951–52, Mrs Sudgen's Report, p. 5. Liverpool Record Office, M326 VIG/3.

Moreover, the notion that Liverpool had a prostitution problem had not gone away between the interwar and post-war years. There was still a sense that a port town, even one that was in a state of decline, would necessarily attract prostitutes because of the abundance of sailors and travellers at the docks. In 1958, the *Daily Mirror* referred to Liverpool as an '"X-certificate" city, with its square-mile of dockland brothels and drug dens', while LVA patroller Mrs Blyth claimed the city was 'One of the sexiest places in the world'.[29] Yet the LVA's defiant assertion of the continuing relevance of their pre-war policies and procedures had begun, by the mid-1950s, to be undermined by state-level interventions. As national attention refocused upon the issue of prostitution, the task of morally policing women on the streets was increasingly taken over by officials and law enforcement, leaving groups like the LVA struggling for room to assert their own authority.

When the Wolfenden Committee was set up in 1954, it was tasked with considering how prostitution and the laws controlling solicitation were influencing urban morality. Following the failure of the Street Offences Committee to bring about a change in the law in the late 1920s, concerns that the laws used to regulate solicitation were too numerous and too complicated persisted. The Wolfenden Committee was supposed to offer clarity, but the committee was preoccupied with assessing prostitution in terms of its visibility. Tim Newburn argues that both the 1951 Festival of Britain and the 1953 Coronation had 'focused the eyes of the world on Britain's streets', giving rise to fears that London was acquiring a global reputation for vice.[30] Much of this concern revolved around the potential for tourists to subscribe to a negative image of the capital and thus Britain as a whole. Writing in 1976, John Wolfenden, the eponymous chairman of the committee, recalled the problem as follows: 'Besides breaking the law they were, by flaunting themselves and pestering passers-by, causing an intolerable degree of embarrassment and giving visitors a deplorable impression of London's immorality.'[31]

29 'Vigil on the Waterfront', *Daily Mirror*, 8 May 1958. LVA, Newspaper cuttings. Liverpool Record Office, M326 VIG/5/2.

30 Tim Newburn, *Permission and Regulation: Law and Morals in Postwar Britain* (London: Routledge, 1992), p. 51. See also Frank Mort, 'Cityscapes: Consumption, Masculinities and the Mapping of London since 1950', *Urban Studies*, 35:5 (1998), p. 889 and Frank Mort, 'The Sexual Geography of the City', in Gary Bridge and Sophie Watson (eds), *The City* (Oxford: Blackwell, 2003), p. 307.

31 John Wolfenden quoted in Tim Newburn, *Permission and Regulation*, pp. 50–1.

The committee utilized the notions of the public and private spheres in order to justify using the law to regulate solicitation.[32] While the Wolfenden Committee supported relaxing regulations on behaviours that happened behind closed doors, they simultaneously acted to increase sanctions on *immoral* behaviours in public spaces.

Though the Wolfenden Committee had been inspired and largely influenced by goings on in London, evidence was heard from representatives from around the country. The exchanges between Chief Constable of Liverpool, Charles Carnegie Martin, and members of the Wolfenden Committee on 31 March 1955 indicate that while officials in the police force saw themselves as occupying a very different role from the moral proselytizing and even amateurism of social purists, their approaches actually had a lot in common.[33] The Chief Constable presented to the committee two competing images of Liverpool. The first was a socially ordered Liverpool, where the police retained control of the city and the streets were free from immoral problems such as prostitution. Chief Constable Martin, no doubt eager to present the effects of his Force in the best possible light, even went so far as to suggest to the Wolfenden Committee that prostitution was 'almost non-existent in many places in the provinces' and that 'it is not a problem outside London'.[34]

Though the LVA preferred to stoke concerns about the potential for prostitution in Liverpool in order to assert their importance, the Chief Constable's references to London were not entirely out of step with LVA rhetoric. One of the tactics that the LVA used in the 1950s to characterize local moral danger was to discuss Liverpool, because of the city's transport connections, as gateway to an immoral life in London. In 1958, the LVA noted:

> London is still the pinnacle of quite a few girls' ambitions as they have a pre-conceived idea that the life there is a dazzling and exciting affair. Whenever girls arrive without a job to go to and with very little money we try to persuade them to stay in Liverpool as we always have a list of employers needing resident domestic helpers.[35]

32   Jeffrey Weeks, *Sexuality and its Discontents: Meanings, Myths and Modern Sexualities* (London: Routledge, 1985), p. 215.
33   C.C. Martin, Transcript of Evidence, Departmental Committee on Homosexual Offences and Prostitution, 31 March 1955. The National Archives, HO 345/13.
34   C.C. Martin, Transcript of Evidence, p. 6.
35   LVA, Annual Report 1958, p. 5. Liverpool Record Office, M326 VIG/3.

Martin, the members of the Wolfenden Committee and the LVA therefore held similar visions of 1950s Liverpool as a much quieter cousin to the more spectacularly immoral London. However, the motivations of Martin and the committee for drawing on this perception of Liverpool were different from those of the LVA. As the quote above shows, the LVA's perception of Liverpool's relationship with London allowed them to convince girls to stay in Liverpool and therefore under their watchful eye. For Martin, his understanding meant that he could claim success in his field. Addressing the committee as the man responsible for policing in the city, it is unsurprising that Martin was keen to present Liverpool's streets as being firmly under his control. From the moment Martin began to address the Wolfenden Committee, he emphasized that prostitution in the sense of 'street walking' was 'not a problem' in Liverpool, with only five convictions for this offence in the previous year.[36] Martin even suggested that the city's docks were free from this type of prostitution 'nowadays', noting that the prostitutes who did frequent this area could be characterized more as 'amateurs … ready to get hold of a sailor and take him home'.[37]

Yet none of this meant that Martin and the Wolfenden Committee considered Liverpool to be a quiet backwater. Just as the LVA associated transience with the potential for immoral transgression, so too did Martin and the Wolfenden Committee. Martin presented the committee with a second, more troubling impression of a hidden Liverpool. In discussing this version of the city, Martin drew connections between the port and the criminal culture of the city. He told the inquiry about more covert, that is to say indoor, forms of sexual trading in Liverpool and about the criminal men involved. He explained that the city was home to 'a good deal of brothel keeping', as well as a 'quite good deal of living on the earnings of prostitution' and much of it by 'coloured men'.[38] Despite his assurances to the committee about the limited nature of street prostitution, Martin did not shy away from presenting his official audience with a picture of Liverpool as home to an underworld of 'shebeens' and brothels, with seafarers inexorably 'attracted to these places' in search of a good time.[39] These hidden prostitutes were situated alongside other criminal

36   C.C. Martin, Transcript of Evidence, p. 1.
37   C.C. Martin, Transcript of Evidence, p. 17.
38   C.C. Martin, Transcript of Evidence, p. 1.
39   Martin defined a shebeen as 'a place where intoxicating liquor is sold without a licence'.

underworld characters in Martin's evidence. He suggested that prostitutes worked 'in league' with men, often pimps, to commit robberies and he observed that prostitutes had been known to associate with murderers.[40] Although he did not claim to have encountered any prostitutes who had themselves committed crimes as serious as murder, Martin's evidence replicated the long-standing idea that the prostitute was located within the world of serious urban criminality.

Martin mapped his imagined sense of a Liverpudlian underworld onto the real, material geography of the city and the wider north-west, with particular emphasis on areas frequented by the working class. When one member of the committee, Mrs Cohen, vice president of the Scottish Association of Girls' Clubs, asked Martin if Liverpool's prostitutes could be characterized as 'high grade' or 'low grade', she and the Chief Constable entered into a discussion about the relationship between a prostitute's hometown and her character.[41] Implicit in this exchange was the assumption that class and moral character were interchangeable attributes, with an individual's geographical origins acting as a measure of both. Martin explained: 'They are tough, the hardcore of prostitutes are tough types. They are Liverpudlians mainly.' He suggested that they were girls from 'squalid districts', though Martin believed that some of the 'tough types' had 'migrated to Liverpool' from other areas of poverty. The discursive ties between poverty and immorality that underpinned Martin's geographical analysis of prostitution were accepted by the committee. For example, Cohen readily assumed that the sorts of prostitutes associated with wider crime in Liverpool were likely to have come from Lancashire, an area associated with working-class employment.[42]

The idea that prostitutes were produced by the supposedly lax morals of down-trodden neighbourhoods was an argument that was easy to accept and propagate for the Chief Constable and members of the committee alike. Since the nineteenth century, the middle and upper classes had criticized the morality of the working class in order to avoid addressing issues of material inequality.[43] Working-class young women, whether they were native to the city of Liverpool or newcomers, were therefore perceived by the committee to lack the appropriate moral fibre required

40   C.C. Martin, Transcript of Evidence, p. 2, 1–2.
41   C.C. Martin, Transcript of Evidence, p. 10.
42   C.C. Martin, Transcript of Evidence, p. 10.
43   Beverley Skeggs, *Formations of Class and Gender*, pp. 43, 46.

to avoid the temptation of the streets.[44] This same moral judgement of working-class women had been central to the formation of the LVA nearly fifty years earlier and it was still a part of the organization's ethos well into the post-war years. Indeed, just as the LVA were concerned about the contagious immorality of working-class women exposed to life near the docks, so too was Liverpool's Chief Constable. Martin told the committee that Liverpool had 'amateur' prostitutes, 'the good-time girls who come in because of the American troops'.[45] For Martin, they were 'not of the same type as the day to day prostitute', but in their pursuit of these foreign men they led what he termed 'a prostitute's life'.[46]

Liverpool's role as a port heightened the sense of danger that surrounded these local amateurs. Cohen asked whether these women would gather at the dock when a Navy ship was in the port. The Chief Constable responded by saying that a 'tremendous number of local girls' would 'crowd round the dock gates, or as near as they [could] to the dock gates' when a domestic or foreign naval detachment arrived. He claimed that when the port was particularly busy with 'a sort of invasion of sailors in the town' there were 'more women of this type knocking about'.[47] The girls were not always from Liverpool either. In one instance, Martin appeared to joke that they came from Manchester, a nod to the rivalry between the two cities, before suggesting some other possibilities. He noted that 'quite a few girls' had arrived 'from places as far off as Leeds and Newcastle' before turning to 'a life of prostitution' in Liverpool.[48] Despite claiming that prostitution was not a problem in Liverpool, then, the Chief Constable contradicted himself by implying that the transient nature of port life could have a negative influence upon the sexual morality of young women. Moreover, for Martin, the prostitute was not simply a social nuisance or petty criminal, rather he imagined her as a signifier of more widespread social disorder and unrest. This ongoing perception of prostitution as a symptom of moral disorder was significant because it allowed the Wolfenden Committee to justify their overall conclusion

44   For more on Victorian middle-class anxieties about working-class women's sexuality and social order, see Judith Walkowitz, 'The Politics of Prostitution', p. 289; Lucy Bland, *Banishing the Beast*, pp. 97–8.
45   C.C. Martin, Transcript of Evidence, p. 10.
46   C.C. Martin, Transcript of Evidence, p. 10.
47   C.C. Martin, Transcript of Evidence, pp. 17–18.
48   C.C. Martin, Transcript of Evidence, p. 18.

that the law did indeed have a part to play in controlling sexual relations between prostitutes and their customers.

The Wolfenden Committee published its report in 1957. Its recommendations to increase the penalties for solicitation and abolish the need for police to provide proof that a citizen had been annoyed by the solicitation became law in the 1959 Street Offences Act. As a result, prostitution was forced off the streets to be replaced by an indoor sex trade, a state of affairs that Wolfenden accepted as preferable and inevitable.[49] Wolfenden defined the nature of the prostitute's offence in terms of her contravention of public order, with her trade supposedly exposing other citizens to immorality.[50] Wolfenden and Martin do not appear to have noticed the overlaps between their ideas and those of social purists who had earlier sought morally to police the streets in an unofficial capacity. Mort argues that the Wolfenden Committee 'privileged the expert witness over the moral campaigner'.[51] He characterizes the post-war period as witnessing a 'generation of state-orientated professionals' move decisively away from 'the 'amateurish' and "unscientific" character of the purity associations'.[52] Amongst some members of the Wolfenden Committee there was a tendency to write off purists as part of a 'lunatic fringe' of campaigners.[53] The supposed expertise of purity groups was called into question by officials who now wanted to bring their own professional politics and career experience to the debate about how to handle prostitution.

Yet the recommendations of the Wolfenden Committee exhibited the same understanding about the moral dangers of public space as social purists in organizations like the LVA had held for decades. Believing that the most useful way of approaching the problem was to attempt to draw a line between prostitution as a moral offence and a criminal offence, the committee essentially deployed the Victorian ideology of 'separate spheres' in order to define the law's interest in prostitution.[54] With the Wolfenden Committee claiming to be uninterested in the private conduct of citizens,

49   Jeffrey Weeks, *Sex, Politics and Society*, p. 244; Helen Self, *Prostitution*, p. 141.

50   Teela Sanders, *Sex Work: Risky Business* (Uffculme: Willan, 2005), p. 94.

51   Frank Mort, *Capital Affairs*, p. 149.

52   Frank Mort, *Capital Affairs*, p. 149.

53   Frank Mort, *Capital Affairs*, p. 147.

54   For more on Victorian gender codes and the separation of public and private, see Catherine Hall, *White, Male and Middle Class: Explorations in Feminism and History* (Cambridge: Polity, 1992), chap. 3 and pp. 153–4.

the price of a relaxation of controls over the private sphere was greater control over the public domain.[55] As such, the law and professional agencies effectively took over the discourses, ideas and in some cases strategies of earlier purists.

The challenge for social purists in the 1950s was, therefore, to stay relevant in a changing social and legal climate. The BVA had attempted to mitigate the effects of official encroachment into their domain with their withdrawal of patrols in 1952 and, it is fair to say, by the end of the 1950s, the BVA considered themselves to have moved on from the approach now being taken by Wolfenden. By the time the Wolfenden Committee made their recommendations, the BVA was critical of proposals that the law should treat prostitutes and customers differently, that the term 'common prostitute' should remain in law and that it should be possible to prosecute solicitation without the need for proof of annoyance. The BVA wrote a memo in response to the Wolfenden Committee which criticized their proposals as 'this driving underground of vice' and argued that the removal of the need to prove annoyance 'discriminates most unfairly between prostitute and customer'.[56] The BVA's concern with the gender disparity in the criminalization of the prostitute signalled a shift away from the earlier NVA approach. Indeed, by the end of the 1950s, the BVA backed proposals to replace the solicitation laws with a 'single uniform enactment' that would 'apply to any person' upon the presentation of evidence by 'the person aggrieved'.[57] This suggests that the BVA favoured the conclusions that had been reached by the Macmillan Committee in the 1920s.

However, it is difficult not to read the shift between the NVA and the BVA in terms of a struggle for relevance rather than as evidence of a deep-seated ideological change. Though the BVA no longer patrolled during the 1950s, they did not entirely cease their support for patrols. After the change in strategy, the BVA noted that, with the help of the

55   Jeffrey Weeks, *Sexuality and its Discontents: Meanings, Myths and Modern Sexualities* (London: Routledge, 1985), p. 215. See also Rosie Campbell and Maggie O'Neill, 'Introduction', in Rosie Campbell and Maggie O'Neill (eds), *Sex Work Now* (Uffculme: Willan, 2006), p. xix.
56   'Memorandum of the British Vigilance Association on the Report of the Wolfenden Committee on Homosexual Offences and Prostitution'. Women's Library, 4BVA/E/5 Box FL349.
57   'The Wolfenden Report. BVA Short Answers to Certain Questions'. Women's Library, 3AMS/B/04/16/12 Box 50.

Salvation Army, they would still 'occasionally' help travellers at stations, and the BVA worked with the LVA to investigate the travels of Irish young women as they arrived in Britain during the 1950s.[58] Furthermore, the local work of the LVA emphasizes that the BVA's attempt to reframe their work cannot be mapped onto other social purity organizations. During the post-war years, the LVA did not abandon their patrols and, even after the introduction of the 1959 Street Offences Act, this local organization continued to implement much the same rhetoric and approach as earlier in a bid to keep Liverpool's streets free from immoral activity. The LVA's practice of patrolling the docks and stations in an effort to intercept vulnerable female newcomers to Liverpool remained a central part of their work during the 1960s.

Morally Policing 1960s Liverpool

During the 1950s and 60s, Liverpool capitalized on increased post-war employment and affluence to become a 'widely acknowledged centre of popular culture'.[59] National figures were unsurprisingly keen to forge associations between themselves and this positive image of the city. Most notably, Harold Wilson linked himself to the city and one of its most famous exports, The Beatles (noting that Ringo Starr was one of his constituents), when running in his successful campaign for the premiership in 1964.[60] By the early 1960s, Liverpool had undoubtedly become an important site in Britain's growing consumer society. Between the 1950s and early 1970s, the economy grew, as did people's disposable incomes.[61] Again, this was a trend that did not pass Liverpool by. Jon Murden notes that lifestyles had changed sufficiently in Liverpool to warrant the sale of an 'ever-increasing range of goods', from washing machines to record players, all of which were available in Liverpool's numerous shopping outlets. Department stores such as George Henry Lee, Owen Owen, Lewis's, T.J. Hughes and Blackler's and

---

58   'Notes of Meeting of Working Part[y] to Consider Future Policy of National Vigilance Assocn. 31 July 1952'; Chapter 8.

59   Paul Du Noyer, *Liverpool Wondrous Place: Music from the Cavern to the Coral* (London: Virgin Books, 2004), p. 14; Jon Murden, '"City of Change and Challenge": Liverpool since 1945', in John Belchem (ed.), *Liverpool 800: Culture, Character and History* (Liverpool: Liverpool University Press, 2006), p. 417.

60   Ben Pimlott, *Harold Wilson* (London: HarperCollins, 1992), p. 307.

61   Paul Addison, *No Turning Back: The Peacetime Revolutions of Post-War Britain* (Oxford: Oxford University Press, 2010), p. 168.

Henderson's all competed with each other as well as with the mail order services of Littlewoods.[62]

Liverpool's port was also given a vital boost as an exporter of British goods, ensuring that by the mid-1950s the city was on the way to recovering the port trade lost in the 1920s and 30s.[63] This period in Liverpool's history was one in which 'civic confidence' in the transformation of the city was high.[64] Tony Lane has suggested that there was a 'brash, mocking and irreverent' mood in Liverpool by the 1960s.[65] Indeed, for Lane, the attitude popularly ascribed to The Beatles is best understood as part of this local disposition. Thus he writes, somewhat romantically, that 'The Beatles were expressive of Liverpool before they were expressive of the 1960s.'[66] Moreover, far from being contained in the cultural hub of the central areas, the communities around the inner city took this identity with them into the outlying areas of the city when clearance programmes directed them to new housing estates during the early part of the 1960s.[67] Under powers granted by the Liverpool Corporation Act 1936, the city developed a number of industrial estates in outlying areas and, in an attempt to diversify the local economy, promoted the development of manufacturing in the city.[68] The social and economic success of these developments was shown to be only ephemeral by the 1970s, but Liverpool certainly began to gain cultural prominence in the 1960s.[69]

62   Jon Murden, 'City of Change and Challenge', p. 417.

63   Jon Murden, 'City of Change and Challenge', p. 402.

64   Jon Murden, 'City of Change and Challenge', p. 402.

65   Tony Lane, *Liverpool: City of the Sea* (Liverpool: Liverpool University Press, 1997), p. 118.

66   Tony Lane, *Liverpool*, p. 118.

67   Tony Lane, *Liverpool*, p. 118.

68   Jon Murden, 'City of Change and Challenge', p. 406.

69   Stuart Wilks-Heeg, 'From World City to Pariah City? Liverpool and the Global Economy, 1850–2000', in Ronaldo Munck (ed.), *Reinventing the City? Liverpool in Comparative Perspective* (Liverpool: Liverpool University Press, 2003), p. 49. For more information on the growth of manufacturing industries in the city, see also Jon Murden, 'City of Change and Challenge', pp. 406–7. On the city's economic downturn in the 1970s, Wilks-Heeg argues that the city had become precariously 'dependent upon a branch-plant economy' by the mid-1970s, with approximately half of Merseyside's workforce working in factories with over 1,000 other employees ('From World City to Pariah City?', p. 49). As a result, unemployment became widespread. Murden suggests that some 350 factories closed or left Liverpool between 1966 and 1977 ('City of Change and Challenge', p. 428).

With this change in the city's image, the LVA restated their concerns about young women who arrived in the city with, in the organization's estimations, little or no consideration for their own moral welfare. In 1964, the Lord Bishop of Liverpool told the LVA's annual meeting that the 'innocent girls' that the organization met on the city's streets needed protecting not only from 'unscrupulous persons', but 'also themselves'.[70] He explained:

> Girls living in comparatively isolated parts of the country believed if they could only get to Liverpool they would find continual glamour and excitement. Having arrived in 'Beatle-land' their day dreams can turn to nightmares and it is then that friendly help is needed.[71]

Though it is unclear from the annual report whether the phrasing used was that of the Lord Bishop of Liverpool or the LVA, it is nevertheless evident that the work of the LVA was placed in direct opposition to the excesses of post-war youth culture and consumerism. For the Lord Bishop and the LVA, there was concern that young women, with little knowledge of what life was like in a large city such as Liverpool, were migrating to the city because of misinformed fantasies about extravagant urban lifestyles. To these supposedly naive youths, Beatle-land represented opportunities for socializing and enjoying consumer pursuits. To social purists, Beatle-land was a dangerous site of social disorder and sexual misadventure. The LVA presented Liverpool's main pop culture export as having achieved such important symbolic status that the city now rivalled London as a site of potential immorality and exploitation, at least where young women were concerned. The lifestyles of young people in the city were derided by the LVA, who feared widespread moral decline. In 1968, the Lord Bishop of Liverpool warned at the LVA's annual meeting that 'permissive morality does not create personal happiness for those who indulge and young people are now expected to take important decisions although lacking knowledge and experience'.[72]

During the 1960s, Liverpool's press and the city's local social purists fretted about young people supposedly seeking Liverpool out as a site of

---

70   LVA, Annual Report 1964. Liverpool Record Office, M326 VIG/3.
71   LVA, Annual Report 1964.
72   LVA, Annual Report 1968, 'General Report', p. 3. Liverpool Record Office, M326 VIG/3.

social and sexual freedom. In April 1965, the front page of the *Liverpool Weekly News* asked the loaded question 'Liverpool – A Street-Girl's Paradise?'[73] The paper warned that there were 'Rumours in Dublin, Belfast and Glasgow, that there [was] easy money for the picking in Liverpool Streets' and that these rumours were 'bringing at least 1,000 girls a year to the city'. In the same article, Mrs Marjorie Osler, Matron of the House of Help, the refuge to which the LVA regularly sent young women, told the newspaper that 'At least half' of the 350 girls that she had helped that year had become or would become prostitutes. Osler lamented that 'nearly every boat from Dublin and Belfast' produced yet more 'penniless' girls who were picked up by the LVA and referred on to the House of Help for shelter.

This proclamation appears to have underestimated the self-sufficiency of the young women who travelled to Liverpool. By the late 1960s, the House of Help had to admit that the 'nature' of its work had 'changed'; the refuge increasingly offered help to women and children being housed for longer periods following 'domestic trouble', new mothers recovering from birth and a 'growing group' of 'elderly or middle-aged' women 'unable to cope with ... everyday life'.[74] As an organization concerned with providing respectable temporary accommodation to morally vulnerable women, the House of Help found that its raison d'être no longer chimed with the needs of young women in the 1960s. The House of Help finally closed in 1969.[75]

The LVA similarly struggled to maintain their influence and explain their value in a world where women were growing in confidence when it came to managing their own occupational and geographical mobility. Warning signs about the future of the LVA had already emerged in the 1950s when the organization's post-war treasurer, Mr R.W. Jones, admitted, while canvassing for funding, that the LVA was 'urgently in need of new capital'.[76] He explained that the Association did not 'undertake any advertising or appeals and for that reason our work is not well known'.[77] With the

---

73 *Liverpool Weekly News*, April 1965. LVA, Newspaper cuttings. Liverpool Record Office, M326 VIG/5/2.

74 House of Help Annual Report 1967, p. 2. Liverpool Record Office, 362/ HOU/3.

75 Administrative history notes for House of Help records, Liverpool Record Office.

76 R.W. Jones, letter to unknown recipient, *c.*mid-1950s. Liverpool Record Office, 362 VIG/7–2.

77 R.W. Jones, letter to unknown recipient, *c.*mid-1950s.

post-war profile of the organization relatively low, the LVA went into the 1960s struggling to adapt to local cultural changes with regards to youth culture and the interest that the Merseybeat phenomenon brought to the city. Moreover, the gulf between the LVA's notions of respectable work and the aspirations of the young women who travelled to the city widened as the LVA remained wedded to the promotion of traditional jobs. As late as 1961, the secretary of the LVA, Mrs Bond, said of the organization's work helping women into employment: 'we are able to put [girls] in touch with local employers needing domestic or factory workers'.[78] That Mrs Bond chose to highlight these areas of work was indicative of the organization's continued focus upon using traditional non-skilled or low-skilled employment in order to deter working-class women from the temptation of earning money via prostitution.

In the mid-1960s, the LVA still helped considerable numbers of people as they travelled through Liverpool. In 1965, LVA workers helped 1,127 people and in 1966 they helped 1,242.[79] However, when the number of people helped dropped to 851 in 1967 the LVA suggested that this was partly because there had been a reduction in the weekly number of boat trips from Dublin to Liverpool and, more worryingly, because their patrol workers had become less reliable. The LVA's secretary complained that during that one year alone the LVA had gone through eleven workers.[80] That the work started early, 6.15 a.m. in the summer and 6.45 a.m. in the winter, as well as the fact that some young women were 'not very co-operative', were thought to sap the commitment of new patrol workers.[81] According to the LVA, 'some people who have been full of enthusiasm and professing that this is just the job they most wanted have stayed only a couple of weeks ... two workers just walked out without even working the month's notice which had been agreed'.[82]

There was a sense by the latter half of the 1960s that social purists were finding it harder and more taxing to exert their authority and make their voices heard. The Bishop of Warrington lamented at the LVA's annual

---

78   Mrs Bond, letter to *Liverpool Daily Post*, December 1961. LVA, Newspaper cuttings. Liverpool Record Office, M326 VIG/5/2.

79   LVA, Annual Report 1965, p. 5 and LVA, Annual Report 1966, p. 5. Liverpool Record Office, M326 VIG/3.

80   LVA, Annual Report 1967, p. 5. Liverpool Record Office, M326 VIG/3.

81   LVA, Annual Report 1967, p. 5.

82   LVA, Annual Report 1967, p. 5.

meeting in 1966 that people lacked 'a sense of belonging', that people had become 'like parcels in transit' but that organizations like the LVA were not given enough credit for protecting these 'fragile' parcels.[83] He suggested that 'vigilant is an honourable word of which people are sometimes suspicious thinking that we look for things which are wrong' when, according to the Bishop, the LVA instead offered a 'positive' alternative to the 'era of smash and grab, broken windows, kiosks and trains'.[84] Yet the Bishop was addressing his comments to the converted. Outside of the community of LVA devotees, the organization was left scrabbling to define their particular contribution to Liverpool life. Social purity organizations had begun to appear increasingly out of date, not necessarily because there was no call for initiatives to help travellers or for controls to guard against prostitution, but because women-led social purity groups were no longer regarded to have sufficient expertise, authority or legitimacy in these areas. In 1965, the Rector of Liverpool and Chairman of the LVA appeared to acknowledge the organization's struggle to complete when he tried to reassure LVA supporters that, 'In these modern times when the State does so much and when there are so many individual agencies at work, it is often the personal thing that counts most.'[85] The Chairman's optimism would see the organization through another decade, but these would be years of struggle and decline for the LVA.

The End of the LVA

Despite the BVA having taken a step back from patrol work in the 1950s, and despite their attempt to show a more modern outlook in their critique of the Wolfenden Report, the BVA actually closed before the LVA. Members of the BVA linked the eventual closure of the organization at the end of 1971 to their failure to modernize successfully. At the emergency meeting on 6 December 1971, where it was ultimately decided to close the BVA, it was noted that the organization's main line of work had been reduced to vetting the employment opportunities of au pairs and that the 'BVA and other societies needed to join together and re-formulate their aims in modern terms'.[86] Others present at the meeting regretted that the BVA no

---

83   LVA, Annual Report 1966, p. 5.
84   LVA, Annual Report 1966, p. 5.
85   C. Edwyn Young in LVA, Annual Report 1965, preface. Liverpool Record Office, M326 VIG/3.
86   'Minutes of the Extraordinary General Meeting of the British Vigilance

longer seemed to concern itself sufficiently with the 'struggle against traffic
in persons'.[87] The BVA's attempt, in the 1950s, to differentiate themselves
from their earlier practices and to cultivate a role that was distinct from the
state's moralizing about prostitution, was, therefore, unsuccessful.

Following the meeting, Joan Vickers, the Chair of the BVA, wrote a letter
to supporters to explain the closure of the organization. She said: 'The
changing pattern of life, the advent of the Welfare State, have … made the
objects for which this Society was originally formed no longer necessary.'[88]
The minutes for the final meeting of the BVA in February 1972 concluded
by drawing a direct line between the solicitation legislation that Wolfenden
inspired and the end of the organization:

> The work done by the British Vigilance Association had been beneficial
> to a great number of women and young persons, but in view of the
> 1959 Street Offences Act and a rather different attitude of society
> towards the role of women in society, it was impossible to raise
> sufficient money to continue the work for which the Association was
> originally formed.[89]

This statement shows that there were more substantial implications to the
state's incursion into the BVA's territory than the tactical difficulties that
this produced for social purists on the lookout for signs of prostitution. As
young women continued to grow in their ambitions and social expectations, the links between prostitution and promiscuity were more subtly
policed by officials who claimed to be free from moralizing. While the ideas
behind older social purity associations like the BVA and the LVA lived on
in the continued policing of prostitution on gendered, moral terms, these
groups could no longer be the vessels for these ideas because their appeals
to authority had, during the post-war years, been fatally diminished.

Association held in the Bishop Partridge Hall, Church House, London, SW1, on
6th December 1971'. Women's Library, 4BVA/E/5 Box FL349.
87   'Minutes of the Extraordinary General Meeting of the British Vigilance
Association held in the Bishop Partridge Hall, Church House, London, SW1, on
6th December 1971'.
88   Letter by Joan Vickers (addressed to 'Dear Sir/Madam'), dated 14 December
1971. Women's Library, 4BVA/E/5 Box FL349.
89   'Minutes of the final winding up of the British Vigilance Association meeting
held on 16th February 1972, at 44 Westminster Gardens, London, S.W.1'. Women's
Library, 4BVA/E/5 Box FL349.

By the time the LVA closed in 1976, it had helped thousands of women who were lost, stranded or looking for work. The organization's aims and practices had changed very little since the early twentieth century. The number one object of the Association in 1976 was still 'To use every means to prevent traffic in women and children.'[90] Figureheads on the board still included the Lord Mayor and Lady Mayoress of Liverpool, as well as local religious leaders. However, the organization was in denial about its influence and its prospects. At the 1976 annual meeting of the board, the Lord Mayor gave no hint of the LVA's imminent closure. Instead, he said that 'so many people were mobile these days with the need to seek new pastures' that 'it was most important that the work of our Association ... continued', while the LVA's treasurer gave an 'optimistic' report to those present.[91]

In terms of the numbers helped, the LVA appeared to be as strong as ever. Between 1975 and 1976, the LVA assisted 1,255 'women, girls, children and youths'.[92] Without doubt, sexuality was still up for regulation, urban spaces were still gendered and sexualized in complex ways. The 1959 Street Offences Act was still used to cleanse the streets of signs of solicitation and shore up the boundary between public and private, and social purists still believed that city life could corrupt the morally vulnerable due to the availability of sex, alcohol and indecent entertainment in urban environments. In 1970, the LVA welcomed Reverend Hester, the Rector of Soho, to their annual meeting. Reverend Hester told those present about 'his work in strip clubs and all-night coffee bars', aligning moral concerns about entertainment with those about promiscuous sex in much the same way as the LVA did.[93] Moreover, young women were still considered to be naive and ignorant of distance, with the LVA suggesting that they encountered young people who arrived in Liverpool and asked about walking distances to 'places as far distant' as Doncaster, Cardiff and Birmingham.[94]

Yet the fact that the LVA had to rely upon stories from Soho was indicative of a broader decline in the sensationalism of their own local work. By the 1970s, the LVA suggested that they were happy to help travellers

90   LVA, Annual Report 1975 and Accounts for 1976, p. 1. Liverpool Record Office, M326 VIG/3.
91   LVA, Annual Report 1975 and Accounts for 1976, p. 2.
92   LVA, Annual Report 1975 and Accounts for 1976, p. 3.
93   LVA, Annual Report 1970, p. 2. Liverpool Record Office, M326 VIG/3.
94   LVA, Annual Report 1970, p. 4.

via gestures 'big and small'.[95] A large part of their work now involved 'looking after children so that parents can collect cars and luggage'.[96] In the organization's final few years, there was also a sense that young women had grown in independence, with even the LVA struggling to muster the same level of concern about women travelling alone on public transport as they had in the early and middle years of the twentieth century. The LVA tried to warn about 'the very real dangers' faced by girls who travelled hitchhiking and their patrollers used 'all their persuasive powers to induce the girls to travel by bus or train', though often to no avail.[97] With young women more confident in their ability to manage their own travel affairs, they were less convinced by the LVA's warnings. In 1971, the LVA encountered two Norwegian girls who were planning a hitchhiking tour of England, Scotland and Wales.[98] Alarmed by the young women's intentions to use strangers' cars to get about, the LVA regretfully reported that the girls 'could not be dissuaded' from their plans. To the LVA's warnings, the girls confidently replied that they had already 'travelled by hitchhiking in every country in Europe'.[99] Such self-assurance was not unusual by the 1970s. Though the LVA attempted to reassure themselves that their warnings about hitchhiking were 'Quite often … heeded', they noted that on just one morning in 1972, their patroller 'tried to persuade 2 girls from Canada, two from Sweden and a girl from Wales to travel by more orthodox means but they were all determined to beg free rides to various parts of the country'.[100]

Having been undermined by official interventions into the gendered policing of vice upon the streets, the authoritative tropes that the LVA had relied upon earlier in the century no longer held sway with the young women that the organization sought to help. The LVA had grown from and been dependent upon middle-class social purity philanthropy in the early part of the twentieth century. By the end of the Association's lifespan, the LVA was more likely to promote the down-to-earth ordinariness of their patrollers in a bid to win support. At their 1972 annual meeting, the LVA welcomed Colonel Bryson, Registrar of Liverpool County Court, who

95   LVA, Annual Report 1975 and Accounts for 1976, p. 3.
96   LVA, Annual Report 1975 and Accounts for 1976, p. 3.
97   LVA, Annual Report 1970, p. 4.
98   LVA, Annual Report 1971, p. 4. Liverpool Record Office, M326 VIG/3.
99   LVA, Annual Report 1971, p. 4.
100   LVA, Annual Report 1972, p. 4. Liverpool Record Office, M326 VIG/3.

praised the workers of the organization by noting: 'when the boats arrive most citizens are asleep and the weather is often wet. This is not too bad if one is earning a fat salary or meeting a loved one but the caseworkers are not doing either of these things'.

According to Bryson, the commitment of the LVA staff was a result of their 'devotion and fortitude'.[101] Indeed, this use of pious language to create a more humble impression of the LVA's work chimed with the LVA's increasing religiosity in later years. Though Christian and Jewish faith leaders had been important figureheads of the LVA since the very beginning, the final reports of the LVA recounted in more detail some of the speeches given by these leaders at the organization's annual meetings. In 1971, the LVA reported that the Bishop of Warrington had compared the Association's work 'to the [biblical] story of Ruth when Naomi tried to persuade Ruth to seek security but Ruth went with her to a strange country and was met with friendliness'.[102] The workers of the LVA were consequently presented as caring, concerned and selfless in their efforts to help others and 'give them a sense of security'.[103]

Alongside these religious accounts were more references to political and religious unrest in Ireland, not least because, from the late 1960s onwards, the Troubles in Northern Ireland increased.[104] But the LVA was still a non-denominational organization and, as such, offered no real reflection on the situation. When the LVA noted that they had 'achieved a record for the number of people met and helped' in 1972, with a figure of 2,067, their report explained that the increase was 'mainly due to families from Northern Ireland arriving to stay with relatives and friends because of the bombings'.[105] Just as in the earlier parts of the twentieth century, the LVA continued to discuss the considerable number of Irish helped in general terms, making no reference to whether those helped were more likely to be Protestant or Catholic. In terms of the LVA's own local religious standing, however, it is clear that they did receive considerable support from the Catholic Community. In 1970, the LVA thanked the Catholic Social Service Bureau for their support and during the 1970s the Catholic Chaplaincy at

101   LVA, Annual Report 1972, p. 2.
102   LVA, Annual Report 1971, p. 2.
103   LVA, Annual Report 1971, p. 2.
104   Erika Hanna, 'Photographs and "Truth" during the Northern Ireland Troubles, 1969–72', *Journal of British Studies*, 54 (2015), pp. 458–9.
105   LVA, Annual Report 1972, p. 3.

the University of Liverpool held an annual coffee morning fund-raiser in support of the LVA.[106]

Rather than attempting to become a more politically engaged, campaigning organization in the mould of the Child Poverty Action Group, and rather than attempting to become more professionalized as a social work outfit, in the 1970s, the LVA clung to their moral and philanthropic heritage. As late as 1972, the organization was still insisting that 'girls' from 'sheltered homes' struggled to 'resist temptations', and the LVA's interwar stereotyping of ethnic minority men as sexually immoral was still part of their philosophy of urban danger.[107] The LVA warned 'guilty men who run houses of ill repute are mostly, if not all, from other countries'.[108] According to the LVA, Britain's 'high moral code' had been undermined by the public's 'separation from both religious and political leaders', and by 'industrial strife'.[109] As such, the reassertion of religious and political authority, along with the small though 'important' work of the LVA, were offered as answers to 'anarchy'.[110] Yet, with the law, in the form of the 1959 Street Offences Act, effectively enforcing a form of gendered moral order on the streets through its treatment of the prostitute as aberrant and immoral, the LVA was without a remit by the mid-1970s. These changes in the law meant that the organization's unofficial street policing was no longer necessary and, even if members of the LVA had wanted to transform the Association from a social purity group into a social work agency with a specific policy agenda, there were other organizations in the city already overseeing practical, rather than moral, social work initiatives.

In a move that served to highlight the LVA's lack of competitiveness in the 1970s, when the organization closed in 1976 the LVA's assets and, in a limited sense, workload were passed to the Liverpool Personal Service Society (PSS). The PSS had existed alongside the LVA for much of the twentieth century, though their work was distinct. The PSS had been set up in 1919 and one of its founders was the MP and social campaigner Eleanor Rathbone.[111]

---

106   LVA, Annual Report 1970, p. 3. See also LVA, Annual Reports for 1973–76. Liverpool Record Office, M326 VIG/3.

107   LVA, Annual Report 1972, p. 2.

108   LVA, Annual Report 1972, p. 2.

109   LVA, Annual Report 1972, p. 2.

110   LVA, Annual Report 1972, p. 2.

111   For more on the work of Eleanor Rathbone, see Susan Pedersen, *Eleanor Rathbone and the Politics of Conscience* (New Haven, Conn.: Yale University Press, 2004), p. 181.

Their volunteers acted as advocates for those in need, ensuring that they received appropriate unemployment benefits and, where relevant, pensions. As such, the PSS was a more explicitly social work-orientated organization that existed to provide help for the city's poor. Their workers helped those in need of accommodation, convalescent treatment or the assistance of the 'Poor Man's Lawyer'.[112] The PSS also took a different approach to those they helped when compared with the attitudes of the LVA and other moral welfare initiatives, such as the House of Help. Volunteers at the PSS did not consider themselves to be particularly distinct from those in need of assistance. In their early years, the PSS explained that their work was 'essentially work for amateurs ... men and women who give their personal service for love – love of God, love of their City, love of the community and love of the individual family'.[113]

By the post-war years, the PSS was increasingly organized and focused on developing 'policies' in line with 'changing situations in the field of Social Service'.[114] The PSS's appropriation of the LVA's work from 1976 took the form of a more general commitment to helping 'young travellers in and around Liverpool' and forging links with organizations like the Young Persons' Advisory Service.[115] Consequently, the survival of the PSS over the LVA was in no small measure because the PSS had been far less concerned with issues of moral edification and informal street policing than the LVA had been, meaning that their work was not rendered outdated by either changes in the law or social changes in women's use of public space.

By the 1970s, there was much that was outdated about the LVA and their practices. Changes in women's attitudes meant that it was harder for patrollers to cajole women into taking their help, and the idea that young women were so morally vulnerable that they could not travel on public transport or through working-class areas without being tempted or tricked into vice no longer gained sufficient traction to garner support for the work of the LVA. However, the LVA's struggle to remain relevant in the 1960s and the ultimate decline of the LVA (and indeed the BVA) should not be read as signs that prostitution and vice were less likely to provoke moral outrage. The enactment of the Street Offences Act in 1959 ensured

112   Personal Service Society Annual Reports 1920–77, Liverpool Record Office, 364 PSS 3/1/1 – 3/1/57.
113   Personal Service Society Annual Report 1921, p. 10.
114   Personal Service Society Annual Report 1962–63, p. 5.
115   Personal Service Society Annual Report 1976–77, p. 4.

that prostitution would continue to be understood and policed as a form of immoral contagion that could be used, albeit more subtly, to code the respectability of female sexuality in terms of women's relationship to public space. Significant elements of the purity discourses endorsed by the LVA had been incorporated into official strategies of regulation at the level of the state. Over the course of the post-war years, the LVA was not diminished because of a rise of permissive attitudes; rather, the LVA had become surplus to requirements and served only as an awkward reminder of a form of street policing that was rendered out of date by the transparency of its moralizing agenda.

Conclusion

We know that, throughout the twentieth century, femininity was culturally codified in problematic terms and that increased social freedom for women came with caveats about the need for women to be demure and to avoid being seen as promiscuous.[1] While Sonya Rose's work reminds us that the idea of female promiscuity as a risk to the nation has a long history of being emphasized at times of national tension and international conflict, this work has sought to add to this by elaborating on the discourses and practices that have given sustenance to these ideas during times of relative peace.[2] Moreover, while important historians of prostitution, such as Laite, Self and notably Walkowitz, have examined the ways that prostitute women have been targeted and marginalized in law, less attention has been given to the historical interplay between the stigmatization and regulation of prostitution and the marginalization of aberrant forms of female heterosexuality more generally.[3] Philippa Levine and Angela Woollacott's work considered this in the context of British society during the First World War, but the wartime 'them-and-us' mentality that Levine notes of women police and the women they monitored was part of a wider culture of socially policing respectable femininity that lasted long after the First World War.[4]

1   Carol Dyhouse, *Girl Trouble*, p. 2.
2   Sonya Rose, 'Sex, Citizenship, and the Nation', p. 1148.
3   Julia Laite, *Common Prostitutes*; Helen Self, *Prostitution*; Judith Walkowitz, *City of Dreadful Delight*.
4   Philippa Levine, '"Walking the Streets in a Way no Decent Woman Should"', p. 54; Angela Woollacott, '"Khaki Fever"'.

By considering longer-term fluctuations in the authority of women who monitored other women, this work has suggested that challenges to and the eventual decline of traditional social purity and moral welfare did not put an end to panic about women's wanderings through urban space. At the same time, the amalgamation of social purity ideas into official forms of prostitution regulation was part of what Hinton has identified as a post-war professionalization of welfare work, as well as being a precursor to the neo-liberal, community-based Neighbourhood Watch policing of the 1980s, recently highlighted by Moores.[5]

This book's focus on Liverpool has indicated that some of the most marginalized women, especially the poor and the immigrant, were affected by the way prostitution and promiscuity were conflated and policed as moral problems during much of the twentieth century. Aspects of Liverpool 'exceptionalism' are evident in the sheer extent to which local social purists and the local press focused on young Irish immigrant women as potential prostitutes.[6] Moreover, associations between transience and immorality meant that Liverpool's port-side, working-class neighbourhoods were scrutinized as problem areas. However, the relationship between young women and urban space in early to mid-twentieth-century Liverpool was heavily shaped by national moral debates about the parameters of respectable femininity. Social purists, the press, politicians and members of the police force subscribed to the idea that prostitution worked like a moral contagion, with the potential to poison the health of the nation. The perceived fragility of the distinction between the respectable young, working-class woman and the prostitute produced a highly gendered understanding of urban space. The Victorian notion that working-class women required moral guidance within the public sphere was restated by social purists, moral welfare workers, police and policymakers in response to changes in women's lifestyles during the interwar and post-war years. The debates conducted by the Street Offences Committee (1927–28) and the Wolfenden Committee (1954–57) revolved around the disjuncture between dominant moral codes of traditional femininity and changing social conditions, especially women's increased use of public space in big cities like Liverpool.

From abstract legal debates among politicians and law-enforcement representatives right down to the moral street policing of the LVA and

5   Hinton, *Women, Social Leadership*; Moores, 'Thatcher's Troops?'.
6   Belchem has argued that Liverpool does not easily fit into typical historical narratives and categorizations. See John Belchem, *Merseypride*.

Women Police Patrols, policies aimed at preventing prostitution had little to do with any objective notion of public order. Instead, they were centred on attempting to shore up the distinctions between *ordinary* women and prostitutes. Nationally and locally, the visibility of prostitution was held in check precisely because female sexual agency within the public sphere was construed by officials and social purists as undermining gendered distinctions between public and private, between respectable and disreputable. Certainly, in Liverpool, it was not uncommon for organizations like the LVA, the Women Police Patrols and the House of Help to offer much-needed help to women at risk of turning to prostitution out of economic necessity. These organizations were instrumental in finding work for working-class women. However, these organizations still formed part of a culture that negatively judged women who already worked as prostitutes; this was a culture that viewed prostitution as a dirty, immoral contagion which was spread not just by loosely defined traffickers but by the indecorous sensibilities of some working-class women. In Liverpool, social purists, women police and moral welfare workers took the paradoxical and even hypocritical approach that women who spent time on the streets were vulnerable to moral corruption. They expressed no interest in challenging the idea that other women were morally weak, and they showed little concern with the physical well-being of women working as prostitutes.

Although a drop in the number of arrests for solicitation in Liverpool during the 1920s suggests that the police were not openly influenced by local social purists' anxieties about prostitution and white slavery during the interwar years, the evidence presented here indicates that local officials nevertheless viewed prostitution in very similar moral and ethical terms to social purity patrollers. The proceedings of the Street Offences Committee clearly illustrate that, despite their efforts to treat prostitution as a legal rather than a moral issue, politicians and lawmakers understood and consequently legislated against the prostitute as a social and cultural other. The Street Offences Committee's extended discussions about the usefulness of the legal category of the common prostitute profiled a dual set of moral arguments. On the one hand, it was suggested that the term legitimated the prostitute's trade by giving these women an official identity and, on the other hand, it was argued that this legal category protected *ordinary* women by ensuring that the police targeted only common prostitutes wandering in public and not all women.

These moral concerns were also in evidence at street level. Local patrollers demonstrated nuanced versions of the broader national obsessions with prostitution and female sexual morality. The LVA and Women Police Patrols perpetuated the notion that young women could be morally corrupted by travelling through the city unchaperoned. In their day-to-day work, the LVA actually had very little to do with the city's prostitutes, despite having been set up to combat white slavery. Once a woman was perceived to have embarked on an immoral lifestyle the LVA's main concern was to keep other young women safe from her corrupting influence rather than to help her. The preventative strategies employed by local social purists therefore meant that they could claim to have a legitimate interest in the lives of women not directly connected to prostitution.

Reflecting earlier purity anxieties about the ability of working-class women to manage their own morality, organizations like the LVA, the Women Police Patrols and the House of Help expressed particular concern about the morality of poor women. Their interest in locating employment for these women was motivated by the belief that women who needed to work outside the home required extra moral guidance. These organizations believed that working-class women needed to be placed in respectable jobs such as domestic service in order to prevent them from turning to vice out of economic necessity. Moreover, late nineteenth-century ideas about the need to protect women from corruption and the dangers of urban space were still being incorporated into official and unofficial responses to prostitution after 1945. The LVA remained active after the Second World War and, once again, concerns about how to regulate the prostitute resulted in the establishment of a government committee.

The proceedings of the Wolfenden Committee highlighted the extent to which earlier purity ideas about the moral dangers of prostitution had been incorporated into official thinking. The Wolfenden Committee represented yet another attempt to find a way to regulate the prostitute without entering into moral debates about this form of commercialized sex. Once again, it was an attempt that failed, and moral perceptions of the prostitute as other remained paramount in this committee's approach to the problem of street solicitation. By arguing for the regulation of the prostitute based upon distinctions between public and private, the Wolfenden Committee and the subsequent Street Offences Act 1959, which implemented the committee's recommendations, incorporated policies which supported the moral outlook if not the practices of the social purity movement. This is despite the Wolfenden Committee being conventionally understood to mark a clean break with Victorian policies of sexual regulation.[7]

Consequently, the decline of the purity movement in the post-war period was not necessarily a sign that their ideas had become outdated. Certainly, the purity movement did lose momentum during these years, insofar as they began to fragment, and their workload became diluted with mundane travel assistance. The survival of organizations such as the PSS over the LVA was indicative of the fact that more professionalized, social work-inspired ideas about the need to alleviate poverty had replaced the activities of social purists. Where local efforts to tackle prostitution were concerned, there is evidence that by the early 1970s, the Liverpool Corporation was working with neighbourhood action groups and housing associations in a bid to regenerate some of the poorer areas of the city; it was thought that such measures would reduce social problems like prostitution and kerb-crawling.[8] The work of the LVA was consequently replaced by the local consultations, reports and investigations of civic leaders, town planners and residents.

At the national level, the Wolfenden Committee and the Street Offences Act 1959 took over the purity movement's policy of keeping the streets morally respectable by implementing preventative policies of social control. I have argued that the legal philosophy underpinning the 1959 Act was significantly influenced by the ideas of social purity campaigners dating back to the Victorian era. By targeting the common prostitute in law, the post-war state reiterated the message that the prostitute was not like other women. By making female sexuality visible, the prostitute's sexual transgressiveness was policed as criminal. Wolfenden's belief that being a *public* woman in this way required regulation was informed by persistent understandings about respectable femininity being confined to the private sphere.

This has had important implications for more recent policies relating to prostitution, with prostitution in England still being regulated according

7   See John Wolfenden, *Turning Points: The Memoirs of Lord Wolfenden* (London: The Bodley Head, 1976); Jeffrey Weeks, *Sex, Politics and Society*, p. 239 and pp. 242–4.

8   See the archives of the Shelter Neighbourhood Action Project (SNAP), established in the 1970s, Liverpool University Archive, D/396/52 and A53/8/1. SNAP was an Association representing residents, the Liverpool Corporation, Housing Associations and Shelter. It was set up in order to allow residents of the Liverpool 8 area to work with the Local Authority on improving environmental conditions there.

to moral distinctions between public and private.[9] New Labour's 'Paying the Price' consultation in 2004 was the 'first attempt since the 1950s' to examine the regulation of prostitution, yet this report did not signify a change in attitudes towards the control of sex work.[10] Prostitution on the streets continued to be the main focus of the discussion and in 2006 the Home Office supported using Anti-Social Behaviour Orders to combat solicitation.[11] More recently, in 2014, an All-Party Parliamentary Group on Prostitution and the Global Sex Trade published their report, 'Shifting the Burden'.[12] This report did recognize that prostitutes have been unfairly stigmatized in law, but by arguing that clients rather than prostitutes should be the focus of prosecutions, the prostitute is still left working at the margins of society, and moral concerns about the visibility of this trade are still prioritized over concerns about safety.[13]

Recent official approaches to prostitution are, therefore, steeped in an extensive genealogy of moral, cultural and legal anxiety about the visibility of women who want, need or are forced to work as prostitutes. Histories of women's presence in public spaces, their relationship to the urban environment and the relationship between the law and other forms of social control are integral to understanding the enduring nature of anxieties about the visibility of prostitution. The historical examination of the relationship between official and unofficial forms of regulation offered in this book demonstrates that cultural anxieties and dominant moral codes about female respectability shaped policy and practice for much of the twentieth century. Prostitution regulation has not just been about the removal of prostitutes from public view; it has also been about protecting the civility of the streets from the supposed moral threat of disreputable female conduct.

9   See Sophie Day, *On the Game: Women and Sex Work* (London: Pluto Press, 2007), pp. 7–8.

10   Teela Sanders, 'Controlling the "Anti-Sexual" City: Sexual Citizenship and the Disciplining of Female Street Workers', *Criminology and Criminal Justice*, 9:4 (2009), p. 511.

11   Teela Sanders, 'Controlling the "Anti-Sexual" City', pp. 511–12.

12   All-Party Parliamentary Group on Prostitution and the Global Sex Trade, 'Shifting the Burden: Inquiry to Assess the Operation of the Current Legal Settlement on Prostitution in England and Wales', March 2014.

13   Helen McCarthy, Samantha Caslin and Julia Laite, 'Prostitution and the Law in Historical Perspective: A Dialogue', *History and Policy* (27 March 2015). See www.historyandpolicy.org/dialogues/discussions/prostitution-and-the-law-in-historical-perspective-a-dialogue [Accessed November 2017].

While social purity organizations no longer appear to have a place in today's moral economy, their ideas about prostitution, promiscuity and women's use of public space continue to resonate in contemporary policy. Social purists' preventative patrol work has, therefore, left a legacy which is by no means concluded.

Bibliography

Archives

Liverpool Metropolitan Cathedral Archive
Catholic Women's League, Liverpool Branch
Letter to Mrs Ryan, 8 December 1977, RAS/S3/1/ABC (Series 3, Box R7, File 9).
Twenty First Report, 1932, RAS/S3/1/ABC (Series 3, Box R7, File 9).
Untitled CWL Notes, undated, RAS/S3/1/ABC (Series 3, Box R7, File 9).

Liverpool Record Office
Diaries of Mary Eileen Rodgers M920 ROD.

Hostel for Girls, Knotty Ash
Annual Reports, H364 5 WOM.

Liverpool House of Help
Annual Reports, 362/HOU/3.

Liverpool Personal Service Society
Annual Reports 1920–77, 364 PSS 3/1/1–3/1/57.

Liverpool Vigilance Association
Annual Reports 1916–75, M326 VIG/3.
'Historical Notes', 326 VIG/9.
R.W. Jones, letter to unknown recipient, c.mid-1950s, 362 VIG/7–2.
National Vigilance Association, Charity Dinner Pamphlet, November 1908,
    M326 VIG/5/1.

Newspaper cuttings (early twentieth century), M326 VIG/5/1.
Newspaper cuttings (post-war), M326 VIG/5/2.
'Notes on the Work of the Liverpool Vigilance Association for His Grace the
     Archbishop of York', undated, 326 VIG/9.
Untitled LVA notes on the history of the National Vigilance Association,
     undated, 326 VIG/9.
Untitled LVA notes on Irish female immigrants, undated (*c.*1954), 326 VIG/9.

Liverpool Women Police Patrols
Annual Report 1924, H364/5 WOM.
Annual Reports 1928–42, 365 WOM/18/1–19.
National Union of Women Workers, Birkenhead Patrol Sub-Committee, Report
     for 1914–15, Liverpool Record Office, H364/5 (719) WOM.
Newspaper cuttings relating to Women Police, 365 WOM/17/1–15.

Liverpool University Archives
Papers relating to the Shelter Neighbourhood Action Project, D/396/52 and
     A53/8/1.

National Archives
Home Office Papers
Departmental Committee on Homosexual Offences and Prostitution (Wolfenden
     Committee), Transcripts of Evidence Hearings, HO 345/13.
     — C.C. Martin, Transcript of Evidence, Departmental Committee on
          Homosexual Offences and Prostitution, 31 March 1955.
Prostitution and Allied Offences: Appointment of Committee to Consider the
     Law and Practice Relating to Soliciting, etc., HO 45/12663.
     — Stuart Deacon, Transcript of Evidence, Departmental Committee on Street
          Offences, 14 January 1928.
     — Home Office Report, 'Public Places (Order) Bill' (*c.*1926), unpublished.
          The National Archives.
     — William Joynson-Hicks, letter to Lady Joynson-Hicks on her appointment
          to the Street Offences Committee, 14 October 1927.
     — William Joynson-Hicks, letter to Ramsay MacDonald on the composition
          of the Street Offences Committee, 19 October 1927.
     — Ramsay MacDonald, letter to William Joynson-Hicks on the composition
          of the Street Offences Committee, 17 October 1927.
     — Minutes of AMSH deputation to the Home Office (Home Office reference
          483.171/21), 13 November 1925.
     — Alison Neilans, letter to William Joynson-Hicks, 6 November 1925. The
          National Archives.
     — Notice issued to the Press, 14 October 1927.

— Parliamentary Debates, House of Lords, 9 December 1926, Official Report, Vol. 65, No. 88.

— Public Places (Order) Bill Memorandum, received by the Home Office, 24 November 1926.

Street Offences Committee, minutes of meetings, 25 October 1927–30 July 1928, HO 326/7.

— Mabel Cowlin and L.D. Potter, Transcript of Evidence, Departmental Committee on Street Offences, 20 April 1928.

North West Sound Archive, Lancashire Record Office

Margaret Butler, oral history interview, 2005.0395 Box 98.

John Mulderigg, oral history interview, 2005.0393 Box 98.

Women's Library

Association for Moral and Social Hygiene

George W. Johnson, *The Need for Repealing the Present Solicitation Laws* (London: Association for Moral and Social Hygiene, 1922), 3AMS/B/04/06.

Public Places (Order) Bill records, 3AMS/B/04/06.

Report of the Departmental Committee on the Employment of Policewomen (1924), Home Office. See Employment of Women Police: Publications, 1908–48, 3AMS/B/12/04.

'The Wolfenden Report. BVA Short Answers to Certain Questions', 3AMS/B/04/16/12 Box 50.

British Vigilance Association

Irish-Girls and Related Problems Sub-Committee, 29 October 1954–4 February 1957, 4NVA/1/7 (Box FL198).

Winding up minutes and documents, 4BVA/E/5.

Periodicals and Newspapers

Aberdeen Press and Journal
British Medical Journal
Hull Daily Mail
Illustrated Police News
Liverpool Echo
The Liverpool Mercury
The Nottingham Evening Post
Sheffield Independent
Thomson's Weekly News
Western Daily Press and Bristol Mirror
Western Morning News and Gazette

Books, Chapters and Articles

Paul Addison, *No Turning Back: The Peacetime Revolutions of Post-War Britain* (Oxford: Oxford University Press, 2010).

Caroline Arni and Claudia Honegger, 'The Modernity of Women: Jenny P. d'Hericourt's Contribution to Social Theory (1809–1875)', *Journal of Classical Sociology*, 8:1 (2008), pp. 45–65.

Rachael Attwood, 'Stopping the Traffic: The National Vigilance Association and the International Fight against the "White Slave" Trade (1899–*c*.1909)', *Women's History Review*, 24:3 (2015), pp. 325–50.

Paula Bartley, *Prostitution: Prevention and Reform in England, 1860–1914* (London: Routledge, 2000).

Caitríona Beaumont, *Housewives and Citizens: Domesticity and the Women's Movement in England, 1928–64* (Manchester: Manchester University Press, 2013).

John Belchem, *Before the Windrush: Race Relations in 20th-Century Liverpool* (Liverpool: Liverpool University Press, 2014).

—— 'Comment: Whiteness and the Liverpool Irish', *Journal of British Studies*, 44:1 (2005), pp. 146–52.

—— 'Introduction: Celebrating Liverpool', in John Belchem (ed.), *Liverpool 800: Culture, Character and History* (Liverpool: Liverpool University Press, 2006), pp. 9–57.

—— *Irish Catholic and Scouse: The History of the Liverpool Irish, 1800–1939* (Liverpool: Liverpool University Press, 2007).

—— *Merseypride: Essays in Liverpool Exceptionalism* (Liverpool: Liverpool University Press, 2006).

Adrian Bingham, '"An Era of Domesticity?" Histories of Women and Gender in Interwar Britain', *Cultural and Social History*, 1:2 (2004), pp. 225–33.

—— *Gender, Modernity and the Popular Press in Inter-War Britain* (Oxford: Clarendon Press, 2004).

Laurence Black and Hugh Pemberton (eds), *An Affluent Society? Britain's Post-War 'Golden Age' Revisited* (London: Routledge, 2004).

Lucy Bland, *Banishing the Beast: Feminism, Sex and Morality* (London: Tauris Parke, 2001).

—— *Modern Women on Trial: Sexual Transgression in the Age of the Flapper* (Manchester: Manchester University Press, 2013).

—— 'The Trials and Tribulations of Edith Thompson: The Capital Crime of Sexual Incitement in 1920s England', *Journal of British Studies*, 47:3 (2008), pp. 624–48.

—— 'White Women and Men of Colour: Miscegenation Fears in Britain after the Great War', *Gender and History*, 17:1 (2005), pp. 29–61.

Anna Bocking-Welch, 'Youth against Hunger: Service, Activism and the Mobilisation of Young Humanitarians in 1960s Britain', *European Review of History*, 23:1–2 (2016), pp. 154–70.

Edward Bristow, *Vice and Vigilance: Purity Movements in Britain since 1700* (Dublin: Gill and Macmillan, 1977).

Michael Brogden, *The Police: Autonomy and Consent* (London: Academic Press, 1982).

Terrence Brown, *Ireland: A Social and Cultural History* (London: Harper Perennial, 2004).

Rosie Campbell and Maggie O'Neill, 'Introduction', in Rosie Campbell and Maggie O'Neill (eds), *Sex Work Now* (Uffculme: Willan, 2006), pp. ix–xxi.

Samantha Caslin, 'Flappers, Amateurs and Professionals: The Spectrum of Promiscuity in 1920s Britain', in Kate Hardy, Sarah Kingston and Teela Sanders (eds), *New Sociologies of Sex Work* (Farnham: Ashgate Publishing, 2010), pp. 11–22.

—— '"One Can Only Guess What Might Have Happened if the Worker Had Not Intervened in Time": The Liverpool Vigilance Association, Moral Vulnerability and Irish Girls in Early to Mid-Twentieth-Century Liverpool', *Women's History Review*, 25:2 (2016), pp. 254–73.

Elizabeth Clement, 'Prostitution', in H.G. Cocks and Matt Houlbrook (eds), *The Modern History of Sexuality* (Basingstoke: Palgrave Macmillan, 2006), pp. 206–30.

H.G. Cocks, 'Saucy Stories: Pornography, Sexology and the Marketing of Sexual Knowledge in Britain, *c.*1918–70', *Social History*, 29:4 (2004), pp. 465–84.

Marcus Collins, 'The Pornography of Permissiveness: Men's Sexuality and Women's Emancipation in Mid-Twentieth-Century Britain', *History Workshop Journal*, 47 (1999), pp. 99–120.

Liz Conor, *The Spectacular Modern Woman: Feminine Visibility in the 1920s* (Bloomington: Indiana University Press, 2004).

Rebecca Conway, 'Making the Mill Girl Modern?: Beauty, Industry, and the Popular Newspaper in 1930s England', *Twentieth Century British History*, 24:4 (2013), pp. 518–41.

Krista Cowman, *'Mrs Brown is a Man and a Brother!' Women in Merseyside's Political Organisations 1890–1920* (Liverpool: Liverpool University Press, 2004).

Pamela Cox, *Bad Girls in Britain: Gender, Justice and Welfare, 1900–1950* (Basingstoke: Palgrave Macmillan, 2013).

Andy Croll, 'Street Disorder, Surveillance and Shame: Regulating Behaviour in the Public Spaces of the Late Victorian British Town', *Social History*, 24:3 (1999), 250–68.

Andrew Davies, 'The Scottish Chicago? From "Hooligans" to "Gangsters" in Inter-War Glasgow', *Cultural and Social History*, 4:4 (2007), pp. 511–27.

—— '"These Viragoes are No Less Cruel than the Lads": Young Women, Gangs and Violence in Late Victorian Manchester and Salford', *British Journal of Criminology*, 39:1 (1999), pp. 72–89.

Sam Davies, Pete Gill, Linda Grant, Martin Nightingale, Ron Noon and Andy Shallice, *Genuinely Seeking Work: Mass Unemployment on Merseyside in the 1930s* (Birkenhead: Liver Press, 1992).

Sophie Day, *On the Game: Women and Sex Work* (London: Pluto Press, 2007).

Enda Delaney, *The Irish in Post-War Britain* (Oxford: Oxford University Press, 2007).

—— 'Transnationalism, Networks and Emigration from Post-War Ireland', *Immigrants & Minorities*, 23:2–3 (2005), pp. 425–46.

Lucy Delap, *Knowing Their Place: Domestic Service in Twentieth-Century Britain* (Oxford: Oxford University Press, 2011).

Laura Doan, 'Passing Fashions: Reading Female Masculinities in the 1920s', *Feminist Studies*, 24:3 (1998), pp. 663–700.

Paul Du Noyer, *Liverpool Wondrous Place: Music from the Cavern to the Coral* (London: Virgin Books, 2004).

Ryan Dye, 'Catholic Protectionism or Irish Nationalism?: Religion and Politics in Liverpool, 1829–1845', *Journal of British Studies*, 40:3 (2001), pp. 357–90.

Carol Dyhouse, *Girl Trouble: Panic and Progress in the History of Young Women* (London: Zed Books, 2013).

—— *Glamour: Women, History, Feminism* (London: Zed Books, 2010).

Lindsey Earner-Byrne, *Mother and Child: Maternity and Child Welfare in Dublin, 1922–60* (Manchester: Manchester University Press, 2007).

Mark Finnane, 'The Carrigan Committee of 1930–31 and the "Moral Condition of the Saorstát"', *Irish Historical Studies*, 32:128 (2001), pp. 519–36.

Kate Fisher, *Birth Control, Sex, and Marriage in Britain 1918–1960* (Oxford: Oxford University Press, 2006).

Trevor Fisher, *Prostitution and the Victorians* (Stroud: Sutton Publishing, 1997).

Derek Fraser, *The Evolution of the British Welfare State: A History of Social Policy since the Industrial Revolution*, 3rd edn (Basingstoke: Palgrave Macmillan, 2003).

John Kenneth Galbraith, *The Affluent Society* (Boston: Houghton Mifflin, 1958).

Juliet Gardiner, *Wartime Britain 1939–1945* (London: Headline, 2004).

Paul Michael Garrett, 'The Abnormal Flight: The Migration and Repatriation of Irish Unmarried Mothers', *Social History*, 25:3 (2000), pp. 330–43.

Judy Giles, 'A Home of One's Own: Women and Domesticity in England 1918–1950', *Women's Studies International Forum*, 16:3 (1993), pp. 239–53.

—— '"Playing Hard to Get": Working-Class Women, Sexuality and Respectability in Britain, 1918–40', *Women's History Review*, 1:2 (1992), pp. 239–55.

—— *Women, Identity and Private Life in Britain, 1900–50* (London: Macmillan, 1995).

Christine Grandy, 'Paying for Love: Women's Work and Love in Popular Film in Interwar Britain', *Journal of the History of Sexuality*, 19:3 (2010), pp. 483–507.

Nicoletta Gullace, *'The Blood of Our Sons': Men, Women and the Regulation of British Citizenship during the Great War* (Basingstoke: Palgrave Macmillan, 2002).

Peter Gurney, '"Intersex" and "Dirty Girls": Mass-Observation and Working-Class Sexuality in England in the 1930s', *Journal of the History of Sexuality*, 8:2 (1997), pp. 256–90.

Catherine Hall, *White, Male and Middle Class: Explorations in Feminism and History* (Cambridge: Polity, 1992).

Lesley A. Hall, 'Impotent Ghosts from No Man's Land, Flappers' Boyfriends, or Crypto-Patriarchs? Men, Sex, and Social Change in 1920s Britain', *Social History*, 21:1 (1996), pp. 54–70.

—— *Sex, Gender and Social Change in Britain since 1800* (Basingstoke: Macmillan Press, 2000).

Jane Hamlett, *At Home in the Institution: Material Life in Asylums, Lodging Houses and Schools in Victorian and Edwardian England* (Basingstoke: Palgrave Macmillan, 2015).

Erika Hanna, 'Photographs and "Truth" during the Northern Ireland Troubles, 1969–72', *Journal of British Studies*, 54 (2015), pp. 457–80.

Robert Hart, 'Women Doing Men's Work and Women Doing Women's Work: Female Work and Pay in British Wartime Engineering', *Explorations in Economic History*, 44:1 (2007), pp. 114–30.

Tony Henderson, *Disorderly Women in Eighteenth-Century London: Prostitution and Control in the Metropolis, 1730–1830* (London: Longman, 1999).

Mary J. Hickman and Bronwen Walter, 'Deconstructing Whiteness: Irish Women in Britain', *Feminist Review*, 50 (1995), pp. 5–19.

James Hinton, *Women, Social Leadership, and the Second World War: Continuities of Class* (Oxford: Oxford University Press, 2002).

Matt Houlbrook, *Queer London: Perils and Pleasures in the Sexual Metropolis, 1918–1957* (London: University of Chicago Press, 2006).

Philip Howell, David Beckingham and Francesca Moore, 'Managed Zones for Sex Workers in Liverpool: Contemporary Proposals, Victorian Parallels', *Transactions of the Institute of British Geographers*, New Series, 33 (2008), pp. 233–50.

Samuel Hynes, *A War Imagined: The First World War and English Culture* (London: The Bodley Head, 1990).

Louise A. Jackson, '"The Coffee Club Menace": Policing Youth, Leisure and Sexuality in Post-War Manchester', *Cultural & Social History*, 5:3 (2008), pp. 289–308.

—— *Women Police: Gender, Welfare and Surveillance in the Twentieth Century* (Manchester: Manchester University Press, 2006).

Louise A. Jackson with Angela Bartie, *Policing Youth, 1945–70* (Manchester: Manchester University Press, 2014).

Sheila Jeffreys, *The Idea of Prostitution* (North Melbourne: Spinifex Press, 1997).

Simon Jenkins, 'Aliens and Predators: Miscegenation, Prostitution and Racial Identities in Cardiff, 1927–47', *Cultural and Social History*, 11:4 (2014), pp. 575–96.

—— 'Inherent Vice? Maltese Men and the Organization of Prostitution in Interwar Cardiff', *Journal of Social History*, 49:4 (2016), pp. 928–58.

Susan Kingsley Kent, *Gender and Power in Britain, 1640–1990* (London: Routledge, 1999).

Marek Kohn, *Dope Girls: The Birth of the British Drug Underground* (London: Granta Books, 2001 [1992]).

Seth Koven, *Slumming: Sexual and Social Politics in Victorian London* (Princeton, NJ: Princeton University Press, 2006).

Julia Laite, 'The Association for Moral and Social Hygiene: Abolitionism and Prostitution Law in Britain (1915–1959)', *Women's History Review*, 17:2 (2008), pp. 207–23.

—— 'Between Scylla and Charybdis: Women's Labour Migration and Sex Trafficking in the Early Twentieth Century', *International Review of Social History*, 62:1 (2017), pp. 37–65.

—— *Common Prostitutes and Ordinary Citizens: Commercial Sex in London, 1885–1960* (Basingstoke: Palgrave Macmillan, 2011).

—— 'Taking Nellie Johnson's Fingerprints: Prostitutes and Legal Identity in Early Twentieth Century London', *History Workshop Journal*, 65 (2008), pp. 96–116.

Sharon Lambert, 'From "Irish Women's Emigration to England 1922–1960: The Lengthening of Family Ties"', in Alan Hayes and Diane Urquhart (eds), *The Irish Women's History Reader* (London: Routledge, 2001), pp. 181–7.

Tony Lane, *Liverpool: City of the Sea* (Liverpool: Liverpool University Press, 1997).

Claire Langhamer, *Women's Leisure in England, 1920–60* (Manchester: Manchester University Press, 2000).

Philippa Levine, '"Walking the Streets in a Way no Decent Woman Should": Women Police in World War I', *Journal of Modern History*, 66 (1994), pp. 34–78.

Stephanie Limoncelli, *The Politics of Trafficking: The First International Movement to Combat the Sexual Exploitation of Women* (Stanford, Calif.: Stanford University Press, 2011).

Maria Luddy, 'Moral Rescue and Unmarried Mothers in Ireland in the 1920s', *Women's Studies: An Interdisciplinary Journal*, 30:6 (2001), pp. 797–817.

—— *Prostitution and Irish Society 1800–1940* (Cambridge: Cambridge University Press, 2007).

Clare Makepeace, 'Male Heterosexuality and Prostitution during the Great War', *Cultural and Social History*, 9:1 (2012), pp. 65–83.

Moira Martin, 'Single Women and Philanthropy: A Case Study of Women's Associational Life in Bristol, 1880–1914', *Women's History Review*, 17:3 (2008), pp. 395–417.

Arthur Marwick, *The Deluge*, 2nd edn (Basingstoke: Palgrave Macmillan, 2006 [1965]).

Helen McCarthy, Samantha Caslin and Julia Laite, 'Prostitution and the Law in Historical Perspective: A Dialogue', *History and Policy* (27 March 2015). See www.historyandpolicy.org/dialogues/discussions/prostitution-and-the-law-in-historical-perspective-a-dialogue [Accessed November 2017].

Leanne McCormick, '"One Yank and They're Off": Interaction between US Troops and Northern Irish Women, 1942–1945', *Journal of the History of Sexuality*, 15:2 (2006), pp. 228–57.

Graeme J. Milne, 'Maritime Liverpool', in John Belchem (ed.), *Liverpool 800: Culture, Character and History* (Liverpool: Liverpool University Press, 2006), 257–309.

David Monger, 'Nothing Special? Propaganda and Women's Roles in Late First World War Britain', *Women's History Review*, 23:4 (2014), pp. 518–42.

Chris Moores, 'Thatcher's Troops? Neighbourhood Watch Schemes and the Search for "Ordinary" Thatcherism in 1980s Britain', *Contemporary British History*, 31:2 (2017), pp. 230–55.

Lydia Morris, *Dangerous Classes: The Underclass and Social Citizenship* (London: Routledge, 1994).

Frank Mort, 'The Ben Pimlott Memorial Lecture 2010: The Permissive Society Revisited', *Twentieth Century British History*, 22:2 (2011), pp. 269–98.

—— *Capital Affairs: London and the Making of the Permissive Society* (London: Yale University Press, 2010).

—— *Dangerous Sexualities: Medico-Moral Politics in England since 1830*, 2nd edn (London: Routledge, 2000).

—— 'Mapping Sexual London: The Wolfenden Committee on Homosexual Offences and Prostitution 1954–57', *New Formations: Sexual Geographies*, 37 (1999), pp. 92–113.

—— 'The Sexual Geography of the City', in Gary Bridge and Sophie Watson (eds), *The City* (Oxford: Blackwell, 2003), pp. 307–15.

—— 'Striptease: The Erotic Female Body and Live Sexual Entertainment in Mid-Twentieth-Century London', *Social History*, 32:1 (2007), pp. 27–53.

Mo Moulton, *Ireland and the Irish in Interwar England* (Cambridge: Cambridge University Press, 2014).

Jon Murden, '"City of Change and Challenge": Liverpool since 1945', in John Belchem (ed.), *Liverpool 800: Culture, Character and History* (Liverpool: Liverpool University Press, 2006), pp. 393–485.

Frank Neal, *Sectarian Violence: The Liverpool Experience, 1819–1914: An Aspect of Anglo-Irish History* (Manchester: Manchester University Press, 1987).

Tim Newburn, *Permission and Regulation: Law and Morals in Postwar Britain* (London: Routledge, 1992).

Lucy Noakes, 'Demobilising the Military Woman: Constructions of Class and Gender in Britain after the First World War', *Gender & History*, 19:9 (2007), pp. 143–62.

—— 'From War Service to Domestic Service: Ex-Servicewomen and the Free Passage Scheme 1919–22', *Twentieth Century British History*, 22:1 (2011), pp. 1–27.

Pat O'Mara, *The Autobiography of a Liverpool Slummy* (Liverpool: Bluecoat Press, 1994).

Debbie Palmer, *Who Cared for the Carers? A History of the Occupational Health of Nurses, 1880–1948* (Manchester: Manchester University Press, 2014).

Susan Pedersen, *Eleanor Rathbone and the Politics of Conscience* (New Haven, Conn.: Yale University Press, 2004).

Ben Pimlott, *Harold Wilson* (London: HarperCollins, 1992).

H.R. Poole *The Liverpool Council of Social Service: 1909–1959* (Liverpool: The Liverpool Council of Social Service, 1960).

Colin G. Pooley, 'Getting to Know the City: The Construction of Spatial Knowledge in London in the 1930s', *Urban History*, 31:2 (2004), pp. 210–28.

—— 'Living in Liverpool: The Modern City', in John Belchem (ed.), *Liverpool 800: Culture, Character and History* (Liverpool: Liverpool University Press, 2006), pp. 171–255.

—— 'The Residential Segregation of Migrant Communities in Mid-Victorian Liverpool', *Transactions of the Institute of British Geographers*, New Series, 2:3 (1977), pp. 364–82.

Jennifer Redmond, 'Immigrants, Aliens, Evacuees: Exploring the History of Irish Children in Britain During the Second World War', *Journal of the History of Childhood and Youth*, 9:2 (2016), pp. 295–308.

—— '"Sinful Singleness?" Exploring the Discourses on Irish Single Women's Emigration to England, 1922–1948', *Women's History Review*, 17:3 (2008), pp. 455–76.

Krisztina Robert, 'Constructions of "Home", "Front", and Women's Military Employment in First World War Britain: A Spatial Interpretation', *History and Theory*, 52 (2013), pp. 319–43.

Alex Rock, 'The "Khaki Fever" Moral Panic: Women's Patrols and the Policing of Cinemas in London, 1913–19', *Early Popular Visual Culture*, 12:1 (2014), pp. 57–72.

Sonya O. Rose, 'Sex, Citizenship, and the Nation in World War II Britain', *American Historical Review*, 103:4 (1998), pp. 1147–76.

—— 'Women's Rights, Women's Obligations: Contradictions of Citizenship in World War II Britain', *European Review of History*, 7:2 (2000), pp. 277–89.

Sheila Rowbotham, *Women in Movement: Feminism and Social Action* (London: Routledge, 1992).

Michael Rowe, 'Sex, "Race" and Riot in Liverpool, 1919', *Immigrants & Minorities*, 19:2 (2000), pp. 53–70.

Teela Sanders, 'Controlling the "Anti-Sexual" City: Sexual Citizenship and the Disciplining of Female Street Workers', *Criminology and Criminal Justice*, 9:4 (2009), pp. 507–25.

—— *Sex Work: Risky Business* (Uffculme: Willan, 2005).

Teela Sanders and Rosie Campbell, 'Criminalization, Protection and Rights: Global Tensions in the Governance of Commercial Sex', *Criminology & Criminal Justice*, 14:5 (2014), pp. 535–48.

Helen J. Self, *Prostitution, Women and Misuse of the Law: The Fallen Daughters of Eve* (London: Frank Cass, 2003).

Louise Settle, 'The Kosmo Club Case: Clandestine Prostitution during the Interwar Period', *Twentieth Century British History*, 25:4 (2014), pp. 562–84.

Lise Shapiro Sanders, '"Equal Laws Based upon an Equal Standard": The Garrett Sisters, the Contagious Diseases Acts, and the Sexual Politics of Victorian and Edwardian Feminism Revisited', *Women's History Review*, 24:3 (2015), pp. 389–409.

Heather Shore, '"Constable Dances with Instructress": The Police and the Queen of Nightclubs in Inter-War London', *Social History*, 38:2 (2013), pp. 183–202.

Margaret Simey, *Charity Rediscovered: A Study of Philanthropic Effort in Nineteenth-Century Liverpool* (Liverpool: Liverpool University Press, 1992).

—— *From Rhetoric to Reality: A Study of the Work of F.G. D'Aeth, Social Administrator*, edited by David Bingham (Liverpool: Liverpool University Press, 2005).

Beverley Skeggs, *Formations of Class and Gender* (London: Sage, 1997).

Stefan Slater, 'Containment: Managing Street Prostitution in London, 1918–1959', *Journal of British Studies*, 49:2 (2010), pp. 332–57.

—— 'Lady Astor and the Ladies of the Night: The Home Office, the Metropolitan Police and the Politics of the Street Offences Committee, 1927–28', *Law and History Review*, 30:2 (2012), pp. 533–73.

—— 'Pimps, Police and Filles de Joie: Foreign Prostitution in Interwar London', *London Journal*, 32:1 (2007), pp. 53–74.

Carol Smart, 'Law and the Control of Women's Sexuality: The Case of the 1950s', in Bridget Hutter and Gillian Williams (eds), *Controlling Women: The Normal and the Deviant* (London: Croom Helm, 1981), pp. 40–60.

—— *Law, Crime and Sexuality: Essays in Feminism* (London: Sage, 1995).

—— 'Law's Power, the Sexed Body, and Feminist Discourse', *Journal of Law and Society*, 17:2 (1990), pp. 194–210.

James M. Smith, *Ireland's Magdalen Laundries and the Nation's Architecture of Containment* (Manchester: Manchester University Press, 2007).

—— 'The Politics of Sexual Knowledge: The Origins of Ireland's Containment Culture and the Carrigan Report', *Journal of the History of Sexuality*, 13:2 (2004), pp. 208–33.

Penny Summerfield, 'Gender and War in the Twentieth Century', *International History Review*, 19:1 (1997), pp. 2–15.

Penny Summerfield and Corinna Peniston-Bird, 'Women in the Firing Line: The Home Guard and the Defence of Gender Boundaries in Britain in the Second World War', *Women's History Review*, 9:2 (2000), pp. 231–54.

Olivier Sykes, Jonathan Brown, Matthew Cocks, David Shaw and Chris Couch, 'A City Profile of Liverpool', *Cities*, 35 (2013), pp. 299–318.

Laura Tabili, 'Women "of a Very Low Type": Crossing Racial Boundaries in Late Imperial Britain', in Laura Levine Frader and Sonya O. Rose (eds), *Gender and Class in Modern Europe* (Ithaca, NY: Cornell University Press, 1996), pp. 165–90.

Pat Thane, 'The Ben Pimlott Memorial Lecture 2011: The "Big Society" and the "Big State": Creative Tension or Crowding Out?', *Twentieth Century British History*, 23:3 (2012), pp. 408–29.

Pat Thane and Tanya Evans, *Sinners? Scroungers? Saints? Unmarried Motherhood in Twentieth-Century England* (Oxford: Oxford University Press, 2012).

Deborah Thom, *Nice Girls and Rude Girls: Women Workers in World War I* (London: IB Tauris Publishers, 1998).

Keith Thomas, 'The Double Standard', *Journal of the History of Ideas*, 20:2 (1959), pp. 195–216.

Penny Tinkler, 'Rebellion, Modernity, and Romance: Smoking as a Gendered Practice in Popular Young Women's Magazines, Britain 1918–1939', *Women's Studies International Forum*, 24:1 (2001), pp. 111–22.

Selina Todd, 'Domestic Service and Class Relations in Britain 1900–1950', *Past and Present*, 203 (2009), pp. 181–204.

—— *The People: The Rise and Fall of the Working Class* (London: John Murray, 2015).

—— 'Poverty and Aspiration: Young Women's Entry to Employment in Inter-war England', *Twentieth Century British History*, 15:2 (2004), pp. 119–42.

—— *Young Women, Work, and Family in England 1918–1950* (Oxford: Oxford University Press, 2005).

—— 'Young Women, Work and Family in Inter-War Rural England', *Agricultural History Review*, 52:1 (2004), pp. 83–98.

—— 'Young Women, Work, and Leisure in Interwar England', *Historical Journal*, 48:3 (2005), pp. 789–809.

Sandra Trudgen Dawson, 'Busy and Bored: The Politics of Work and Leisure for Women Workers in Second World War British Government Hostels', *Twentieth Century British History*, 21:1 (2010), pp. 29–49.

Alison Twells, '"Went into Raptures": Reading Emotion in the Ordinary Wartime Diary, 1941–1946', *Women's History Review*, 25:1 (2016), pp. 143–60.

Judith R. Walkowitz, *City of Dreadful Delight: Narratives of Sexual Danger in Late-Victorian London* (London: Virago Press, 1992).

—— 'Going Public: Shopping, Street Harassment, and Streetwalking in Late Victorian London', *Representations*, 62 (1998), pp. 1–30.

—— *Nights Out: Life in Cosmopolitan London* (New Haven, Conn.: Yale University Press, 2012).

—— 'The Politics of Prostitution', in Stevi Jackson and Sue Scott (eds), *Feminism and Sexuality: A Reader* (Edinburgh: Edinburgh University Press, 1996), pp. 288–96.

—— *Prostitution and Victorian Society: Women, Class, and the State* (Cambridge: Cambridge University Press, 1980).

Bronwen Walter, *Outsiders Inside: Whiteness, Place and Irish Women* (London: Routledge, 2001).

Chris Waters, '"Dark Strangers" in Our Midst: Discourses of Race and Nation in Britain, 1947–1963', *Journal of British Studies*, 36:2 (1997), pp. 207–38.

Wendy Webster, '"Race", Ethnicity and National Identity', in Ina Zweiniger-Bargielowska (ed.), *Women in Twentieth-Century Britain* (Harlow: Pearson Education, 2001), pp. 292–306.

Jeffrey Weeks, *Sex, Politics and Society: The Regulation of Sexuality since 1800*, 2nd edn (London: Longman, 1989).

—— *Sexuality and its Discontents: Meanings, Myths and Modern Sexualities* (London: Routledge, 1985).

John Welshman, *Underclass: A History of the Excluded Since 1880* (London: Hambledon, 2006).

Charlotte Wildman, 'Miss Moriarty, the Adventuress and the Crime Queen: The Rise of the Modern Female Criminal in Britain, 1918–1939', *Contemporary British History*, 30:1 (2016), pp. 73–98.

—— *Urban Redevelopment and Modernity in Liverpool and Manchester, 1918–1939* (London: Bloomsbury, 2016).

—— 'Urban Transformation in Liverpool and Manchester, 1918–1939', *Historical Journal*, 55:1 (2012), pp. 119–43.

Stuart Wilks-Heeg, 'From World City to Pariah City? Liverpool and the Global Economy, 1850–2000', in Ronaldo Munck (ed.), *Reinventing the City? Liverpool in Comparative Perspective* (Liverpool: Liverpool University Press, 2003), pp. 36–52.

John Wolfenden, *Turning Points: The Memoirs of Lord Wolfenden* (London: The Bodley Head, 1976).

Angela Woollacott, '"Khaki Fever" and its Control: Gender, Class, Age and Sexual Morality on the British Homefront in the First World War', *Journal of Contemporary History*, 29 (1994): 325–47.

—— *On Her Their Lives Depend: Munitions Workers in the Great War* (Berkeley: University of California Press, 1994).

Reference Texts

Who Was Who (London: A & C Black, 1920–2016; online edition, Oxford University Press).

Unpublished Theses

David Justham, 'A Study of Nursing Practices Used in the Management of Infection in Hospitals, 1929–1948', PhD thesis, University of Manchester, 2014.

Charlotte Wildman, 'The "Spectacle" of Interwar Manchester and Liverpool: Urban Fantasies, Consumer Cultures and Gendered Identities', PhD thesis, University of Manchester, 2007.

Gaynor Diane Williams, 'Women in Public Life in Liverpool between the Wars', PhD thesis, University of Liverpool, 2000.

Index

amateur prostitution 41, 44, 63, 126, 165, 192, 194
America 36, 118, 119, 141, 157–8
American Consul 20–1
American troops 167, 194
Anomalies Act 1931 89
Association for Moral and Social Hygiene (AMSH) 66–8, 72–3, 108

The Beatles 197–9
Belfast 95, 150, 157n55, 168, 200
Birmingham 176, 204
Blackpool 103, 175
British Vigilance Association (BVA) 174–5, 184–5, 187–9, 196–7, 202–3, 208
see also National Vigilance Association (NVA)
Buenos Aires 21, 95
Butler, Josephine 22–3, 39n112
Butler, Margaret 153

Cardiff 4, 107n4, 132n27, 133, 204
Catholic Aid Society 98, 151
Catholic Social Service Bureau 177, 206

Catholic Women's League (CWL) 10, 16–17, 27–30, 34, 39–40, 44, 56–8, 61
children 18, 31, 37, 50, 53, 56–7, 75, 90, 117, 132, 167, 172, 173n47, 176, 181, 200, 204, 205
and brothels 135
Irish children 157
and race 133
cinema 36, 86, 102, 169, 170
A-rated films 57
pictures 47
consumerism 44–7, 163, 169–70, 178, 197, 199
contraception 45, 56
convalescence 155n47, 208
Coote, William Alexander 23–4
Cork 95, 157n55
Cowlin, Mabel 74–83, 93
Criminal Law Amendment
of 1885 25
of 1912 25

dating 169–71
Deacon, Stuart (Stipendiary Magistrate, Liverpool) 65

department stores and retail outlets
46, 197
docks 1, 20, 32, 44, 48–9, 53, 87, 89,
110, 190, 192, 194, 197
Domestic Servants' Registration
Department 97
domestic service 11, 18, 43, 50,
54–7, 60–1, 85–90, 93,
97–101, 105, 108, 110, 128,
129, 146n5, 160, 175, 179, 191,
201, 213
domesticity and the private sphere
14–17, 32–3, 41–3, 49, 56, 60,
129–32, 154, 180, 191, 196,
214
and class 31, 39–40, 42, 61, 86,
105
and contrast with city life 21, 44,
57
'feminine' skills 29, 38, 40, 55, 85
Dublin 57, 95, 98, 100, 150, 157n55,
164, 168, 173, 179, 200, 201

factory work 37, 45, 85, 88, 101, 103,
201
feminism 4, 11, 22–3, 25, 43, 47, 49,
67, 73–4, 108, 121n50, 143
see also suffrage
First World War 1, 16, 28, 32–40,
42n1, 87, 92, 96, 118, 130, 210
flappers 35, 43, 44–5, 55, 63
The Fletcher Report 133
The Free Passage Scheme, 1919–22
87

glamour 13, 21, 46, 53, 103, 199
see also Hollywood; performing arts
work
Glasgow 95, 200

health 18, 99, 131, 157
hitchhiking 53, 103n61, 105, 205

Hollywood 102–3
Home Office 4, 66, 69–73, 118, 135,
172n41, 174, 188, 215
hospital work 55, 75, 85, 86, 90, 100,
129, 146–7
House of Help
domestic chores 57
links to Liverpool Vigilance
Association (LVA) 19, 28, 44,
85, 95, 200
links to Women Police Patrols in
Liverpool 28, 44, 59–60, 165–6
moral outlook 17–18, 46–7, 57–9
origins of 18
religiosity 17, 19

International Convention for the
Suppression of the White Slave
Traffic (1902) 111
internationalism 22, 87, 94, 106–7,
110–11, 116–22, 125–6, 140–1,
168, 172, 188–9
interracial relationships 127–36,
155n45
Irish immigration 8, 12, 119, 148–55,
160, 161, 164, 166, 172–80

Johnson, George 67–8
Jones, Caradog 90
Joynson-Hicks, William 69–73

khaki fever 35–6

Ladies' Associations for the Care of
Friendless Girls 109
Lancashire 60, 102, 112, 159, 160,
193
Landing Stage 30, 32, 48, 60, 95, 98,
102, 116, 120, 145
Leeds 194
Lime Street 1, 30, 32, 48, 77, 87, 95,
103, 110, 139

Liverpool 7–9, 211
   interwar economy 46, 87–9
   perceptions of 15, 18, 48, 51, 64,
      94, 115, 190–2, 197, 199
   postwar economy 197–8
   and prostitution 65–6, 77, 135,
      190, 192–4, 212
   and race 131–4, 192
   and religion 19
   and white slavery 21, 110, 120,
      121–2, 126
Liverpool and County Catholic Aid
   Society 98, 151
Liverpool Personal Service Society
   207–8
Liverpool Vigilance Association
   (LVA)
   dependence upon Irish female
      immigration 119, 154–5, 166
   links to Catholic Women's League
      28
   links to House of Help 19, 28, 44,
      85, 95, 200
   links to Women Police Patrols in
      Liverpool 28, 31
   name changes ix, 106
   relationships with employers
      96–7, 155–6, 174–5, 179–80,
      191, 201
   relationships with transport
      representatives and companies
      36–7, 49, 118, 146
Liverpool Women's Industrial
   Council 33
London 3–4, 8, 11, 31, 36, 63, 90, 93,
      94, 95, 110–11, 121, 123, 133,
      139, 147, 154, 171, 176, 189,
      190–2, 199

Macmillan, Hugh 69, 78, 80–2
Manchester 37–8, 42, 53, 66, 94, 95,
      103, 128, 184, 194

Martin, Charles Carnegie (Chief
      Constable of Liverpool)
      191–4, 195
Maxwell Fyfe, David 187–8
Maxwell Fyfe, Lady 187–9
men
   as clients of prostitutes 62, 73,
      128, 215
   as pimps 126, 128, 193
motherhood (idealisation of) 16–17,
      38, 56, 86, 141

National Council of Women 30, 75
National Union of Women Workers
      30n68, 74
National Union of Women's Suffrage
      Societies 30
National Vigilance Association
      (NVA) 20–6, 31, 32, 66, 72–3,
      83, 91, 93, 95, 106, 107, 108,
      109–13, 116, 117, 121, 137–8,
      139, 156, 165, 174, 184, 188–9,
      196
   see also British Vigilance
      Association (BVA)
Newcastle 95, 134, 194
Northern Ireland (The Troubles)
      206
Nugent House 95

Paris 95, 111
performing arts work 53, 88, 103–5
permissive society 185, 187, 199,
      209
pornography 71, 186
Public Places (Order) Bill 1926
      68–9

Report of the Departmental
      Committee on the Employment
      of Policewomen, 1924 50
Rose, Edith 25, 31, 117, 166, 167

sailors, seamen and seafarers 18, 37–8,
    120, 129–30, 133, 190, 192, 194
Salvation Army 68, 123, 197
Scotland Road 30, 155
Second World War 12, 25, 120–1n50,
    123, 154n40, 162–3, 165–72,
    181
smoking 44–5, 80
solicitation laws 63–4, 66–9, 72, 74,
    84, 185, 187, 196
Stanley, Sophia 79
Stead, W.T. 25
Stopes, Marie 56, 130n18
Street Offences Act 1959 12–13, 184,
    195, 197, 203–4, 207–9, 213–14
suffrage 27, 30, 43, 67
    see also feminism

Toxteth 18, 127, 136

unemployment 7, 18, 47, 88, 91,
    132n31, 198n69, 208
    female unemployment 29, 89, 94,
        181
    links to prostitution 11, 86, 88,
        91–5, 100, 104, 108, 175, 180,
        201
    male unemployment 89, 94

Vagrancy Act 65
Vickers, Joan 203

Victorian period (later continuities
    with) 2–3, 6–7, 17–19, 22–3,
    25, 27, 33, 36, 40, 42, 62–3,
    74, 95, 105, 115, 130, 140,
    153, 184, 186, 193, 195, 211,
    213–14

Wolfenden, John 190
Women Police Patrols in Liverpool
    funding 50
    Knotty Ash Hostel 59–61, 134,
        155n45
    links to Catholic Women's League
        (CWL) 28
    links to House of Help 28, 44,
        59–60, 165–6
    links to Liverpool Vigilance
        Association (LVA) 28, 31
    moral expertise 79, 81–4
women's war work
    First World War 16–17, 32–4, 37,
        50, 96
    Second World War 120, 121n50,
        162–3
Wyles, Lillian 79

Yorkshire 28, 97, 159
Young Women's Christian Association
    68
youth 6, 35–6, 41, 47, 53, 76–7, 82,
    140, 176–7, 180, 199, 201, 204